D1279152

# SOUTHERN HISTORY ACROSS THE COLOR LINE

# SOUTHERN HISTORY ACROSS THE COLOR LINE

## NELL IRVIN PAINTER

The University of North Carolina Press  Chapel Hill & London

© 2002

The University of North Carolina Press

All rights reserved

Set in Carter Cone Galliard and Mantinia types

by Keystone Typesetting, Inc.

Manufactured in the United States of America

The paper in this book meets the guidelines for

permanence and durability of the Committee on

Production Guidelines for Book Longevity of the

Council on Library Resources.

Library of Congress

Cataloging-in-Publication Data

Painter, Nell Irvin.

Southern history across the color line / Nell Irvin Painter.

p. cm. — (Gender and American culture)

Includes bibliographical references and index.

ISBN 0-8078-2692-8 (alk. paper) —

ISBN 0-8078-5360-7 (pbk.: alk. paper)

1. Southern States — Historiography. 2. Southern

States — Race relations. 3. Southern States — Social

conditions. I. Title. II. Gender & American culture.

F208.2 .P35    2002

975'.007'2 — dc21        2001053070

Cloth  06  05  04  03  02   5  4  3  2  1

Paper  06  05  04  03  02   5  4  3  2  1

TO JOHN HOPE FRANKLIN

*who showed it could be done*

# CONTENTS

# SOUTHERN HISTORY ACROSS THE COLOR LINE

# Introduction

## SOUTHERN HISTORY ACROSS

## THE COLOR LINE

• • •

Fruit of many years' thought and living, *Southern History across the Color Line* points across and beyond a color line once all too solid in southern public life and still discernible in scholarship and everyday life. Preserved by residential segregation, class barriers, and the old bogey of "social equality," the color line seems practically indelible. It outlasted the legal framework and institutional superstructure erected in the wake of the U.S. Supreme Court's 1896 ruling, in *Plessy v. Ferguson*, permitting the existence of racially "separate but equal" establishments. The mid-twentieth-century civil rights revolution dismantled the laws separating the races, yet two generations later, southerners of all races still must go against the grain of their culture to reach for equals outside the churches, clubs, and habit-places of their own race.

Those habit-places house intellectual production, for an all-too-firm conceptual barrier still bisects the world of scholarship. Oh, yes, much has changed—thankfully. Before my time, but within the lifetime of John Hope Franklin—born in 1915 and a graduate student and young scholar during the 1940s and 1950s—the color line interfered materially with the pursuit of history. Legal segregation and traditions of unwelcome restricted the places where a historian could do research and eat lunch. Colleges segregated by race and gender offered unequal opportunities for professional advancement. Even the process of dismantling the color bar turned a black scholar's presenting a paper in a scholarly meeting into a public curiosity, as John Hope Franklin discovered at a meeting of the Southern Historical Association in the late 1940s.

Most historians followed (and all too often still follow) segregation's decree and wrote about the South as though people of different
races occupied entirely different spheres. First, white historians made
up a lily-white southern history that included no blacks, or only those
blacks who loved serving whites, loved being enslaved or at least benefited from the institution, and who missed slavery after it was gone.
Then, in the wake of the civil rights revolution, black historians and our
allies tried to redress the imbalance by publishing the history of blacks
as though white people existed only as faceless oppressors. My first
book appeared in that era. My primary sources — full of the details
characteristic of individual day-by-day experience lived according to
necessity, not society's larger rules — showed me southerners tracking
across the color line. But as a beginning historian, I lacked the writing
skill to present a thoroughly racialized, steeply hierarchical, utterly re-
pressive society in which some black and white people nonetheless
looked and stepped across the line. I expressed my doubts only timidly
and resolved better to capture nuance in future. Nowadays more and
more historians write about southerners of many races as fully realized
historical actors. The old habit of writing only or mainly about white
people or only or mainly about black people dies hard, but it never
fettered John Hope Franklin.

In a segregated world, Franklin received accolades in abundance as
the author of *From Slavery to Freedom*, first published in 1947 and still,
after ten revisions, in print and flourishing. Franklin very rightly deserves honors for this finest and most enduring history of black Americans. He also deserves recognition for a good deal else he has written.
In addition to contributing a distinguished oeuvre in American history,
Franklin also thought and wrote across the color line and probed the
meaning of southern history as a whole.

Segregation may have encumbered Franklin's conditions of research, but it never shuttered his vision. He wrote perceptively of white
as well as black southerners and of all Americans.[1] How much richer
would history be if historians of all races followed his lead and peered
beyond their own allotments! This is beginning to happen: I love the
breaching of the conceptual color bar in southern history into which
many now step. There are too many for me to name them all here, but I
cannot resist the desire to mention some with whom I've had the

opportunity to work closely: Crystal Feimster, Glenda Gilmore, and Walter Johnson, for example.[2] Much more work remains to be done, especially to keep black women as well as black men in view as full-fledged southerners. But, happily, the work is well launched.

In one sense, the very fact of my writing about white southerners lofts this book across the color line. While white historians often write about black people, black historians still rarely write about whites.[3] I regret this imbalance, if only because black historians are more likely than whites to read the vast literature of African American studies. The bibliography of this field, consisting of work by scholars from all racial-ethnic backgrounds, contains trenchant analyses of American culture from a black point of view ordinarily lacking in American scholarship. Unfortunately, the color line endures in the world of footnotes and citations and still distorts the intellectual history of African Americans and Americans generally. I lament the tendency of scholars of all races to overlook the publications of authors who were or are black.

In another, larger sense, I want to cross the color line by looking beyond color and race. I do *not* mean *not* looking at color and race. Race matters enormously and must figure in any analysis of American history, doubly so for southern history. For too long we have normalized whiteness, as though to be white were to be natural, and only those people not counted as white had racial identities. "Southerner" used to mean only "white southerner," as though black southerners somehow were not part of the South. Along the same line, "the South" and "the Confederacy" used also to seem interchangeable, as though the only people who counted as "southerners" supported the Confederacy. Yes, especially in southern history, race matters a lot. But race is not all there is to life or to history. Much more remains to be said. Playing with the vogue for quantification, I used to joke that race constitutes 49 percent of a southerner's human life: as the crucial factor, it counts for a plurality, but not the totality, of causes and effects. (Now that cliometrics has faded into historiography's mists, I must find another, up-to-date little formula.)

Responsible historians cannot halt their analyses at the color line, and now they can draw upon a generation's worth or more of new scholarship for guidance. African American studies and women's studies tell us — and rightly — to think through race, class, and gender simultaneously. No one goes through life as simply a unit of race, for race's significance varies according to one's class and gender. Womanliness or manliness means different things for people of different races. Wealth and poverty play out according to the race and gender of the subject(s) at hand. But even race, class, and gender together miss much in life and history. Keeping all three in mind always, historians must transcend them.

Race, class, and gender constitute three essential but blunt tools of analysis. Each contains a plethora of subcategories and variations: region, chronology, cultural context, sexual orientation, physical ability, education, and so on. Within race lies color, for instance. The shade of color of an African American woman's skin affects her life's chances, so that one black woman's experience with people of all races cannot simply be interchanged with another's. We are less likely to assume that all white women are identical to one another, but we need always to keep in mind their differences according to class-inflected levels of education and standing, even within the same region, the same era, and the same generation.

Beyond even the most finely tuned categories lies something exceeding race, class, and gender: individual subjectivity. Biography, if you wish. From the very beginning of my career in history, biography captured my attention. Even my purest work of social history, *Exodusters: Black Migration after Reconstruction*, contains biographies of the two leading Exodusters, Henry Adams and Benjamin "Pap" Singleton, both southerners, both former slaves, both men cognizant of the imperatives of manhood, but each distinct from the other in ideology and behavior. After *Exodusters* I wrote about another singular southern black man, Hosea Hudson, who reminded me of a sort of latter-day Henry Adams. But Hudson, a twentieth-century urban working man, was a radical in ways Adams was not. Having studied such superficially similar but profoundly singular men, I remain curious about individual lives. I have never assumed that one person's experience determines the experiences of another — even someone of the same race, class, gender, or region.

The pursuit of individual subjectivity has taken me to psychology and psychoanalysis.[4] As a historian of the nineteenth and early twentieth centuries, I recognize that my interest in psychology and other social sciences inspires a certain wariness among my colleagues. Some doubt the applicability of a field invented in turn-of-the-twentieth-century Vienna by an upper-middle-class Jew to poor southerners. They wonder whether "white" psychology works on "black" people. My psychologist sister-in-law warned me that you "can't psychoanalyze the dead." A kindly editor reminded me to let readers know quite clearly that I recognize the difference time-bound culture makes.

I have tried to heed all these warnings but still keep going. Because psychology and psychoanalysis only make sense within a particular culture's own orientation, at a given times and places, I use them sparingly. But I remain convinced that historians should keep in sight the fundamental lessons of psychology and psychoanalysis: that all people, even people who describe themselves primarily as raced or gendered, are individuals; that individual subjects develop within families; that families need not be related biologically; that attachment does not necessarily connote positive feeling; that attachment and grief do not stop at social barriers of color or class. Within southern history, the families of the oppressed have offered a haven to the physically afflicted, a bulwark against psychological assault. Families at every economic level inculcate the finest and the basest of values. Without attempting to psychoanalyze the dead, I want to read the people in historical texts with my eyes wide open. From psychoanalysis, psychology, and the other tools I borrow from the social sciences, I draw questions, not answers.

Three themes wind through the essays that follow, all related but worthy of individual mention. I entered the historical profession in the 1970s under the sign of Herbert Gutman, who when I first met him was immersed in — no, consumed by — the source material for what would become *The Black Family in Slavery and Freedom, 1750–1925* (1976).[5] He validated my interest in the 1879 Exodus to Kansas, making it available to me as a dissertation topic. Gutman's early Marxism bequeathed him an interest in working people and a focus on their roles as historical actors (what came to be summed up as historical "agency" in the 1980s). He excavated the history of ordinary black people and rightly recognized the novelty and value of his investigation. Considering myself a person of the Left, I was and remain attentive to material conditions: wealth and income, work, the distribution of power in the political economy, patriarchy, and white supremacy. These concerns bear the imprint of a Marxist or "materialist" orientation. But Marxist or not, they are matters every historian would do well to heed, even in these post-post-structuralist times. Thinking about class, however, can be even harder than thinking clearly about race. We Americans generally find it difficult to deal with class, preferring, to the detriment of historical analysis, to use race as a handy surrogate.

Another material theme in these essays that differs from traditional Marxist concerns is that of the body, particularly the body subject to torture. Before I could focus on personal violence, I had to learn a great deal more than what my graduate education had provided. My first big, post-dissertation auto-education took me through feminist scholarship, with its attention to the gendered body.[6] Physical violence and physical pain play a role in activist feminist literature, but this activism does not deal with the nineteenth-century evils of slavery. Southern historians, too, have averted their eyes from slavery's inevitable bodily torment. The mopping up of blood occurs between the historian's research in primary documents and publication.

Any sojourn in southern archives covers the researcher in blood, and slavery, particularly, throws buckets of blood in the historian's face. Yet violence and pain seldom appear in historical writings, for professionalism prompts historians to clean up the mess before going into print. I have tried not to wipe up so thoroughly as to lose what the enslaved wanted us to recall: that slavery rested on the threat and the abundant use of physical violence. Contrary to the images from nineteenth- and twentieth-century American popular culture and even from American popular history, slaves had to be coerced into playing their roles in involuntary servitude. Coercion meant physical beating and the anger it incites. Both the beaten body and the political economy belong to the materialist theme in these essays.

Culture, including cultural symbolism, constitutes my third main theme. While hierarchies of race and gender produce material consequences, some of the more obvious manifestations of patriarchy and white supremacy are cultural: assumptions that the concerns of men and white people take precedence over the concerns of women and people of color.[7] Persons and events bear more than just one meaning, depending on the identity of the witness and the point of view. Networks of meaning, symbols, and semiology acquire lives of their own, complementary to (but not substitutes for) material meaning. In my research I have found two examples of nonmaterial culture particularly striking: first, the religious faith in the rightness of slavery and the secular belief in the social hierarchy, both shaken by the fact of emancipation after the Civil War and given life in the journal of Gertrude Thomas; second, the potency of the notion of "social equality" during the era of segregation that emerges from Charles Manigault's autobiographical musings and the bloody work of Atlanta rioters in 1906. These cultural manifestations of racial hierarchy produced psychosexual consequences.

My fourth theme is sexuality, which led me straight to Freud. Writings by black southerners in the late nineteenth and early twentieth centuries focus far less obsessively on sexuality than do the works of their white contemporaries, because whites were less able than blacks to face up to the consequences of unsanctioned sexual desire. The telling difference has to do with secrecy, for a lot of white people were keeping secrets from themselves in ways black people simply could not. Because people of mixed race were classified as Negroes, African Americans lived with the literal consequences of patriarchy and racism. The children of rape or other forms of sex across the color line became black southerners' own children, parents, grandparents, uncles, and aunts. Harriet Jacobs, for instance, the North Carolinian author of *Incidents in the Life of a Slave Girl* (1861), hesitated before exposing her intimate history but ultimately took it into print. For the great majority of white people, however, interracial sex remained a strange kind of secret: a secret as big as the elephant in the living room. Facing up to that secret tormented Gertrude Thomas and, I suspect, Wilbur J. Cash. Considering the potency of secrets, I would not be surprised if twenty-first-century historians discovered that black women, having been the most obscured people in southern history, hold the keys to that history.

The six essays in this book date mainly from the late 1980s and early 1990s, written (with the exception of "Hosea Hudson") between

*Standing at Armageddon: The United States, 1877–1919* (1987) and *Sojourner Truth: A Life, a Symbol* (1996). They chronicle a transformation from relatively pure social history to a methodology more imbued with psychology and semiology. The most heavily political essay here is also the oldest. But even as I examined Hosea Hudson's life as a Negro Communist in Birmingham, Alabama, in the 1930s and 1940s, I investigated his psychology by looking at his youth: his family attachments, his fears, his quartet singing. I cannot draw lines of causality between the hardship of Hudson's childhood and his fractured relationship with his father. But I tried to convey his individuality, his working-class urban culture, and his personal triumphs and tragedies. Hudson became the sort of figure who is still largely invisible in southern history, an urban industrial worker. (I am still amazed at how rarely enslaved and segregated workers figure in American labor history.) His experience reveals much about the twentieth-century South, even as he remained a uniquely tough-minded radical until his death in 1988.

An early product of my move into interdisciplinarity, " 'Social Equality' and 'Rape' in the Fin-de-Siècle South" tries to do too much to succeed fully. If I were to take on its themes today, I would expect to write a book rather than a single essay, for the topic needs much more fleshing out. This essay touches on the material, symbolic, and psychological consequences of white supremacy, running through laws, customs, dreams, literature, and lynching with the aim of exposing both the material and symbolic components of segregation. I wanted to show that white supremacy is more than ideology — more personal, more intimate, more psychological. Segregation burrowed into the psyches of southerners of all races and affected their gut-level feelings about themselves. If historians overlook the importance of symbols and what this essay terms "pornographic" domination, we cannot understand or explain the tenacity of white supremacy in southern, or actually in all of American, life.

"The Journal of Ella Gertrude Clanton Thomas" came out of systematic study in 1988–89 at the Center for Advanced Study in the Behavioral Sciences in Palo Alto, a haven for psychologists. Colleagues there helped me find scholarship on intimate relationships and adultery, the keys to parsing hidden meanings within Thomas's 1,380-page journal. Once immersed in the literature of psychology, I never re-emerged. Three essays in this collection and *Sojourner Truth: A Life, a Symbol* (as well as my editions of the *Narrative of Sojourner Truth* and Harriet Jacobs's *Incidents in the Life of a Slave Girl*) attest to that immersion. At Stanford I also attended the excellent seminars of the Institute for Research on Women and Gender. There I found feminist collegiality — usually in short supply in the academic world and always appreciated — along with assistance in reading and thinking through the works of feminists from several disciplines.

"Three Southern Women and Freud" grew directly out of my work on Gertrude Thomas. While Thomas fascinated me, I sought an opportunity to round out her experiences and place them in historical context. As a more historical treatment of the themes of sexuality and gender in the antebellum Low Country of the Carolinas and Georgia, "Three Southern Women and Freud" complements the exclusively biographical character of the Gertrude Thomas piece.

One characteristic inherent in personal testimony is the blocking out of references to people painful to the author. In the hundreds of pages of Gertrude Thomas's journal, the woman whose existence caused her so much pain — her husband's other intimate partner — never once appears. I wanted to tell her side of the story using the testimony of another woman who had been in the invisible woman's situation, though not, of course, in her place. Harriet Jacobs cannot stand in for this invisible woman whom Thomas saw as a competitor, but Jacobs can at least begin to balance the scales historiographically. In "Three Southern Women and Freud" I deal with three characters: Lily establishes the widespread nature of Thomas's personal preoccupation with competition between women; Harriet Jacobs offers a view from the other side of the color line. And Freud? Freud examines through an ostensibly unraced lens the masculine phenomena that appear in all societies with a sexual double standard.

I doubt I would have written the essay on Wilbur J. Cash had Paul Escott not invited me to participate in Wake Forest University's celebration of the fiftieth anniversary of the publication of *The Mind of the South*. As a white southerner obsessed by sex and an amateur Freudian, Cash presented me with a likely subject. In the end, he fit in perfectly with my existing cast of characters. At the time, though, I annoyed some members of my audience. My paper especially piqued the reporter from the *Raleigh News and Observer*, who took me to task for insufficiently appreciating a great man and a fine book—and for powdering my nose before a televised interview.

My most popular essay, "Soul Murder and Slavery," opens this book. Appearing originally in hard-to-find places, "Soul Murder and Slavery" has consumed endless e-mails between me and readers wanting to secure a copy of an article that seeks to reckon the wider meanings of slavery. In this essay, I focus on the results of what historians usually gloss over: personal violence and its psychological sequelae. Pulling together social science scholarship on child abuse and other forms of torture, I figure up the accounts of damage on both sides of the color line. My attempt to bring psychology to bear on slavery may seem initially to go down a path scorched and burned by Stanley Elkins and his critics. I separate myself from Elkins by citing slaves' sources of strength, principally family and religion, and by bringing the families of owners into the picture as well. Elkins's denatured victims and unscathed tyrants do not appear in my piece.

Younger historians wondering about the rewards and perils of working across the color line sometimes ask me about my intellectual trajectory. Some years ago in Toronto a couple of my accomplished younger colleagues wondered how I dealt with not having received adequate recognition for my work. The question took me quite by surprise, and my honest answer came out as astonishment: With a chair in history and several books in print (*Southern History across the Color Line* and two edited books bring the total to seven), I felt, I said, quite nicely acknowledged. In fact, I did feel recognized; further, the image of so affirmed a figure's whining about a lack of recognition struck me as unseemly. Any Princeton professor who snivels about professional lack has lost all sense of proportion, considering the less conducive conditions of research, teaching, and remuneration offered to colleagues at other institutions. Such was my answer in Toronto. But questions regarding my career have not subsided.

Sometimes questioners mean to solicit basic how-to answers: When and where do you work? Answer: Regularly, and usually in my study at home, but sometimes in the wonderful Firestone Library. Sometimes, as in Toronto, the questioners see themselves in my career and wonder about their own careers: How does one keep writing when so much in American culture seems to say to people like me, "Shut up"? At this level of inquiry, questioners want me to transcend material considerations of rank and institution. To take those next steps, I adjusted my usual focal length and looked past the mentors, colleagues, editors, and agents who have so generously helped me along. I peered into the obscure field of American culture and confronted something else: my own feelings of hurt, anger, and recrimination.

Having been so blessed—so fortunate with regard to parents, opportunities, friends, husbands, professional advancement, and publication—I realized that any expression on my part of that same hurt, anger, and recrimination would run two big risks: I would appear not to appreciate my own enormous good fortune; and I would appear to underestimate the achievements of my peers who have overcome adversity. Better, I thought, considering the emotional dimension of an intellectual itinerary, to leave out my professional autobiography.

Pressed now again with the query, I will once again attempt a response, beginning with the admission that despite much success, I have experienced my work as struggle against the conventions of American education and scholarship. I feel I have wrestled for half a century with what I have been taught. For this black woman, at least (and I do not pretend to speak for any but myself) Western knowledge is not to be trusted. Everything in it needs careful inspection for insults and blind spots, which turn up all too often, diminishing the authority of prominent authorities in my eyes. Such a critical process means that education proceeds slowly and patchily. But I have kept at the struggle.

Therein lies the key to what kind readers see as my originality. I question (nearly) everything, and so many questions produce some good answers. Fresh, perceptive insight exhilarates me and my readers. At the same time, I have also met refusal and accusation: my work is not history, is not good enough, is wrong-headed, is just plain wrong. The hard part lies in separating needed criticism—for anyone's work, mine included, can in fact be not history, not good enough, wrong-headed, just plain wrong—from criticism in bad faith. How, in the formula of the late poet Audre Lorde, does one try to dismantle the master's house using the master's tools? Lorde decided that feminists, especially feminists of color, could not take down the master's house with the master's tools, and she may prove right in the end. But I can try to tell you a little of how I chipped away at the building with the tools I had at hand.

I spent some of my formative years outside the United States (in Ghana, France, and the West Indies), an escape I recommend to every black person in America. Unremitting existence in the situation of despised minority drives one crazy, and I marvel that any African American who has not lived in a majority black country can keep his or her sanity. (Actually, every nonblack American would also do well to live for some time in a black place.) Ghana allowed me to peer past race and see class and much else that was not-race that the American obsession with race had hidden from my view. Ghana led to *Exodusters*, in which poor southerners took the making of history into their own hands, and *The Narrative of Hosea Hudson*, in which a southern worker formed his own class analysis of the southern political economy. The power of the working-class and farming people at the center of those two books led me to the analysis in *Standing at Armageddon*, in which the impetus for positive reform comes from below.

*Exodusters* had encouraged me to write southern history across the color line, for my research revealed a South more racially complex than any that appeared in the then-current historiography. In the mid-1980s, my southern social history research took me to the Duke University archives, where I found the journal of the Georgia plantation mistress Gertrude Thomas. This long, rich document begged for a psychological analysis I did not then know how to undertake. Much of my later work grew out of questions in Gertrude Thomas's journals.

The southerners herein led me to themes that preoccupied me throughout the late 1990s and that appear in *Sojourner Truth: A Life, a Symbol* and the books now in my pipeline. With the Truth biography, I wanted to explore history and memory — in this case, the relationship between historical existence and legend, both "the life" and "the symbol." Writing about Truth, who did not herself write, brought me to the analysis of photographs. Not only did I dedicate a whole chapter of *Sojourner Truth* to her photographic portraits, but I remain situated in visual analysis as a facet of the study of history and memory. In the late 1990s, for example, I wrote an essay on the figures of Honest Abe and Uncle Tom in Civil War memory.[8] My current work in progress concerns the visual expression of African American history and a discussion of personal beauty. I am also writing a history of white people, partly as a means of repossessing Western knowledge, partly to embed in the new field of whiteness studies the views of African Americans, the world's experts on white people as a race.

Ending this autobiographical excursion recalls the pleasure I have always taken from research and writing. I entered the historical profession because I liked the work. I still like the work. Despite my love of the field, I am ready for a new vocation. After I finish my book on beauty, I am going to art school. Scholarship will give way to artistic creation.

Berlin, April 2001

# I

## *Soul Murder & Slavery*

### TOWARD A FULLY LOADED

### COST ACCOUNTING

• • •

We all know on a certain, almost intuitive level that violence is insepar-
able from slavery. Historians rarely trace the descent of that conjunction, although several of them answered a journalist's questions about
high homicide rates in the late twentieth-century South. In a 1998
article in the *New York Times*, Fox Butterfield addressed the South's
permanently high murder rate. Butterfield notes the existence of sharp
differences in homicide across the regions of the United States. The
states of the former Confederacy all figured in the top twenty states for
murder, with the highest rate in Louisiana: 17.5 murders per 100,000
people. Overall, the southern murder rate nearly doubles that of the
Northeast.[1]

Butterfield advanced several explanations, based on the views of
nineteenth-century observers such as Alexis de Tocqueville and Frederick Law Olmsted, who blamed the prevalence of guns and a frontier
mentality. Historians pointed to the Scotch-Irish culture of many
southerners, which disposed them toward whisky drinking and family
feuding, a system of "primal honor," and a touchiness that slavery reinforced. None indicted the long-standing ideals of obedience and submission, the values of slavery, and the acceptance of violence as a means
of enforcement.

In this essay I accept the unhappy task of probing slavery's legacy of
violence. My aim is to examine the implications of soul murder (a
phrase to which I will return momentarily) and use them to ques-

tion the entireness of historians' descriptions of American society during the era of slavery. My hope is that a more complete accounting — what bookkeepers would term a "fully loaded cost accounting" — of slavery's costs, most notably the tragic overhead costs that were reckoned in the currency of physical abuse and family violence, will yield a fuller comprehension of our national experience. With the broad geography of American slavery in mind, I take as my theme "Soul Murder and Slavery."

This work is interdisciplinary, drawing on the history of American slavery, feminist scholarship on women, the family, and the workplace, and on the thought of sociologists and psychologists regarding children. My questions have their roots in second-wave feminism of the 1960s, which influenced the rewriting of history generally. By focusing attention on women's lives, feminist scholarship has made women visible rather than taken for granted and queried the means by which societies forge gender out of the physical apparatus of sex. While some feminist thinkers have analyzed women's writing and gender, recently other intellectuals and activists have turned a spotlight on a protected, potent social institution: the family. Even though families, as the site of identity formation, shape the elaboration of politics, and even though public policy profoundly influences families, family dynamics have generally been treated as private and separate from the public realm and have not traditionally figured prominently in the writing of history.

Historiographical blindness toward families still persists, even though the source material is abundant. Turning new eyes on evidence that has been at hand forever, feminist historians are able to hear subaltern voices and recognize phenomena that had not previously been investigated seriously.[2] What were long termed "discipline" and "seduction" of the young and powerless, who were described as feckless and oversexed, we can now call by their own names: child abuse, sexual abuse, sexual harassment, rape, battering. Psychologists aggregate the effects of these all-too-familiar practices in the phrase *soul murder*, which may be summed up as depression, lowered self-esteem, and anger.

Soul murder has a long genealogy, going back to folk beliefs in Europe and Africa about the possibility of stealing or killing another person's soul. Soul murder appeared in connection with the 1828 story of Kaspar Hauser, who, having spent his childhood imprisoned alone in a dark cellar, emerged as an emotionally crippled young adult unable to talk or walk. Before emerging into the light, Hauser had glimpsed only one other person, his jailer, to whom he wished to return. Within psychoanalytic literature, the classic, anguished phrasing of soul murder as the violation of one's inner being, the extinguishing of one's identity, including sexual identity, comes initially from Anselm von Feuerbach's 1832 account of Hauser and from Daniel Paul Schreber's 1903 *Memoirs of My Nervous Illness*, inspired by Feuerbach and commented on, in turn, by Sigmund Freud and Jacques Lacan. Schreber's memoir made him the world's most famous paranoid.[3]

More recently, soul murder appears in the title of a book by a professor of psychiatry at the New York University School of Medicine, Leonard Shengold (*Soul Murder: The Effects of Child Abuse and Deprivation*). The "abuse" in the subtitle can be violent and/or sexual, which presents children with too much sensation to bear. "Deprivation," as in the case of Kaspar Hauser, refers to neglect that deprives children of enough attention to meet their psychic needs.

Sexual abuse, emotional deprivation, and physical and mental torture can lead to soul murder, and soul-murdered children's identity is compromised; they cannot register what it is that they want and what it is that they feel. Like Kaspar Hauser, they often identify with the person who has abused them, and they may express anger toward themselves and others. Abused persons are more at risk for the development of an array of psychological problems that include depression, anxiety, self-mutilation, suicide attempts, sexual problems, and drug and alcohol abuse.[4] Victims of soul murder do not inevitably turn into abusers — there is no direct or predictable line of cause and effect — but people who have been abused or deprived as children grow up at risk psychologically.

We surely cannot translate twentieth-century psychology directly into the mentalities of eighteenth- and nineteenth-century societies, because many aspects of life that we regard as psychological were, in earlier times, connected to religion. Spirituality then, as now, varied considerably from person to person and from group to group; with the passage of time, religious sensibilities were subject to fundamental alterations. American religion generally changed in the aftermath of the Great Awakening of the early eighteenth century and the Second Great Awakening of the early nineteenth century. The various evangelicals, especially Methodists and Baptists, deeply influenced what we would call the psychology of Americans, as well as the terms in which they envisioned and communicated with their gods.

Despite differences of mentality wrought by greater or lesser religiosity, psychology — when used carefully, perhaps gingerly — provides a valuable means of understanding people and families who cannot be brought to the analyst's couch. Ideally historians could enter a kind of science fiction virtual reality in which we could hold intelligent conversations with the dead, then remand them to their various hells, purgatories, and heavens and return to our computers. Lacking this facility, we can only read twentieth-century practitioners and enter the archives with our eyes wide open.

Even without the benefit of an esoteric knowledge of psychology, we readily acknowledge the existence of certain conventions associated with slavery: the use of physical violence to make slaves obedient and submissive, the unquestioned right of owners to use the people they owned in whatever ways they wished. But we may need to be reminded that these habits also translate into a set of ideals that were associated with white women in middle- and upper-class families and into another set of ideals identified with evangelical religion. Submission and obedience, the core values of slavery, were also the key words of patriarchy and piety.

Because the standard of slavery calibrated values in other core institutions, slavery deserves recognition as one of the fundamental influences on American family mores and, by extension, on American society as a whole. Religion, democracy, the frontier, patriarchy, and mobility are all recognized as having played their part in the making of American families and American history. Slavery also counted, and not merely for Americans who experienced it as captive, unpaid laborers.

No matter how much American convention exempts whites from paying any costs for the enslavement of blacks, the implications of slavery did not stop at the color line; rather, slavery's theory and praxis permeated the whole of slave-holding society. Without seeking to establish one-to-one relationships or direct lines of causality, I will pose questions and suggest answers that may foster more comprehensive and feminist thinking about American history. Ironically, perhaps, names that have only recently been coined help reinterpret the past.

The fields of study focusing on child abuse, sexual harassment, and sexual abuse were born in the 1960s and 1970s. In the last quarter century or so these fields have grown and supplied therapists, medical doctors, recovering victims, lawyers, and feminists, some of whom were looking for the roots of women's impaired self-esteem, others of whom were seeking to right the wrongs that women have suffered in patriarchal families and in the workplace. I suppose the appearance of professionals who profit from suits over child abuse, sexual abuse, and sexual harassment is inevitable in a capitalist society. Nonetheless, the profit-making aspect of the phenomenon of recall has provoked a good deal of commentary about suppressed memory and false memory. The debate now centers mainly on women who can afford therapists and lawyers and whose family mores and career chances have encouraged the suppression rather than the reporting of unacceptable memories. Much commentary on child sexual abuse — currently the most discussed form of violence against the young — involves what the skeptical philosopher, Ian Hacking, terms "memoro-politics." His and psychologist Carol Tavris's doubts are institutionalized in the False Memory Syndrome Foundation, founded in Philadelphia in 1992.[5] With all its visibility, the controversy over false memory obscures the subjectivity of enslaved people, whose victimization is well documented and uncontested.

American habits of thought — what Marxist philosopher and critic Louis Althusser and Pierre Macherey call "ideology" — have rendered the experience of slaves utterly invisible in the literature of child abuse. No one at all disputes the fact that these children and women endured hurts that they did not forget, yet these victims do not currently figure in the consideration of the effects of child abuse and sexual harassment. An example is to be found in the widely acclaimed work of Judith Herman, one of the premier analysts of sexual abuse. Herman includes a chapter entitled "Captivity" in her second book, *Trauma and Recovery*. Here the captivity in question is figurative rather than literal. She does not acknowledge the history of the literal captivity of millions of American slaves over several generations.[6]

For most scholars of child abuse and sexual abuse, slavery possesses neither a literal meaning nor consequences; it serves only as a potent, negative metaphor. As a historian familiar with the institution that existed throughout most of American territory into the early nineteenth century, I *do* want to think literally: I want to investigate the consequences of child abuse and sexual abuse on an entire society in which the beating and raping of enslaved people was neither secret nor metaphorical.

The first step is to think about slaves as people with all the psychological characteristics of human beings, with childhoods and adult identities formed during youthful interaction with others. As ordinary as is the assumption that white people evolve psychologically from childhood to adulthood, to speak of black people in psychological terms can be problematical. This history has a history. Much of scholars' and readers' reluctance to deal with black people's psychology goes back to the 1960s debate over Stanley Elkins's *Slavery: A Problem in American Institutional and Intellectual Life* (Chicago: University of Chicago Press, 1959), which provoked extensive criticism and revision.

Acknowledging the "spiritual agony" inherent in American slavery, Elkins compared slavery in the American South with Nazi concentration camps, in which, he thought, an all-encompassing system of repression infantilized people who had been psychologically healthy. Elkins wrote that on southern plantations and in Nazi concentration camps, inmates "*internalized*" their masters' attitudes. Drawing a flawed analogy between concentration camps, which existed for a few years, and slavery, which persisted over many generations and was psychologically more porous, Elkins argued that the closed system of slavery produced psychologically crippled adults who were docile, irresponsible, loyal, lazy, humble, and deceitful, in short, who were Sambos. With regard to both slavery and concentration camps, Elkins's methodology was more psychological than archival, and he also overlooked resistance in both contexts. In the American South, Elkins ignored the significance of slave families and communities and the long tradition of resistance and revolt, as chronicled in Herbert Aptheker's *American Negro Slave Revolts* (New York: International Publishers, 1943).[7]

The scholarship appearing in the 1970s and 1980s provided a more complete view of slaves and slave families than Elkins had presented in the broken-up character of Sambo. Yet since the thunder and lightning of the Elkins controversy — even after the appearance of extensive revisionist writing—scholars and lay people have avoided, sometimes positively resisted, the whole calculation of slavery's psychological costs. The Sambo problem was solved through the pretense that black people do not have psyches.

Prevailing wisdom says that strong black people functioned as members of a group, "the black community," as though black people shared a collective psyche whose only perception was racial, as if race obviated the need to discuss black people's subjective development. Within this version of the black community, the institution of "the black family" appears as preternaturally immune to the brutality inherent in slavery. Black patriarchy with a human face appears in much of this post-Elkins writing, particularly in the case of the well-intentioned work of Herbert Gutman, which refuted a 1965 report by Daniel Patrick Moynihan that blamed poverty and criminality on black families.[8] In family groups or as individuals, slaves emerged from historians' pages in the pose of lofty transcendence over racist adversity. Any analysis hinting that black people suffered psychological trauma as a result of the vicious physical and emotional practices that slavery entailed seemed tantamount to recapitulating Elkins and admitting the defeat of the race at the hands of bigots.

Rejecting that reasoning is imperative, because denying slaves psychological personhood impoverishes the study of everyone in slaveholding society. Historians already realize that including enslaved workers as part of the American working classes recasts the labor history of the United States; similarly, envisioning slaves as people who developed psychologically sheds new light on the culture of violence in which they matured.

Societies whose economic basis rested on slave production were built on violence, and the calculus of slavery configured society as a whole, as nineteenth-century analysts realized. When proslavery apologists spoke of owners and slaves as belonging to the same family, they were acknowledging the relationship between modes of production, politics, family, and society that three other nineteenth-century commentators, Karl Marx, Frederick Engels, and Alexis de Tocqueville, also perceived. From very different vantage points and with quite different emphases, Tocqueville in *Democracy in America* and Marx and Engels in *The German Ideology* recognized the influence of the political economy on civil society. For Marx and Engels, "the production of ideas, of conceptions, of consciousness, is at first directly interwoven with the material activity and the material intercourse of men," which they totaled up as "the language of real life." Material existence, they said, shapes the relationships between husbands and wives and between parents and children that we term *"family"* and that they underlined in the original.[9]

Peering through the lens of political economy, Marx and Engels spoke in the interest of workers, but Tocqueville, who was more comfortable with people of his own privileged class, unabashedly admired the democracy of the United States. Moving among Americans who had flourished since the American Revolution, Tocqueville in his appraisal of the consequences of American institutions was generally positive. He credited American political arrangements with the creation of more democratic relationships within American families, but he also traced democracy's limits. Where there was slavery, he noted, democracy could not do its salutary work. Slavery was "so cruel to the slave," but it was "fatal to the master," for it attacked American society through opinions, character, and style and devalued the ideals that undergird democratic society.[10]

Marx and Engels may have overestimated the ramifications of the dominant mode of production, and Tocqueville may have held too sanguine a view of the consequences of political democracy within the household, but all three remind us that political and economic life shapes families and households. This point has been rephrased by more recent authorities. Twentieth-century commentators like Louis Althusser modify Marx and Engels's analysis of relations between the economic base and the social superstructure but nonetheless relate the institutions of civil society, including the family, to the political economy. Psychoanalyst Jacques Lacan indicates the crucial role of the family — the role of the father, in particular — in reproducing on a subjective level the power relations of the political economy.[11] When the household was also a work site, the influence of labor relations within families would have been magnified.

### Child Abuse and Slavery

Slave owners, slaves, jurists, abolitionists, and historians all have recognized personal violence as a component of the regulation of owned labor; as Charles Pettigrew, a slaveholder, wrote to his son: "It is a pity that . . . Slavery and Tyranny must go together and that there is no such thing as having an obedient and useful Slave, without the painful exercise of undue and tyrannical authority." Tyrannical authority there was in abundance, and slave children's parents, even when they were present, could not save their babies. It was as though a slave mother's children were not her own, a former slave recalled: "Many a day my old mamma has stood by an' watched massa beat her chillun 'till dey bled an' she couldn' open her mouf."[12]

From an entirely different vantage point, southern judiciaries acknowledged that owners needed and should lawfully exercise total power over their slaves. The central legal tenet of slavery was summed up by a southern judge: "The power of the master must be absolute, to render the submission of the slave perfect." Kenneth Stampp entitled the fourth chapter of *The Peculiar Institution*, "To Make Them Stand in Fear."[13]

On the personal level, the evidence of this kind of discipline is heartbreaking, whether between master and slave, slave parent and child, or across the generations. When he was a child, fugitive slave narrator William Wells Brown witnessed the harrowing scene of his mother being flogged for going late into the fields. Years later Brown recalled that "the cold chills ran over me, and I wept aloud." Sojourner Truth, who was beaten as a slave in New York's Hudson Valley in the early nineteenth century, beat her own children — to make them obedient and to stop their hungry cries when her work prevented her from feeding them.[14]

One of the most vivid testimonies of the intergenerational effect of child beating in slavery appears in oral testimony gathered one hundred years after the abolition of slavery. In Theodore Rosengarten's *All God's Dangers*, an old black Alabamian, Ned Cobb (alias Nate Shaw), laments that his father, Hayes, who had been a slave for his first fifteen years, beat his children and his wives as he himself had been beaten.[15] Cobb testifies to two kinds of hurt, for in addition to himself having been flogged, he was haunted by his father's brutal attacks on his mother and stepmother.

Masters beat slave children to make them into good slaves. Slave parents beat children to make them regard obedience as an automatic component of their personal makeup that was necessary for survival in a cruel world, a world in which they were to be first and always submissive. In other words, slave parents beat slave children to make them into good slaves. The underlying motives of parents and owners did not overlap, but in practice, their aim coincided.

Parents and owners taught slave children to quash their anger when they were beaten, for anger was a forbidden emotion for slaves to display before owners. A Virginia owner summed up the prevailing wisdom among his peers in these phrases: "They Must obey at all times, and under all circumstances, cheerfully and with alacrity." Suppression of this kind of anger is one of the characteristics of what psychologist Alice Miller terms the "poisonous pedagogy" of child abuse, and it has certain fairly predictable effects on its victims: feelings of degradation and humiliation, impaired identity formation, suppression of vitality and creativity, deadening of feeling of self, anger, hatred, and self-hatred on the individual level and violence on the social level.[16]

Slave children, particularly those whose mothers worked in the fields, were also very likely to suffer physical and emotional neglect, because their mothers were allowed only a minimum of time off the job with their children. Child care by people other than mothers could be adequate, as in the case of the young Frederick Douglass, who began his life in the custody of his maternal grandmother. But in other situations, the caretakers of children might be too old, too young, or too infirm to provide adequate supervision. Ex-slave narratives illustrate child-rearing patterns that forced hardworking parents to neglect their children and that, as a consequence, often denied babies the opportunity to attach to a parent or parental figure securely.[17]

The slave trade, which disrupted an estimated one-third of all slave families in the antebellum South, weighed heavily on children and young adults under thirty, when they were most likely to be the parents of young children. Such trauma took a devastating emotional toll, as antislavery writing and iconography illustrate.[18] As a young child in New York State, Sojourner Truth lived with her own parents, but they were chronically depressed as a result of having sacrificed their children to the market, one after the other. Such forfeiture would have been tantamount to having one's child die, and Truth's grieving parents lost ten children to this callous trade.

In slave societies, neglect was routine, abuse was rampant, and anger was to be suppressed. The question regarding the neglect and physical abuse of slave children is not whether they took place—everyone agreed that they did—but rather, what they meant to the children and adults who experienced them. Did the whipping that was so central a part of child rearing and the enforcement of discipline among slaves affect them and their families as child abuse traumatized twentieth-century victims?

There is evidence that the child abuse of slavery imposed enormous costs. The relationship between abuse and repercussion is not simple or predetermined, but the damage is frequent enough to be recognizable. For countless women and children, these injuries were magnified by the intimate nature of the abuse.

### Sexual Abuse and Sexual Harassment

Like child beating in slavery, the sexual torment of slave women and children has been evident for more than a century. Some of this mistreatment occurred in situations that we now recognize as sexual harassment on the job, and some occurred within households—which were work sites for hundreds of thousands of slave women—and with overtones of incest. One well-known figure exemplifies both patterns.

While many ex-slave narratives mention master-slave sexuality, the most extended commentary on the sexual harassment of slave women comes from Harriet Jacobs, who was a slave in Edenton, North Carolina. Writing under the pseudonym Linda Brent, Jacobs published a narrative in 1861, entitled *Incidents in the Life of a Slave Girl*. Jacobs's character, Linda, becomes the literal embodiment of the slave as sexual quarry in the testimony of slaves. We know from the work of critic Jean Yellin that *Incidents in the Life of a Slave Girl* is autobiography, and that Jacobs's master harassed her sexually from the time she was thirteen. Her narrative is a story of pursuit, evasion, and, ultimately, escape, although in order to evade her owner Jacobs had to spend seven years closed up in her grandmother's tiny attic crawl space, unable to stand up straight, sweltering in the summer, cold in the winter. As portrayed in *Incidents in the Life of a Slave Girl*, much of Jacobs's life in North Carolina revolved around avoiding her master's advances.

Jacobs says that without her master's having succeeded in raping her, he inflicted injuries that young female slaves frequently suffered and that we would consider psychological. As she became nubile, she says, her master began to whisper "foul words in my ear," which robbed her of her innocence and purity, a phenomenon that psychologists call inappropriate sexualization, which encourages a child to interpret her own value primarily in sexual terms. Describing the effect of her master's "foul words" and the angry and jealous outbreaks from her mistress, Jacobs says she became, like any slave girl in her position, "prematurely knowing in evil things," including life in a household cum work site that was suffused with predation, infidelity, and rage.[19]

Jacobs commits an entire, highly charged chapter of *Incidents in the Life of a Slave Girl* to "The Jealous Mistress." The angry figure of the jealous mistress, frequently ridiculed, never seriously investigated, is so common in the literature of slavery as to have become a southern trope. Perhaps because I have my own jealous mistress, so to speak, I am certain that the figure deserves a longer, much longer look. My jealous mistress is Gertrude Thomas, of Augusta, Georgia, who kept a journal from the time she was fourteen years old in 1848 until 1889, when she was fifty-five.

Although she was a jealous mistress, Gertrude Thomas may also be understood as a victim of adultery. According to the ostensible mores of her community, she stood near the pinnacle of society (as a woman, she was denied space at the very top). She was a plantation mistress in a society dominated by the minuscule proportion of white families that qualified as planters by owning twenty or more slaves; she was an educated woman at a time when only elite men could take higher education for granted; and she was white in a profoundly racist culture. Yet neither Gertrude Thomas's economic or educational advantages nor her social status protected her from what she saw as sexual competition from inferior women. She knew, as Mary Chesnut and her friends knew, that they were supposed to pretend not to see "what is as plain before their eyes as the sunlight."[20] The deception did not ease the discomfort, for Thomas knew and wrote that white men saw women — whether slave or free, wealthy or impoverished, cultured or untutored, black or white — as interchangeable. She and other plantation mistresses failed to elevate themselves sufficiently as women to avoid the pain of sharing their husbands with their slaves.

Preoccupied by the issue of competition between women, Thomas realized and recorded with tortuous indirection a central fact of her emotional life: that female slaves and female slaveholders were in the same sexual marketplace and that in this competition, free women circulated at a discount due to the ready availability of women who could be forced to obey. The existence in the same market for sex of women who were literally property lowered the value of Gertrude Thomas and her mother as sexual partners. The concept of women as property has long been evident to feminists as a powerful means of keeping women subjected.

*The traffic in women*, a phrase coined by the early twentieth-century American anarchist, Emma Goldman, is shorthand for cultural practices that anthropologists (such as Claude Lévi-Strauss) and psychoanalysts (such as Jacques Lacan) have seen as basic to human nature but that feminists have identified with patriarchy and considered devastating to women. The phrase reappears in a classic 1975 essay by feminist anthropologist Gayle Rubin, who analyzes the sex/gender system of several different cultures.[21]

Although Rubin uses the concept of the traffic in women allegorically when she turns to American society, the notion of such a traffic is useful both literally and metaphorically with regard to American society during its nearly three centuries of slavery. Over the course of those ten or more generations, rich white women saw themselves in competition for the attention of husbands whose black partners were ideal women: Slave women had to be present when summoned and were conceded no will of their own. Gertrude Thomas knew moments of despair over her husband's infidelities, but if she contemplated suicide, she censored the thought. Testimony from Kentucky captures marital strife more vividly.

Andrew Jackson, an ex-slave narrator (not the president of the United States), had belonged to a fiery preacher he called a "right down blower." Though the owner's preaching moved his congregation to tears, at home he and his wife quarreled bitterly over his attraction to their enslaved cook, Hannah. Jackson recalled hearing the wife accuse the preacher of having gone into the kitchen expressly to be with Hannah, which the preacher denied. "I know you have, you brute," Jackson quotes the wife crying, "I have a great mind to cut my own throat!" To this, Jackson says, the preacher replied, "I really wish you would." The wife understood his meaning: "Yes I presume you do, so that you could run to the kitchen, as much as you please, to see Hannah." Andrew Jackson concluded that slaveholders "had such bad hearts toward one another" because they treated their slaves so brutally.[22]

At the same time that jealous mistresses were angry over their husbands' adulterous conduct, slave women like Harriet Jacobs who were the husbands' prey realized fully that mistresses saw themselves (not the slaves) as the victims in such triangles. Slave women resented what they envisioned as their mistresses' narcissistic self-pity, and they returned their mistresses' anger in kind. Jacobs's outrage at her mistress is part of a larger phenomenon, for other ex-slave narrators, like Sojourner Truth, and historians, like Kenneth Stampp, Elizabeth Fox-Genovese, and Eugene Genovese, corroborate the existence of a good deal of resentment at jealous mistresses on the part of slave women. Slave women's anger has etched yet more deeply the unsympathetic portrait of women who held slaves. Today we can see that more was at stake than contention over the ultimate title of victim.

What slaves could seldom acknowledge and historians have not seen is that attachment often lay at the core of slave women's resentment. With slave families constantly subject to disruption, mistresses often functioned as mothers — good or bad — to their young female slaves. In this sense, the bitterness that Linda Brent felt as the prey of her master emerged against her mistress, just as victims of incest often hate their mothers for not saving them from the sexual advances of fathers and stepfathers. Psychiatrist Judith Herman says that many sexually abused children feel deeply betrayed because their mothers or mother figures are not able to protect them. Victims who do not display anger at their abusers may displace their rage on to nonabusing but impotent parental figures: mothers.[23] The psychological dynamics of the heterogeneous households of slavery explicate attitudes and behaviors that cannot be explained if we deny to slaves the personhood that we grant to our own contemporaries.

It has been difficult for historians to view interracial households as families and slaves as workers and as people, but such understanding places the sexual abuse of slave women and children (including boys) within categories that are now familiar and that we now term sexual harassment. One of the founders of the field, Catharine A. MacKinnon, noted in the 1970s that poorer women seem more likely to suffer physical harassment than middle-class and career women, whose abuse is more often verbal.[24] This should alert us to the triple vulnerability of slave women; they were among the poorest of working women and members of a race considered inherently inferior, and, if they were domestic servants like Harriet Jacobs, they spent long hours in the company of the men who had power over them.

Psychologists say that children and young women who are sexually abused, like children who are beaten, tend to blame themselves for their victimization and consequently have very poor self-esteem. They may also see their sexuality as their only means of binding other people to them as friends or allies. Recent scholarship outlines a series of long-term psychological repercussions of sexual abuse and incest: depression, difficulty sleeping, feelings of isolation, poor self-esteem, difficulty relating to other people, contempt for all women including oneself, revictimization, and impaired sexuality that may manifest itself in behaviors that can appear as frigidity or promiscuity.[25] I doubt that slaves possessed an immunity that victims lack today.

It is tempting to see all slaves as strong people who recognized the injustice of their treatment and were therefore able to transcend the savagery to which they were subjected from very early ages. However, ex-slave narratives also bear witness to much psychological hurt. What today's psychologists call anger, depression, and problems of self-esteem come through ex-slave narratives and attest to slaves' difficulty in securing unqualified trust. Theologian Benjamin Mays discerned the theme of personal isolation that pervaded black slave religion and that spiritual songs expressed so movingly. Their titles are embedded in American memory: "Sometimes I Feel Like a Motherless Child," "Nobody Knows the Trouble I've Seen," "I'm a Long Way from Home."[26]

We are used to hearing such sentiments as poignant artistry, but they are also testimonies of desolation. Slaves' situation within a system built on violence, disfranchisement, and white supremacy was analogous to that of twentieth-century victims of abuse, and some slaves, like people today, responded with self-hatred, anger, and identification with the aggressor. As understandable as such responses would have been, they are not all there is to the story.

Were this analysis to stop here, it might seem to invite a rerun of the controversy over Stanley Elkins's *Slavery*, for I might seem to be saying, like Elkins, that slavery inflicted psychic wounds so severe that slaves were massively disabled psychologically. This is *not* a recapitulation of Stanley Elkins, because my arguments exceed Elkins's in two important ways: I insist, first, that slaves had two crucial means of support that helped them resist being damaged permanently by the assaults of their owners and their fellows; and second, that owners also inflicted the psychic damage of slavery upon themselves, their white families, and, ultimately, on their whole society.

## Enslaved People's Means of Survival

Since the 1959 publication of Elkins's *Slavery*, historians such as John Hope Franklin and Earl E. Thorpe have presented evidence of the ways in which slaves seized the initiative and found "elbow-room" within a system that was meant to dehumanize them.[27] Once historians began to seek it, confirmation of slaves' resistance and survival appeared in abundance. The testimony comes from slaves and from owners, and it affirms that most slave women and men were able to survive slavery in a human and humane manner, particularly if they lived where they were surrounded by people who were actual or fictive kin. Historians have concentrated their attention on the half or so of slaves in the antebellum South who lived on plantations with twenty or more bondspeople, the people more likely to belong to a community of slaves. Plantation slaves did not, however, represent the totality of Americans who were enslaved. So far, unfortunately, the other half of southern slaves and virtually all northern slaves, who were surrounded by mostly white people, have received little scrutiny.[28] Slaves living in isolation would hardly have benefited from the psychological support that a slave community could provide.

John Blassingame sees slave families as a source of psychic protection from slavery's onslaught and considers families "an important survival mechanism." (Had he been critiquing Elkins's whole argument, Blassingame might have extended this insight to concentration camps, where actual and fictive kin and comrades helped inmates resist their dehumanization.) Deborah White, writing as a feminist, is more explicit, and she explores slave women's own community in far more detail. White entitles one chapter of her book on plantation slave women "The Female Slave Network," in which she shows how slave women working together created their own internal rank ordering. Although their owners and other whites might dishonor and mistreat them, slave women forged "their own independent definition of womanhood" through their own web of women's relationships, which functioned as an antidote to slavery's degradation.[29]

White and Blassingame are supported by psychologists such as Gail Wyatt and M. Ray Mickey, who explain that the existence of a countervailing value system helps people who are abused resist internalizing their oppressors' devaluation of their worth.[30] Ex-slave narratives from the nineteenth and twentieth centuries make it clear that slaves rejected their masters' assumptions that slaves were constitutionally inferior as a people and that they deserved to be enslaved.

Historians like Deborah Gray White and John Blassingame have shown that plantation slaves' psychic health depended largely on another essential emotional counterweight to owners' physical and psychological assaults besides the slaves' own families. That second bulwark consisted of a system of evangelical religious beliefs that repudiated the masters' religious and social ideology of white supremacy and black inferiority. Slave religion also buttressed a countervailing belief system by promising that equity would ultimately prevail in God's world.

During and after slavery, religion was an important means through which powerless people preserved their identity. Scholars such as Albert Raboteau, Gayraud S. Wilmore, and James Cone have shown how black people forged their own evangelical religion, which could be apocalyptic and reassuring. Wilmore, especially, indicates that a belief in the impending apocalypse, a perennial theme in American evangelicalism, served the particular needs of the black poor by promising that there would soon come a time when God would judge all people, that he would punish the wicked, who were the slaveholders, and reward the good, who were the slaves. Cone stresses slaves' identification with the crucifixion, which symbolizes Jesus' concern for the oppressed and his repudiation of the hierarchies of this world.[31]

Psychologists have noted that in situations where the individual is totally powerless, faith in a greater power than the self becomes a potent means of survival. Slaves with a firm religious belief were able to benefit from this nonmaterial source of support, which we recognize today in the methodology of twelve-step programs for overcoming addiction that begin by putting one's fate in the hands of a greater power than the self.[32]

In their appeal to countervailing ideologies, supportive communities, and spirituality, slaves were, in a sense, behaving like good feminists seeking means of lessening the power of oppression and sexual abuse in their lives. Having been identified and set apart as a despised race, slaves found it easier to create alternative ideologies than the white people—including women—who owned them and who told them what to do. There is no denying that white ladies were able to oppress slaves, but even so, the ladies lacked access to much of their society's other kinds of power. Of all the people living in slave-holding societies who might have benefited from an alternative system of values, rich white women were least likely to forge one. In the words of Catherine Clinton, plantation mistresses, unlike plantation slaves, "had no comparable sense of community."[33]

### Damage across the Color Line

Owning as well as owned families paid a high psychological and physical cost for the child and sexual abuse that was so integral with slavery. First, despite what black and white scholars assume about the rigidity of the color bar, attachment and loss often transcended the barriers of race and class and flowed in both directions. The abuse of slaves pained and damaged nonslaves, particularly children, and forced those witnessing slave abuse to identify with the victim or the perpetrator.

Second, the values and practices of slavery, in particular the use of violence to secure obedience and deference, prevailed within white families as well. The ideals of slavery—obedience and submission—were concurrently and not accidentally the prototypes of white womanhood and of evangelical piety, which intensified the prestige and reinforced the attraction of these ideals. Caroline Howard Gilman, for instance, wrote in the antebellum era as both a "New England bride" and a "southern matron." She recommended that the former "[r]everence" her husband's wishes; to the latter she advised not only "submission," but also silence when self-defense was called for. The southern matron may know the rightness of her position or suffer painful illness, but she must always smile, smile no matter what the circumstances.[34]

Nineteenth-century evangelical religion meant various things to its many believers. It could compel them toward startlingly different ideological conclusions, as exemplified in the North in the Jacksonian era. After the abolition of slavery in the North, evangelicalism fostered a profusion of convictions, including abolitionism and feminism; in the region still committed to slavery, however, evangelicalism produced no reforming offshoots that were allowed to flourish. Instead, unquestioning evangelical piety was more valued, and piety was another word for submission and obedience, terms that also figured prominently in the language of the family.

The imageries of religion and family have much in common, rhetorically and structurally, and scholars have repeatedly stressed the crucial role of human families as structural models both in religion and in slavery. Christians speak of God the Father, the Son, and the Holy Ghost, and Christians, Jews, and Muslims trace the origin of humankind to the family of Adam and Eve. Religions routinely evoke the language of kinship when sketching out holy relationships between gods and people.

Slavery and the family are just as inextricably intertwined, for the etymology of the word *family* reaches back to the Latin words *familia*, meaning a household, and *famulus/famula*, meaning servant or slave, deeply embedding the notion of servitude within our concept of family. As the ideals and practices of servitude, family, and religion are so firmly linked in this cultural system, a search for cause and effect is bound to prove frustrating. Even without recourse to relations of causality, however, the confluence of values is noteworthy.[35]

Slavery accentuated the hierarchical rather than the egalitarian and democratic strains in American culture, thereby shaping relations within and without families and polities. Patriarchal families, slavery, and evangelical religion further reinforced one another's emphasis on submission and obedience in civil society, particularly concerning people in subaltern positions.

Despite the existence of a wide spectrum of opinion on slavery and feminism, agreement exists on the close relationship between the concepts of the white woman and slavery. Proslavery apologists often insisted that the maintenance of slavery depended on the preservation of patriarchy within white families, arguing that white women, especially rich women, must remain in their places and be submissive to their fathers and husbands so that slaves would not conceive notions of equality. Similar motives prohibited white men from acknowledging publicly that white women commonly labored in southern fields at tasks that the culture reserved rhetorically for women who were enslaved.[36] The reasoning of proslavery apologia ran from women's honor to gender roles to black men–white women sex, skipping over the reality of white men's sexual use and abuse of black women in a manner that I find remarkable: for its silences, its intertextuality, and its unabashed patriarchy. Of course, there is nothing at all contradictory between family feeling and hierarchy, between attachment and the conviction that some people absolutely must obey others.

Hierarchy by no means precludes attachment. Just as young slaves attached to the adults closest to them, white as well as black, so the white children and adults in slave-owning households became psychologically entangled with the slaves they came to know well. When Peter, Sojourner Truth's son, was beaten by his owner in Alabama, his mistress (who was Sojourner's mistress's cousin) salved his wounds and cried over his injuries. That story concluded with Peter's mistress's murder by the very same man, her husband, who had previously abused Peter. Like Peter's murdered mistress, other slave owners, especially women, grieved at the sight of slaves who had been beaten.[37]

Abolitionist Angelina Grimké recalled scenes from her life as a privileged young woman in Charleston, South Carolina. When Grimké was about thirteen and attending a seminary for wealthy girls, a slave boy who had been severely battered was called into her classroom to open a window. The sight of his wounds so pained Grimké that she fainted. Her school was located near the workhouse where slaves were sent to be reprimanded. One of her friends who lived near it complained to Grimké that the screams of the slaves being whipped often reached her house. These awful cries from the workhouse terrified Grimké whenever she had to walk nearby.[38]

As slave-owning children grew into adults, their identification with victims or victimizers often accorded to gender. Elizabeth Fox-Genovese shows that mistresses could be cruel tormentors of their slaves.[39] But in comparison with masters, white women were more likely to take the side of the slaves, while white men nearly unanimously identified with the aggressor as a requisite of manhood. Becoming such a man did not happen automatically or painlessly. Playing on the patriarchy inherent in Western cultural institutions, which are also rooted in Christian religion, Jacques Lacan terms this socialization "the name-of-the-father."

Fathers ordinarily did the work of inculcating manhood, which included snuffing out white children's identification with slaves. In 1839 a Virginian named John M. Nelson described his shift from painful childhood sympathy to manly callousness. As a child, he would try to stop the beating of slave children and, he said, "mingle my cries with theirs, and feel almost willing to take a part of the punishment." After his father severely and repeatedly rebuked him for this kind of compassion, he "became so blunted that I could not only witness their stripes with composure, but *myself* inflict them, and that without remorse."[40] The comments of Thomas Jefferson on this whole subject are revealingly oblique.

Thomas Jefferson, Founding Father, slave owner, author of the Declaration of Independence, and acknowledged expert on his own state of Virginia and the United States generally, wrote *Notes on the State of Virginia* in response to a questionnaire from François Marbois, the secretary of the French legation at Philadelphia. Between 1780 and 1785 Jefferson codified his social, political, scientific, and ethical convictions. Jefferson did not have a very high opinion of Africans, though American Indians, he thought, would display their real and substantial worth when afforded decent opportunities. Jefferson found African Americans stupid and ugly, a people more or less well suited to the low estate they occupied in eighteenth-century Virginia. Contrary to facile assumption, Jefferson's appraisal of the capacities of Africans did not make him an unequivocal supporter of slavery. Nonetheless, as a gentleman whose entire material existence depended on the produce of his slaves, he was never an abolitionist. In fact, his reluctance to interfere with slavery hardened as he aged. By 1819, as the Missouri Compromise was being forged, Jefferson was warning American politicians not, under any circumstances, to tamper with slavery, even though he realized that by preserving slavery, the United States was holding "a wolf by the ears."[41]

Jefferson's reservations about slavery pertained to the owners of slaves, not to the slaves themselves. Being the property of other people was not noxious to blacks, he thought, but owning slaves entailed great drawbacks for whites. Jefferson recognized that the requirements of

slave ownership "nursed, educated, and daily exercised" habits of tyranny, and he observed that "[t]he man must be a prodigy who can
retain his manners and morals undepraved by such circumstances." In
this part of his discussion, Jefferson's customary verbal talent and intellectual suppleness turned into obfuscation. He veiled his explanation of
the bad things that slavery did to slaveholders and was only able to
write, intriguingly, of slavery's breeding "odious peculiarities."

Jefferson's phrasing does not appeal to today's family systems theorists and psychoanalysts, who use instead the language of triangles to
explain family relationships, including those that are violent. Children
who are observers of abuse are likely to assume the position of the other
members of the triangle: either by becoming victims themselves or by
abusing others, especially younger siblings or children in positions of
relative weakness.[42] This is the kind of repercussion that eighteenth-
and nineteenth-century observers like Thomas Jefferson were deploring through euphemism.

So far in this discussion, only slaves have figured as the victims of
physical and psychological abuse. But the ideals of slavery affected
families quite apart from the toll they exacted from the bodies and
psyches of blacks. Thanks to the abundance of historical scholarship
that concentrates on antebellum southern society, it is possible to reach
some generalizations regarding whites. But even in the slave South,
historians have been much less aware of the abuse of white women than
of the oppression of black slaves. Abuse there was, as the diary of
Baltimorean Madge Preston indicates.[43]

Petitions for divorce and church records show that wife beating was
a common motive for the attempted dissolution of marriages and the
expulsion of men and women from church membership. Doubtless this
was true in nonslave-holding regions as well. What is noteworthy in
this context, as Stephanie McCurry shows for the South Carolina low
country, is that legislators and church leaders routinely urged women
to remain in abusive unions and to bear abuse in a spirit of submission.[44] In the hard-drinking antebellum South, which was well known
for rampant violence against slaves and between white men, white
women had little recourse when their husbands beat them, for, in general, the southern states were slow to grant women the legal right to
divorce or to custody of their children in cases of separation. Until the

1830s, southern states lacked divorce laws, and state legislatures heard divorce petitions on a case-by-case basis. The result was a small number of divorces granted inconsistently and according to the social and economic status of the petitioner.

The disposal of the small number of cases of incest that came before judges also illuminates the reasoning of the men who exercised power in the slave South. As in instances of wife beating, so in cases of incest, judges preferred to investigate the flaws of the female petitioner, who, even despite extreme youth, usually came to be seen as consenting. Not surprisingly, incest seldom became public, but when it entered the criminal justice system, the girls in question were likely as not seen as accomplices in their own ravishment.

In the interests of preserving patriarchy, victims of incest, like victims of wife abuse, were abandoned by law and sacrificed to the ideal of submission. Legal historians like A. Leon Higginbotham and Peter Bardaglio have discovered that the southern lawmakers and judges who were anxious to regulate racialized sexuality were loath to punish white men for sexual violence against white or black women and children.[45]

Incest and wife beating do not usually appear in general studies of the antebellum South, where the received wisdom, as in histories like Daniel Blake Smith's study of eighteenth-century planter society in the Chesapeake, is that planter families came to be child-centered and companionate.[46] Such a vision fails even to allow for the level of familial abuse that psychologists see as usual in twentieth-century households, where, according to the American Medical Association, one-quarter of married women will be abused by a current or former partner at some point during their lives.[47] Were planter families more straightforwardly loving than we? I doubt it.

## Keeping Secrets from Historians

Aristocrats were skilled at keeping secrets and preserving appearances, as I know from experience with Gertrude Thomas. Only by reading her 1,380-page journal repeatedly was I able to discover her secrecy and self-deception. In this case, the secret I discovered was adultery, for both her father and her husband had outside wives and children. Her journal never reveals her other family secret, her husband's drunkenness, which was only preserved orally in family lore.

Then and now, family violence and child sexual abuse are usually concealed, and the people with the most privacy, the wealthy, are better at preserving their secrets than poor people, who live their lives in full view of the world. Scholars have connived with wealthy families to hide child sexual abuse among people of privilege, which one psychologist concludes is "most conspicuous for its presumed absence."[48] This is an old, old story.

In the 1890s Sigmund Freud discovered the prevalence of incest as a cause of hysteria; when his professional colleagues objected to what he had found, he reworked his theory into fantasy and the oedipal complex. In 1932 Freud's friend and protégé, Sandor Ferenczi, reestablished the facts that childhood sexual trauma was common in the best of families and that it was devastating to emotional development. A few months after he presented his paper, "Confusion of Tongues between Adults and the Child," to the International Psycho-Analytic Congress in Wiesbaden, Ferenczi died, and his theory died with him. In the 1980s Jeffrey Masson revealed Freud's about-face and was drummed out of psychoanalysis.[49] Historians who have taken their sources at face value have missed the family secrets of slave-owning households, but in their unwillingness to see, they find themselves in distinguished psychological company.

Some historians are ready to examine their sources more critically. Works by Richard Bushman and critic Jay Fliegelman alert us that by the late eighteenth and early nineteenth centuries, wealthy Americans had come to prize gentility so highly that they spent enormous amounts of time and energy creating pleasing appearances. Bushman and Fliegelman say, and I concur, that the letters, speeches, and journals that historians have used as the means of uncovering reality and gauging consciousness ought more properly to be considered self-conscious performances intended to create beautiful tableaux. People with sufficient time, space, and money modeled themselves on characters in novels and acted out what they saw as appropriate parts. What was actually taking place at home was another story entirely, which was not necessarily preserved for our easy investigation.[50] If historians are to understand the less attractive and deeply buried aspects of slave society, the scales will have to fall from their eyes. They will have to see beyond the beauty of performance and probe slavery's family romance more skeptically.

Once we transcend complete reliance on the written record, deception clues are not hard to see. They include the murderous rage Fox Butterfield highlights in his 1998 *New York Times* article, but also the eloquent alcoholism and invalidism of the eighteenth- and nineteenth-century South that could not be concealed. Murder, alcohol, and illness hint at the existence of compelling family secrets. In the 1940s southern author Lillian Smith summed up the society in which she lived in a phrase that applies to slave societies. Smith said that her thoroughly segregated South, with its myriad instances of bad faith, was "pathological."[51]

Historians need to heed the wisdom of psychologists, take Lillian Smith to heart, look beneath the gorgeous surface that cultured slave owners presented to the world, and pursue the hidden truths of slavery, including soul murder and patriarchy. The task is essential, for our mental health as a society depends on the ability to see our interrelatedness across lines of class and race, in the past, as in the present.

# 2

## *The Journal of Ella Gertrude Clanton Thomas*

### A TESTAMENT OF WEALTH, LOSS, & ADULTERY

. . .

In true autobiographer's style, Ella Gertrude Clanton Thomas exists twice: once in her own lifetime, from 1834 to 1907, when she flowered into a belle, married a man who betrayed her, faced Confederate defeat, lost her wealth and standing, went out to work, paid the bills, and became a feminist. Thomas also exists as a rich personal text: the journal she generated between 1848 and 1889, which offers a glimpse into a privileged private life marked by material ease and adultery.

To an extent unusual in autobiographical literature, Gertrude Thomas the life and Gertrude Thomas the text disaccord. The journal, its last entry dated Friday, 30 August 1889, ends on a somber note. Thomas's life began anew with her move to Atlanta in 1893 and her embrace of woman suffrage. She gained prominence as a public figure and died relatively happy.[1]

Unlike the published memoirs of Myrta Lockett Avary or the revised diaries of Mary Boykin Chesnut, the Thomas journal presents unretouched, day-to-day tussles with the contingencies of life.[2] Speaking through words and communicating through silence, Thomas's journal permits its readers to gauge the emotional costs of the South's peculiar institution on a wife of the planter class. It speaks, even as it strives to keep its secrets. Its torrent of words washes away the false truisms of slave society and reveals its most intimate wounds.

Respecting the distinction of life from text, I will discuss them sequentially. The first, biographical section of this essay narrates Thomas's life.[3] The second section discusses the journal's main themes: identity, gender and sexuality, religion, race, labor, and the journal's great and painful secret of adultery.

## A Life of Ease

Gertrude Clanton was born in Columbia County, near Augusta, Georgia, in 1834. Her family belonged to the approximately 6 percent of southern whites who made up the Deep South planter elite.[4] Clanton's mother, the former Mary Luke (born in 1812), was from a wealthy rural family living near Augusta. Mary Luke married Turner Clanton in 1829. Born in 1798 in southside Virginia, where the ambitious rather than the First Families scrambled for wealth, Turner Clanton had already improved his sizable inheritance and reinforced his own claim to gentility by serving two terms in the Georgia legislature. Mary Luke and Turner Clanton had eleven children, seven of whom lived past the age of five: Anne, born in 1831; Ella Gertrude, born in 1834; Mary, born in 1841; James, born in 1843; Cora, born in 1846; Nathaniel Holt, born in 1849; and Catherine, born in 1855. When he died in 1864, Clanton's estate was valued at some $2,500,000 in Confederate dollars, and he was reckoned as one of the wealthiest planters in the state.[5]

As a girl, Gertrude Clanton slept late, read voraciously, visited friends, dressed prettily, and wrote letters. But her time became more regimented in January 1849, when she went away to Wesleyan Female College in Macon, Georgia. Gertrude was the first Clanton daughter to go away to school or college and one of a tiny minority of southern women of her generation with access to higher education. Schools for women were few, and those that existed — for example, Clanton's Wesleyan, Salem Academy in Salem, North Carolina, and Mme Talvanne's in Charleston — cost anywhere from $200 to $700 per year. Wesleyan, which formed part of the antebellum movement in the South toward more rigorous education for women, was a Methodist institution that had been chartered in 1836, during a fertile period in southern evangelical education.[6]

Seventeen-year-old Clanton graduated from Wesleyan after three years, in 1851. An active and enthusiastic alumna, she twice held office in the Wesleyan Alumnae Association and returned to Macon several times for reunions. Over the years she remained in regular touch with many of her school friends. One, Martha (Mat) Oliver, was particularly close. Gertrude Clanton grieved when Mat Oliver married for the first time, but then, as the years passed, she gradually lost interest in Mat's fate. Another school friend, Julia (Jule) Thomas, became family.[7] When Jule's charming and handsome brother, James Jefferson Thomas, began courting Gertrude in the spring of 1851, he was completing his undergraduate work at Princeton, and in the fall he pursued medical studies in Augusta.

In a milieu that venerated romantic love, courtship was the great and public moment in the life of the belle, a smooth and glamorous ritual. Clanton strove to fill her role, though Jeff Thomas proved perplexing. While she did her best to keep her composure, he kept her off balance and insecure.[8] She pretended, even to her journal, not to be upset by his absences, silences, and suspicious maladies, but Jeff Thomas caused her distress as well as delight. Turner Clanton's lukewarm approval of the match also proved wrenching. To aggravate matters further, Jeff fell ill in 1852 and delayed the wedding for nearly a month. Ella Gertrude Clanton and Jefferson Thomas married in December 1852, then honeymooned with her family in New York City. At some point during their betrothal, Jeff had decided to abandon his medical studies, an unexplained decision that both later came to regret.

Jefferson Thomas came from a Burke County, Georgia, plantation family in the Augusta environs. With both of them bringing wealth to the marriage, Gertrude and Jeff were well off. When they married, Turner Clanton gave Gertrude and Jeff a house, plantation, and slaves worth nearly $30,000. In the years that followed, her father remained in the financial picture. Even during the prosperous years of the mid-1850s, he furnished luxuries — such as the addition of a piazza on the Thomases' house — that his daughter had earlier taken for granted. Turner Clanton also gave gifts of money and supplies, such as animal fodder, that eased the Thomases' economic situation. That such gifts were so welcome indicates a degree of financial stringency. As early as 1855 Gertrude Thomas began to write about, if not to attempt seriously to reduce, her level of spending.[9]

During the 1850s, however, money did not unduly worry the young matron, and she and Jeff began their family. Between the ages of nineteen and forty-one, Gertrude Thomas bore ten children, seven of whom lived past the age of five: Turner Clanton (1853–1917); Mary Belle (1858–1929); Jefferson Davis (1861–1920); Cora Lou (1863–

1956); Julian Pinckney (1868–1928); James Clanton (1872–79); and Kathleen (1875–1968).

Thomas was in her late twenties when the Civil War broke out. Like other Confederates—indeed like her northern counterparts—she rejoiced (momentarily) at the prospect of warfare: "Our country is invaded—our homes are in danger—We are deprived or they are attempting to deprive us of that glorious liberty for which our Fathers fought and bled and shall we tamely submit to this? Never!" She reveled in the thought that her husband, brother, and brother-in-law would sign up immediately, thereby redeeming their and the South's white manhood. With many other Confederates, Thomas welcomed warfare as proof "that southern blood has not degenerated in consequence of the life of luxury and ease we have been living." She looked forward to teaching her sons of their father's glorious martial exploits.[10]

Throughout the war years, she pondered the meaning of southern national identity and worried that "the South" continued to be too indolent and too dependent upon the North intellectually. Thomas followed the progress of the war closely, was a director of the Augusta Ladies' Aid Society, sewed uniforms, made cartridges, and visited military hospitals repeatedly. During the war and after, she spoke of the Confederacy as "we."[11]

In 1861, during her period of flag-waving Confederate nationalism, Gertrude gloried in Jefferson Thomas's military service and played mid-August parting like a scene in an opera. But by October 1861, Jeff was back home to purchase uniforms, sell Confederate bonds, and visit his plantations. His mother's and his own illnesses delayed his return to the front until November 1861. In early 1862 Gertrude began to hope that he would leave the army, and by late February 1862 he was back at home, this time to recruit volunteers and purchase supplies in Augusta and Atlanta. Jeff was in Virginia again from April to June 1862. In mid-1862 he became one of scores of Confederate officers who resigned their commissions, complaining of favoritism and low morale.[12] Jeff purchased a substitute and joined a local militia unit that would hardly take him far from Augusta.

Until the war lost its focus as memory, Jefferson's record proved more a source of ambivalence to Gertrude than of pride. All told, Jefferson Thomas spent about nine months at the front.[13] His spotty war record did not prevent his embrace of the role of Confederate veteran. As an old man he rode about at reunions of Confederates and Princeton alumni on his favorite horse "Dixie Will Go."

Three years into the war, the glamour of the Confederate cause wore thin for Gertrude. Weary of the war with its shortages, inflation, and social upheaval, by 1864 she preferred to keep her husband safe at home, even if it meant losing Atlanta to the Yankees. Wearing cotton instead of linen, complaining of the discomfort of the town house they were renting, she wondered, "Oh God will this war never cease?"[14] The war came close to home in 1864, when Gen. William T. Sherman's army burned buildings on one of the Thomas plantations in Burke County and looted the storehouses and cotton-gin houses. Contemplating the possibility of Confederate defeat, Thomas began to question the deeper significance of the war.

The enduring personal meaning of the Confederate defeat for Thomas was financial, and in the loss of wealth her experience was characteristic of the planter class.[15] Like every other slaveowning family in the South, the Thomases lost every cent they had invested in slaves; the C$15,000 they had invested in Confederate bonds also became worthless.

To compound the tragedy of Confederate defeat, Thomas had sustained another crippling loss before the end of the war, this one personal as well as financial. The death of her father figures larger than any other event in her journal, spreading over twelve pages in the typescript for 1864 and reappearing in the years that followed. Turner Clanton, a source of moral and financial support over the years, died in 1864. Gertrude assumed she would receive a handsome inheritance, but this was not to be the case. Sixteen years after Clanton's death, his will was finally settled, but Gertrude received relatively little from it. Without her knowledge, her husband had over the course of ten years resorted to the (not uncommon) expedient of borrowing from his father-in-law, substituting liabilities for Gertrude's inheritance. In the postwar years, Jeff went deeper into debt to Gertrude's family and his own siblings. During the hard financial times of the late 1860s and the 1870s, Gertrude missed her father keenly.

At the moment of Confederate defeat, Gertrude experienced a serious crisis. She fainted, miscarried, and tormented herself with doubts. Although she did not see things so starkly, her standing in her own eyes and that of her kin and neighbors had depended, before the war, on their owning many slaves — together with the wealth that slaveowning symbolized — and on the refinement that came with higher education.[16] Without slaveownership as a social marker, her identity collapsed. Emancipation shook her to the point of threatening her physical health, her religious beliefs, and her certainty about her position as a woman. The end of the war, which she described as "the turning point, the crisis with me," changed Gertrude Thomas's life profoundly.[17]

She recovered quickly, and accepted the permanence of emancipation. Despite the despondency and doubt that plagued her from time to time, she was able to look ahead and plan to bring money into the family. By the summer of 1866 her health was good, but Jefferson's was still terrible.

At his best, Jefferson Thomas was an attractive and generous gentleman whom Gertrude loved deeply. But after the war, he fell apart physically and emotionally, a far-from-unique failing of the time. He brooded over the Confederate defeat and denied the justice of emancipation. Jeff Thomas had actually suffered bouts of nervous stomach and shortness of breath since 1859. But the immobilizing depressions he suffered after the war marked deterioration in his mental as well as physical health. In her journal entry of 29 November 1868, Gertrude speaks of Jeff's depression and the terrible "strain upon his nerves & physical system." On 7 December 1870, she writes that her husband "talks about being a fit subject for the Lunatic Asylum." His psychosomatic illnesses, his chronic mismanagement of his plantations and his business, his bitterness at the Confederate defeat and emancipation, and his habit (acquired during the war) of swearing before his pious Methodist wife severely strained the marriage.[18]

## An Adjustment to Loss

The postwar era fundamentally altered relations between men and women in the South, as both natives and visitors observed. Southern white women seemed generally to have more energy and intelligence than men, and they were suing for divorce, going out to work, and speaking up in public for the first time.[19] The thought that she might earn money had never crossed Gertrude Thomas's mind before the Civil War. But afterwards, as financial losses began to afflict the Thomases, she appreciated her education anew.[20] Contemplating salaried work as a teacher for the first time and taking advantage of women's new employment opportunities, Thomas entered the universe of paid labor, both as employee and employer.

To a certain degree, Thomas gloried in the new order. "I think and think boldly," she wrote, "I act — and act boldly." Unaccompanied by a man, she walked in the streets of Augusta and journeyed by train to a postwar Wesleyan reunion. In Macon she read aloud a piece of her own writing with sufficient aplomb to think on her feet. In 1869 she sought to publish her writing for money. The temptation of writing professionally never disappeared.[21] Without remuneration, she proudly published her account of the improvements in her church, not as Mrs. Jefferson Thomas, but as Mrs. Gertrude Thomas. Even as she regretted the motives for her moving out into the world as a woman of affairs rather than as a lady, she relished her increased individuality.[22]

Reconstruction — in the strictly political sense of the term — was a brief affair in the state of Georgia (1867–70), but it did bring political upheaval accompanied by a perceptible increase in black self-confidence among women as well as men. Black political independence alarmed Jefferson Thomas, the head of the local Democrats. Gertrude Thomas, to the contrary, was not threatened by blacks in politics. She praised the abilities of Aaron Bradley, a black politician, and realized that were she black, she, too, would support the Radicals.[23]

Because women could neither vote nor hold office, politics was not the stuff of Thomas's day-to-day life. Nonetheless, she resented the economic ramifications of Reconstruction: Free workers seized their new mobility and changed jobs in pursuit of better wages and working conditions. While her husband's adjustment to emancipation and Reconstruction took place largely in the more public worlds of politics and farm employment, hers was a far more intimate accommodation. Thomas's accommodation to free labor took place within the private household, unmediated by the power of the state. No laws regulated household employment, in which there were no Freedmen's Bureau contracts, liens, or prosecutions for debt. For the first time, she lost unconditional access to her own reliable and experienced workers. Like many other formerly prosperous former slaveowners, she gritted her teeth at the thought of the "low class of people," the nouveau-riche whites (some of whom had migrated from the North) now benefiting from the service of workers whom she and her class had trained but could no longer afford to employ.[24] She further had to adjust to her husband's difficulties in business.

Jefferson Thomas's retail business, established during the war, failed in 1868. His New York creditor forced Jefferson and his partners to declare bankruptcy and sell off what was left of their inventory at a publicly advertised sale that embarrassed both of the Thomases. Just as Gertrude faced the fact of the bankruptcy of Jefferson's business, he announced more bad news: Belmont, their home, might well be sold for debt.[25] Between 1868 and the early 1890s, the Thomases gradually lost much of their property. City lots, plantations in Burke County, and, finally, their residence in Augusta were auctioned off for debt in the early 1870s. Their remaining properties—Belmont (which, in the event, was not sold), Dixie Farm, and the Road Place—were heavily mortgaged. In 1875 or 1876 Belmont burned, and Gertrude lost the home in which she had lived during most of her married life. In the face of so much loss, Gertrude Thomas faltered, and she wrote the word "humiliation" in her journal many a time.[26]

Financial ruin meant shabbiness: the worn-out carpets, carriages, and clothing the Thomases could not afford to replace, the sight of her property advertised by the sheriff in the newspapers for sale at auction, and the realization that her children lacked the status only wealth supplied. Her husband's business failures and crushing debts became public knowledge in the late 1860s, exposing their financial difficulties to everyone who read the local newspapers. Rather than let her neighbors see her in reduced circumstances, Thomas refused to go to town. She would not let her neighborhood literary club meet at her house until she could buy new carpets, noting sadly that she could no longer afford to replace the worn-out velvet tapestry.[27] With the passage of time, however, Thomas discovered that she no longer felt the sting so acutely. By mid-1880 the public disclosure of bankruptcy no longer mortified her.[28]

She never learned to swallow what she saw as her children's lack of social advantages. Early in 1880 she cried at the thought that she could not give her children the wealth and prestige she had enjoyed.[29] None of her children attained planter status, and the Thomas family descendants never regained the status that accompanied landed wealth. Toward the end of the journal, Thomas writes of her three adult children: Turner is selling insurance; Jeff works for an express company; and Mary Belle, married, lives in Atlanta.[30]

Downward mobility sums up Gertrude Thomas's postwar experience, and she felt it keenly. Resenting poverty and everything it implied in her life, she tortured herself by listing her expenses down to the penny, yet took pride in her ability to pay off creditors, bit by bit, week by week.[31] Throughout this scrimping and close figuring, she recalled the luxury in which she had been raised and which she had for so long taken for granted. At times she was amazed that she, "the child of wealth and pride," should suffer "such degradations" and saddened that hardship had prevented her oldest child, Turner, from drinking from the "golden cup" that had been held to his lips at birth.[32]

Hard times impaired Gertrude's relationship with her husband. She realized his inability to support the family delegated the task of providing for her children to her. To preserve her family's integrity, she used her salary to pay taxes and wages on the farms — obligations that before the war she took to be her husband's responsibility. Yet for all her unquestioned commitment to the nuclear family, she distinguished rhetorically between her husband, on one side, and herself and her children, on the other, as though hard times stripped the family down to its matrifocal core.[33] In a revision of the traditional roles she had once accepted for herself and her husband, she was now the breadwinner. Gertrude became the pillar of the family, as her husband, with his debts and bad management and ill temper, became ever more peripheral.

Money problems also created difficulties between Gertrude Thomas and her mother, her siblings, and her in-laws, all of whom were her husband's creditors. Homestead legislation passed in 1868 allowed Jefferson Thomas to shelter $2,000 worth of real estate and $1,000 worth of personal property from seizure for debt. In the late 1860s and early 1870s, he often considered declaring one or another of their plantations a homestead. But Gertrude found this plan distasteful, as so many of their creditors were their own relatives. As she saw it, sheltering their property meant cheating their families. Over the years the Thomases argued about the homestead law, with Gertrude opposing its use on the ground that her brother, her sister, and her brother-in-law would be injured for incurring financial risks on Jefferson Thomas's account.[34]

Even as she reproached her husband for endangering their siblings financially, she lashed out at her family. She complained to her mother that it hurt to be sued by one's own sisters; she accused her family of avoiding her presence entirely.[35] As in so many human affairs, poverty strained the bonds of family, but not, in this case, to the breaking point. Thomas remained close to her husband, children, mother, and siblings, and her mother contributed generously to the support of the Thomases' children for a decade and a half.[36]

Gertrude Thomas experienced pain and anguish, but she also coped with catastrophe. Her progress was uneven, but she grew strong and independent as she wavered between growing assurance in her abilities and doubts about her proper role as a wife. With the instinctive knowledge that as a mother she must provide for her children and the growing confidence in her business sense, her self-esteem increased. At the same time, she was subject to conflicting pressures. Jeff detested her giving him advice—however sound—and asked her, as his wife, to defer to his judgment. Had she been permitted, she would doubtless have managed their affairs more efficiently, certainly more vigorously.[37] But she would not subject her marriage to the strain such a role reversal would have imposed.

The trauma of publicly advertised bankruptcy and her husband's emotional decline made for tough times, but Thomas had to endure one last tragedy. In 1879, in the midst of economic ruin and declining status, her six-year-old son Clanton died, a loss that symbolized the death of her grand old self and her future's bleakness. Thomas grieved over Clanton as intensely as she had mourned her father.

Jeff Thomas let his wife down financially and emotionally. He often failed to meet his economic obligations, and in 1880 he was able to continue planting only after Gertrude arranged for credit.[38] He no longer gave his wife the moral support he had offered, for instance, when a premature baby had died in late 1855. Now she complained that he never appreciated her sacrifices and his grouchiness got on her nerves. For a while in the early 1870s they ceased sleeping together, because he—not she—was afraid of having more children they could

not afford to support. Intimacy between the two resumed in the early
1870s, for Clanton was born in 1872 and Kathleen in 1875. By 1880
they were again occupying separate bedrooms.[39]

The Civil War had made teaching acceptable for respectable women,
and Gertrude had decided in 1865 that she wanted to teach, but Jeff
resisted her plan to work for wages.[40] Finally their desperate need
converted him, and she began teaching elementary school in 1878.
Through all the six years that she kept school, Thomas fought off
competition from other hard-up, educated women. Her teaching salary
of $30 per month enabled her to pay wages and property taxes on their
farm, but she still had to borrow money from her aunt and her mother
to meet other expenses.[41]

Gertrude Thomas found teaching elementary school tiring and frustrating, even though she took a sincere interest in the welfare of her
pupils. Charmed by the hope that she could write for money, she
regretted wasting her abilities on the very young. She wanted to quit
teaching in 1880, but her husband persuaded her to persevere, for the
family depended on her salary.[42]

The year 1879, when she was forty-five, marked Gertrude Thomas's
lowest point, financially and emotionally. Feeling old and poor and
alone, she had by this point lost hope of collecting any inheritance from
her father's estate. "I only felt that Mr. Thomas could not help me, the
children could not," she wrote. "I had not one friend upon whom I
could rely and before me seemed a dense high wall."[43] During the 1870s
and 1880s she winced at the physical decline of middle age.

She stayed in the classroom until her mother's death in 1884. The
Thomases then moved to the Clanton mansion in Augusta, where they
took in boarders. In these further reduced circumstances, Gertrude
suffered a long, debilitating illness, which she suspected was related to
the lack of privacy and to the emotional strain the boarders imposed.
While she was physically and emotionally vulnerable, a series of earthquakes in 1886–87 proved terrifying. In the spring of 1888, when she
was about to turn fifty-four, she lamented that she was not even good
for $50 worth of credit.[44] With the earthquakes and the meetings of her
local literary society the journal stops.

Were Thomas's life to have ended with her journal, it would embody
the ruin of the antebellum planter class. Thomas would stand as a fe-

male counterpart to Thomas Chaplin of the South Carolina low country, who also went from planting to teaching school. Unlike Thomas,
who grappled with hardship and wrote about it almost unblinkingly,
Thomas Chaplin avoided the fundamental truths and tragedies of his
postwar existence.[45]

But this was not Gertrude Thomas's end.

### After the Journal Ends

Even before she stopped writing in her journal, Thomas had begun to
rally. As an officer in the Richmond County Grange, she occasionally
published essays on matters of especial concern to women, one of
which won a prize. Following a pattern that typified white southern
women of her class and generation, she also joined women's groups.[46]

Without jettisoning the Wesleyan Alumnae Society, in the mid-
1880s Thomas became active in four organizations of the sort then
easing formerly cloistered southern white ladies into public life: the
Ladies' Missionary Society of St. John's Methodist Church in Augusta;
the Hayne Circle, a literary club in Augusta (that included men as well
as women); the Ladies' [Confederate] Memorial Association of Augusta; and the Woman's Christian Temperance Union (WCTU).

In the South, women's missionary societies were an innovation of
the 1870s and 1880s, beginning with those sponsored by the Southern
Methodist church in 1878. Such societies allowed women active in
churches—a perfectly acceptable activity for middle- and upper-class
southern women—to work outside their homes, families, and neighborhoods. Thomas had been an enthusiastic Methodist ever since her
conversion at Wesleyan College, and missionary work grew naturally
from that lifelong allegiance.[47] Respectable women across the South
were forming women's clubs, often as a means of furthering their education.[48] Similarly, Thomas figured among hundreds of white southern
women who had been ardent Confederates and who, in the 1880s,
organized memorial associations to commemorate the Civil War dead.
Like many others, Thomas went from holding office in the Augusta
Ladies' Memorial Society into the United Daughters of the Confederacy (UDC), formed in 1894. In the middle and late 1890s she served as
recording secretary and national treasurer of the UDC.

Thousands of southern women, many of whom, like Thomas, had
become accustomed to working together in missionary societies and

women's clubs, took their giant step beyond familiar bounds when they joined the Woman's Christian Temperance Union in the 1880s. When her socially prominent kinswoman in Augusta, Jane Thomas Sibley (Mrs. William Sibley), founded the local WCTU, Thomas also became active. Legions of southern women flocked to the WCTU either as followers of Frances Willard or out of an abstract belief in the cause. Thomas had additional, personal reasons for advocating temperance.

There is little question that Jefferson Thomas had a drinking problem, which by the 1880s was of long standing. Years earlier, before the marriage, Jeff's father had asked Gertrude what she would do were Jeff to get drunk. Her own father harbored reservations toward her fiancé doubtlessly rooted in finances, personal morality, or both. During their courtship, Gertrude extracted an unspecified promise from Jeff that she hoped he would keep.[49]

National policy as well as individual initiative attracted Thomas to the WCTU.[50] Frances Willard, second president of the WCTU, made a special effort to conciliate educated white southern women who had been Confederate supporters. Willard's nine southern tours between 1881 and 1896 brought into the WCTU white and some black respectable southern women worried by social changes and appalled by widespread male drunkenness. Adopting a version of Henry Grady's New South rhetoric, Willard toured the South with a broad-gauged and ladylike brand of feminism, attracting white southerners like Caroline Merrick, a New Orleans clubwoman; Belle Kearney, a teacher from Jackson, Mississippi; and Rebecca Latimer Felton, a controversial lecturer from Atlanta who would become Thomas's colleague.[51]

Thomas served as secretary and vice president of the Augusta chapter of the WCTU. Heeding Willard's motto of "Do Everything," southern WCTU women went beyond temperance. The WCTU led Thomas to concerns she shared with Rebeca Felton and Felton's sister, Mary Latimer McLendon: penal reform, industrial education for girls, and woman suffrage, causes that enriched her last decades.

By the time Gertrude and Jefferson Thomas had mortgaged everything they owned in and around Augusta, their fifth child, Julian (born 1863) had grown up and graduated from the Augusta Medical College in 1887. After completing a residency in New Jersey, Julian moved to Atlanta to specialize in dermatology and preventive medicine. His parents accepted his invitation to move in with him in 1893. At age fifty-nine, Thomas left Augusta and Richmond County, where she had spent her entire life.

In Atlanta she continued to develop as a feminist, helping Mary Latimer McLendon found the Industrial School for Girls in Milledgeville, Georgia. Thomas followed McLendon and Felton into local and state woman suffrage organizations. During the 1890s she spoke frequently in public, traveled to WCTU, UDC, and suffrage conventions throughout the nation, and wrote for publication. In 1895 Thomas attended the meeting of the National American Woman Suffrage Association (NAWSA) in Atlanta as a delegate from the Atlanta WCTU.[52] In 1899, at the age of sixty-five, she was elected president of the Georgia Woman Suffrage Association (GWSA). In 1903 she became a life member of the NAWSA and received a letter of acknowledgment from Susan B. Anthony. Such honors would not have seemed possible in her dismal decades after the war.

Thomas died in 1907 after a stroke, and her obituaries bore witness to her prominence in public life. She had never realized her old ambition of becoming a professional writer, but she had established herself as a leading Georgian. By the end of her life, Thomas had become a full-fledged suffragist whose stature was recognized throughout her state and region. Having begun her woman's life as a belle, she ended it a feminist.

During her maturity, Thomas's life fortunes rose from the ashes. With the return of more sunny times, however, she neglected her journal. Over the years her writing had changed from performing a ritual of the elite to recording family history for her children to seeking a confidante in times of trouble. After her emergence as a public figure in the 1890s and 1900s, no new motive appeared.

## Gertrude Thomas's Journal

Journal-keeping among the elites of the Old South was a fairly common pastime, a convention that lent weight to individual experience but that required more discipline than most could summon over the long haul. Even the best-known nineteenth-century southern journal, that of the indomitable Mary Boykin Chesnut, encompasses only the Civil War years. Other extended journals lack the detail and candor that

Gertrude Thomas sustained for over two decades.[53] The journal of Gertrude Thomas is, therefore, unique. Spanning forty-one years, it presents one intelligent woman's responses to the upheavals of her times. Because Thomas was unusually articulate, her journal illuminates experiences that she shared with thousands of women but that only she documented in a persistent fashion.

Considering Thomas's keen sense of gender, it is fitting that her journal owes its survival to her female descendants. Cora Lou Thomas Farrell, Thomas's daughter, became the guardian of the thirteen extant manuscript journals until her death in 1956. After Farrell's death, the journals remained in her home in Atlanta, where her niece, Gertrude Ingraham Threlkeld (Gertrude Thomas's granddaughter), and Gertrude Threlkeld Despeaux (Threlkeld's daughter and Gertrude Thomas's great-granddaughter) lived. At least three volumes of the journal, covering the years 1849–51, 1859–61, and 1871–78, had disappeared. All other lacunae reflect years in which Thomas did not write. According to Virginia Burr, the volume(s) from 1859 to 1861 were obviously lost. However, the volume(s) from 1871 to 1878, in which Thomas was writing candidly about hard times, may have been destroyed by Thomas or by one of her daughters in an act of censorship.

The process by which the journals were transferred from private possession to the Duke University Library Manuscript Department in 1957 is not entirely clear but seems to have occurred at the instigation of the historian Katherine M. Jones. Researching *The Plantation South* (Englewood Cliffs: Bobbs-Merrill, N.J., 1957), Jones became the first historian to use the Thomas journals. Jones knew both the curator of manuscripts at Duke, Mattie Russell, and Thomas descendant Gertrude Threlkeld Despeaux.

Despeaux deposited the journals in the Manuscript Department at the Duke University Library, where a pioneer in southern women's history, Mary Elizabeth Massey of Winthrop College in South Carolina, discovered them. Massey commissioned the journals' transcription. The typescript of the extant volumes runs to approximately 1,350 pages. Until the publication of *The Secret Eye: The Journal of Ella Gertrude Clanton Thomas, 1848–1889* in 1990, historians generally worked from Massey's typescript.[54] Unfortunately, the typescript is far from accurate, for Thomas's handwriting is difficult to decipher, and the typists were not historians.

Mary Elizabeth Massey was elected president of the Southern Historical Association in 1972, and her presidential address, "The Making
of a Feminist," presents a brief biography of Thomas based upon the
journals and scrapbooks. Massey doubtless intended to publish more
on Thomas, but her untimely death in 1974 cut short her career. Massey's essay represented the most sustained published scholarship on
Thomas and her journal until 1990.

Gertrude Thomas was an intelligent, independent thinker whose
strength of character and perseverance against enormous obstacles set
her apart from ordinary folk. More important for southern history, she
captured her thoughts in writing. Her ability to record (most of) her
thoughts in clear and honest phrasing renders her journal exceptional.
The utility of her journal is not simply personal, for in many ways
Thomas represents broader phenomena in southern history. As an unusually wealthy and well-educated young woman, she belonged to a
small but extremely influential cohort of antebellum southerners, many
of whom also lost their wealth after the Civil War. Other contemporary
journals, diaries, and letters indicate that her reactions to loss were
neither more rigid nor more racist than her peers' — on the contrary. In
view of the racial and economic ideologies prevailing among her fellow
citizens, North and South, she showed herself in many instances to be
surprisingly open-minded. She peeled back the layers of conventional
utterance to put into words what others left unspoken. This is not to
say that the journal represents an artless record of Thomas's thoughts
and experiences. It is, rather, a performance through which Thomas
composes what she reveals and hides what she cannot face. Although
the Thomas journal's great historical contribution lies in its revelations,
its secrets are also of enormous interest.[55]

## Why Write?

Throughout Thomas's journal runs the overarching theme of personal
identity that binds together her self, family, religion, gender, class, and
race. In the dialectic of thought and language, her definition of self
begins with the existential question: Why write?

Fourteen-year-old Gertrude began her journal in 1848 without posing that question. Her journal represented literate self-consciousness as
an accouterment of her style of life. Other classmates also kept journals,

and when her own daughter Mary Belle reached twelve years of age, she, in turn, began a journal of her own. Thomas's journal started as an emblem of her standing as an educated person; a record of her days, her reading, and her associates, it lent her life a larger reality. She wanted the journal to reflect only the sunny side of life, and even long after she began to write in almost complete honesty, she still sought to hide unflattering truths about her family.[56]

Between 1848 and early 1852, the journal presents a chronology of activities, visits, reading, and wearing apparel. Assuming that the journal requires a more formal language than ordinary speech ("How I wish I could wander o'er these old woods again"), Clanton often finds writing a chore, and she notes her dereliction of duty many times over.[57]

She first questions her motives in the entry for 7 March 1852, acknowledging the neglect of one aspect of her journal: recording her thoughts. She wonders what journals are for and how other people use them. In the midst of her courtship with Jefferson Thomas, she begins to doubt the use to which she had been putting her journal for nearly four years.[58]

She wants to record her feelings more openly but fears they will be read by others. In the spring of 1852 this concern was plausible, for she was living in her parents' house with several other literate people. But the fear of discovery persisted, even in the house where she lived with her husband, whom she knew was not interested enough in her journal to pry, with her children, who were very young, and with her slaves, who were illiterate.[59]

Her fear, I suspect, was not so much of discovery but of self-revelation, of an admission of the existence of an uncontrolled and disordered self that violated the ideals of her class and race. Children and servants expressed emotions they could not master. Educated adults did not. Thomas's reluctance to write down her turmoil reflected an attempt to avoid painful knowledge and an unwillingness to admit that she was not always serenely in control.[60]

Like her peers, Thomas placed enormous importance on appearances, particularly on the appearance of self-mastery. Mary Boykin Chesnut's mother-in-law, Mary Cox Chesnut, represented this kind of elite ideal, for with perfect good manners and seeming effortlessness she ran a household of twenty-five servants and an extended Chesnut family of six adults.[61] Just as Mary Boykin Chesnut tried but was unable to match that paragon of self-discipline, Thomas also struggled to maintain the proper facade.

As a young woman, Thomas knew that she must present a cool front and seems to have done so with remarkable success. Later, when the disappointments and tragedies accumulated, presenting an immobile countenance (in company or in the journal) became more difficult, yet she persevered. During the extremely disordered wartime — which made normal domestic management virtually impossible — she felt shame for not keeping her household running smoothly. Self-mastery came more easily when, infuriated, she presented an impassive front to offensive Yankees and departing servants alike. The need to appear controlled persisted, for even as her property was being sold at auction and her husband was proving exasperating, she strove to mask her distress.[62] For whom was this performance necessary? In part it was for her children, the journal's ostensible readers. Her other audiences were not spelled out, but the journal offers clues.

In her reluctance to express herself openly, even in her journal, Thomas indicates that her ultimate judges are herself and God. Hence the necessity for self-control is absolute and independent of external witness. But the journal also shows self-control as an act to be performed before inferiors, whether children, servants, or Yankees (whose claims to gentlemanliness Thomas doubts). In this sense, self-control becomes an aspect of self-definition, a means of marking oneself off from the audience of undisciplined and therefore inferior others.[63] Thomas addressed two sorts of audiences, journal/self/God and children/servants/Yankees, and before the latter she preserved appearances to the end. But for the former audience, she nearly freed herself to voice and therefore to feel loss of control, relating particularly to lack of money, labor problems, and downward mobility in the years following the war, when her world fell apart.

## A Spiritual Record

God is present throughout Thomas's journal, in prayers and appeals to his mercy and examinations of the state of her faith. Her religion was woven into her life and her ideology, so that any cause or ideal in which she believed, any value she cherished, became God's as well. She measured her virtue as an individual by her worth as a Christian.

Without designating the journal a spiritual record, as did so many devout nineteenth-century Protestants, Thomas uses her journal to measure her progress as a Christian. After the death of her infant Anna Lou in 1855, she prays God will enable her "to live during this year more in the performance of duty, with a more devout and earnest heart than heretofore." On the last day of each year she reflects on the year gone by, figuring up a spiritual evaluation such as that in 1865, when she terms her journal the "quiet monitor which urges me by the memory of recorded vows to fulfill my promises to live nearer to God."[64] Many entries mention her falling on her knees beside her bed to pray, particularly as she confronts ever-more-unsettling realities. This is her religion of times of trial. The early pages of the journal record her conversion.

Thomas's years at Wesleyan coincided with a wave of Methodist and Baptist revivals extending from 1846 to 1849. Another round of revivals among Methodists and Presbyterians followed in the mid-1850s, culminating in the Great Revival of the late 1850s.[65] Southern evangelicals — especially Baptists and Methodists — rededicated themselves to the values of dissenting Protestantism, employing the highly emotional camp-meeting style of the Second Great Awakening of the early nineteenth century. Although Thomas came along somewhat after the vogue of a Quaker-like Methodist simplicity of style, she did retain one aspect of Methodism's ideal of a "peculiar people": She did not dance.

Her Methodism grew out of the early nineteenth-century revivals, and even in the middle of the century she participated in an evangelical Protestantism characteristic of the decades before her birth. In her journal entries of the late 1840s and early 1850s, Thomas describes a religion shared by young people, women, and African Americans in terminology that evangelical Christianity still employs.[66]

Two emblematic phrases of the twentieth-century evangelical vocabulary are missing from Thomas's lexicon: Jesus and the Lord. Although she uses imagery associated with Jesus Christ (twice she mentions not wanting to roll the stone away from the sepulcher of her hopes), "Jesus" and "Christ" do not appear in her journal except when she is quoting others. Her concern is with God, whom she calls "God" (not "the Lord") and with the world of spirits. Three times she notes her attraction (fleeting) to Catholicism, embodied mainly in the figure of the Virgin Mary—Mary, a mother, rather than Mary, the mother of Jesus. Jesus simply does not figure very centrally in her Methodism.[67]

Revealing the older connections between antebellum black and white evangelical religion in the South, Thomas often mentions attending black services and appreciating one especially gifted preacher.[68] After the war, however, she became disenchanted with the political themes that Reconstruction brought into black religion.[69]

Thomas's Methodism was highly emotional, favoring prayer meetings in which preachers "exhorted" "seekers after religion." "Mourners" who "struggled" might "get" religion. When they succeeded, they "shouted" the "praises of God" and were "happy." Only women shouted in church.[70] The opposite of getting religion was failing to make the connection with God and remaining "cold and indifferent," a phrase Thomas uses repeatedly to indicate a turning away from God.[71] She employs evangelical terminology most intensely during her years at Wesleyan, when she and her fellow students were preoccupied with the state of their souls. The central feature of this style of religion is an emotional commitment to a personal God.

As the white evangelical churches became more reserved during the late antebellum era, shouting fell out of fashion. By 1855 Thomas cites a woman's shouting in her church in Augusta as "unusual."[72] Torn between fervor and respectability, Thomas flirted with Episcopalianism. But even though she deplores the lack of refinement and culture of her Methodist church and is attracted to the ritual and solemnity of the Episcopalian church, preaching at the latter bores her. At bottom an evangelical Christian, Thomas says she prefers sermons that move her in her heart: "Oh gospel preaching is the most effective after all," she writes. "Give to me the preaching that touches the heart."[73]

Religion of the heart always appealed to Thomas, but not to her husband. For most of their married life she longed for his conversion. When he went to the altar to accept God in 1870, she described the scene in loving detail, though his falling away from her religion she reported only briefly.[74]

Confirmed Methodist though Thomas was, she conceived her Christianity broadly. Like many respectable southerners, she saw nature (which she identified as female) as closely allied with God. Her Christianity being highly literal, she took natural phenomena, such as the clearing of the sky ("a smile direct from Heaven") or the sound of thunder ("God's voice"), as indications of God's immediate presence.[75] She also belonged to the thousands of educated men and women in the nineteenth-century United States, including many feminists and abolitionists, who believed it possible to establish contact with a spirit world.[76]

Although northern intellectuals and reformers had known about the writing of Emanuel Swedenborg in the 1840s, Thomas did not discover his thought until 1857, when she began investigating spiritualism.[77] Like many others, her interest in establishing contact with the spirit world increased with personal loss, in this case the deaths of her father and her children. She worried whether they were happy and repeatedly (and mostly in vain) attempted to contact them, by herself or through human mediums. Her belief in the possibility of communicating with the world of spirits shows that for Thomas, Methodism and spiritualism did not conflict. Hers, however, was a highly evangelical brand of spiritualism. Her visits to spiritualists in New York City demonstrate the limits of her willingness to stray from Methodist orthodoxy.

In the fall of 1870, Thomas accompanied her mother and older sister to New York, where they visited a medium who put them in touch with the spirit of her late father Turner Clanton. The medium did not offend Thomas, for he presented himself as a man with a useful skill rather than as a religious practitioner. But the religion she discovered at a self-proclaimed spiritualist church did put her off. She found the pastor of the Strangers Church at Apollo Hall at once attractive and repellent. He reinforced her hope that spirits did visit the world, but he also advanced doctrines antithetical to "our religion." The section of his sermon on spirits persuaded her, but as a whole Thomas found this no proper church: "It was good so far as it went, but there was no religion there. No acknowledgement of a personal God." In the final analysis, the spiritualist minister's hands and feet were too big, his boots were coarse, and his clothes were common, shortcomings that weighed heavily in Thomas's system of values. Apollo Hall did not extinguish Thomas's attraction to spiritualism, though, and she continued to write of wanting to talk with the dead over a period of nearly twenty-five years.[78]

Given the depth of her commitment to her religion and its constant presence in her life, Thomas's spiritual record is most poignant in moments when she loses faith. For any Christian, particularly one so devout as she, doubting God is highly disturbing, as Thomas makes clear. Her religion briefly failed to sustain her when she feared that her son Julian was about to die, but her worse religious crises — and therefore, her strongest psychological and ideological perturbations — were three in number. The first occurred in 1864, when her father died. The second followed emancipation in 1865, and the third accompanied the first awful round of financial failures in 1869–70. She wondered why God would send the earthquakes that frightened her so in the 1880s, but this constituted a query rather than a loss of faith.[79]

The doubts associated with her father's death were many: How could God take away her strongest support, her admired and generous father? Turner Clanton had been ill in the past, and in 1858, when Jefferson Thomas's father died, Gertrude had faced the possibility of her own father's dying. Yet the actual event unnerved her. Thomas believed that Turner Clanton, when he died, not only belonged to no church but also had contravened the sixth commandment with women he owned. Desperately striving to prevent his going to hell, Gertrude sent for the Episcopal prayer for the dying and prayed with him on his deathbed.

After Turner Clanton's death, doubts as to his whereabouts tortured her "as with the whip of scorpions" in relation to his greatest sins: Not only had Clanton broken the commandment against adultery, but he had owned, and therefore willed to his heirs as property, his own children. The moral monstrosity of treating his own children as things made Thomas "cold and indifferent to spiritual things." In her anguish, she wrote (and later tried to erase) the pain of recognizing the provenance of part of her inheritance:

Pa's will [illegible] giving of spirit [illegible] making a most liberal provision for all of us children but as God is my witness I would rather never of had that additional increase of property if [illegible]

I would have been afraid the knowledge which was communicated at the same time, how hath the mighty fallen![80]

The crisis passed within a few months, but only after attenuating her faith. It established a metaphor in the journal for ineffectual prayer: It did not ascend "higher than my head." She employed this image again after her second great moment of crisis: emancipation.[81]

Thomas's remarks on emancipation reveal what thousands of former slaveowners must have felt in the spring of 1865. Unlike most, Thomas wrote about the effect of emancipation on her religion. Confederates had attached God to the Confederacy. They had prayed earnestly, confident that God would respond to their entreaties. When the Confederate cause was lost, all that faith seemed to have been wasted. She admits that "my faith in revelation and faith in the institution of slavery had been woven together."[82]

This disappointment she shared with every partisan who has ever championed war in the certainty that God is on her side. But for Confederates, whose cause finally came down to a defense of slavery, failure had an additional religious dimension. The Bible sanctioned slavery, and proslavery rhetoric had made much of that. In 1864, when Thomas tried to convince herself that slavery was right, she consulted the Bible. Once slavery actually was abolished, she admitted her quandary: "If the *Bible* was right then slavery *must be*—Slavery was done away with and my faith in God's Holy Book was terribly shaken." Employing language that she would use again when faced with insurmountable financial problems that also taxed her religious faith, Thomas was "bewildered."[83]

Crisis after crisis beat down her convictions and a flood of frustration eroded her faith. By 1870 she no longer lashed out at God in defiance. Struggling to regain her old, fervent religion, she admitted "I cannot, I cannot."[84]

Thomas remained in the Methodist church even after her children and grandchildren moved into more formalist denominations in the late nineteenth and early twentieth centuries. But hers was no longer the unquestioning faith of an innocent. It may be that Thomas's loss of religious conviction was implicated in the way she lived the last twenty or so years of her life. Without sufficient religion to sustain her, she may have found it impossible to continue her journal. Or the social activism of her mature years may have taken the place of her earlier religious faith. In either case, she left no clues.

Thomas embedded her identity as a Christian within her identity as a woman. In 1855, she was shocked when a woman spoke up in church, for St. Paul had said that women should not speak in public. When she questioned the Methodist church's provision for confession and counseling, she spoke of the inability of male class leaders to fathom a woman's nature. And in her respect for the power of nature, she spoke repeatedly of a gendered, female Nature.[85] Beyond religion, her female identity was of a piece with her identity as an individual.

### *"A Woman Myself"*

From the moment she finished Wesleyan, Thomas wrote of herself as a woman and, over the years, exhibited an acute consciousness of gender. A young wife and mother, she defined womanhood through these roles, as they were shaped by their attendant gratification and suffering — especially suffering.[86]

With the fulfillment of her woman's role came certain pains, most of which she did not seek to conceal. She grieved for each of her children who died, whether it was a tiny infant whose life ended within a few weeks, or Clanton, who lived to be nearly seven years old. She cherished her children but hated the early weeks of pregnancy, when she felt depressed and tired. Three times she expresses ambivalence toward childbearing.

Despite loving her children and giving birth with comparative ease, she did not want children too frequently. An interval of less than two years between pregnancies seemed insufficient, and she pitied an acquaintance who had had children only thirteen months apart. Motherhood was a joy, the mission of woman's life, but the lucky woman spaced out her blessings.[87] For Thomas conception was a matter of chance. Unlike many northern women, and along with her fellow southerners of both races, she did not attempt to limit the size of her family, through either abstinence or contraception.[88]

To be a woman also meant overcoming the frustrations inherent in marriage, which Thomas terms the "matrimonial quicksands against which my wayward barque has sometimes drifted."[89] She expresses solidarity with other women in need or in trouble, even when they belonged to classes and races other than her own. Before the Civil War she writes that, as "a woman myself," she can sympathize with slave women who are pregnant.[90] (Thomas's sentiments toward her female employees hardened after emancipation, when she was paying them wages that represented scarce cash in the Thomas household. In a wage economy, the old gender solidarity vanished. Thomas resented the drag that young children imposed on household workers and dismissed a young mother who was about to give birth.) During the war she gave money and food to a poor white woman refugee who was living in a railroad car.[91] Throughout the journal she writes sympathetically of poor seamstresses forced to support their children and husbands when the latter were drunkards or otherwise unable to provide for their families. Women, she believed, were entitled to support from their husbands.[92]

Thomas deplored separation or divorce even when men failed to maintain their families or the marriages were miserable. At the same time, she repeatedly records such occurrences, particularly during the 1850s, when she questioned the soundness of her own marriage. She calls divorce a disaster and, posing a hypothetical choice that may also have been part of an argument with herself, prefers widowhood to divorce.[93] Thomas's peers shared her views and only reluctantly conceded that separation and divorce actually occurred, an attitude particularly strong before the Civil War, when the ideology of romance captivated wealthy southern women.

In the 1850s Thomas saw gender hierarchy as natural and right. She calls her husband as her "master," to whom she looks up, and mentions her "woman's weakness protected by man's superior strength."[94] Such remarks do not indicate a blind acceptance of the conventions of mid-century gender relations. Although she distanced herself from the northern movement for women's rights, Thomas held clear ideas about injustices women suffered in the areas of education and sexuality. Having received far more formal education than most southern women, she knew women could absorb more learning than they were allowed. She believed women should be able to stay longer in school for purely intellectual reasons. Higher education need not be aimed toward moral ends, for southern women (i.e., white women from respectable families) received sufficient moral instruction within the home. Men were another matter. Men required as much education as possible to instill in them the correct notions of right and wrong, particularly in regard to sex.[95]

Before the war, Thomas condemns the sexual double standard. She insists that women should maintain the highest standards of sexual purity, yet recognizes that they might be raped or seduced or led astray by men. Outraged, she denounces the acquittal of a local rapist who had taken advantage of his wife's friend, a woman of his own class.[96] Thomas did not judge unchaste women more harshly than free loving men. She reckoned that nearly all men, particularly southern white men, were morally depraved — after carefully excepting her own husband.[97] Like most social purity advocates, Thomas wanted to confine sex to marriage. Her reasoning, unacknowledged in her journal, was highly personal.

The journal does not clarify whether Thomas's female purity phrasing came from her evangelical Methodism or drew on the female purity movement in the antebellum North. She does not mention the northern movement, perhaps because its adherents tended toward abolitionism. Nonetheless, Thomas's wide-ranging reading of current literature would have brought her into touch with moral reform thought. Without a doubt, her mid-century convictions made the Woman's Christian Temperance Union doubly attractive to her in the 1880s, for one of the organization's basic goals was elevating men to women's standards of sexual purity. Working for temperance in the 1880s in the WCTU extended Thomas's long-standing concern for social purity and a single sexual standard.[98]

Before the war, Thomas has but little comment on the morals of blacks.[99] The slaves (termed "servants") appearing in the antebellum section of the journal are virtually all women. They are as likely to appear in the roles of women in black families as they are to appear as workers. As workers, too, they often serve in familial roles. One job Thomas mentions several times during her antebellum childbearing years is that of wet nurse. She does not note that although these mother surrogates filled the most maternal of roles, they were bought, sold, and lent as chattel.[100]

As befit their lofty status, Thomas and the other women in her family took a maternal, noblesse oblige interest in the weddings of their slaves, providing the cloth and supplies from which the celebrants made bridal costumes and party food. Even after emancipation, the custom of giving household workers wedding provisions endured, although in attenuated fashion. The weddings of female slaves appear as special events, which Thomas describes in more detail than she does the weddings of her family, friends, and neighbors.[101]

The salient identity of female slaves in the journal is as mothers — mothers of many children, devoted mothers, mothers of the children of white men. One striking journal entry fondly describes a slave woman whose "maternal affection is the most strongly developed feeling she has."[102] Thomas describes households in which black and white women share far more than a work site. Her slaves are, like her, mothers and daughters of whom she sometimes grows fond. Thomas describes enslaved women with varying amounts of affect; sometimes slaves appear within the setting of physical scenes, occasionally they come to life as individuals with whom Thomas is engaged. Thomas's experience with one of her female slaves illustrates both the boundaries and the attractions of an ambiguous relationship.

Isabella, whom Thomas ultimately came to regard as a thief and a runaway, appears as her son Turner's baby nurse in many entries between the spring of 1855 and the winter of 1859. Most citations are brief, but three are longer, including a confession, which Thomas finds "strange," of "a feeling amounting nearer to attachment than to any servant I ever met with in my life." After Isabella has been banished from the household, her memory haunts Thomas, who gets the blues in the kitchen where Isabella had worked.[103]

When the time came to name her baby girl, Thomas invoked the name Isabella, but sought more acceptable antecedents. The baby became Mary Belle, "Mary" after Thomas's mother and sister. To explain "Belle," Thomas recalled a girlhood friend from her own race and class, Isabel Morrison Harrington. However, the chronology of events mentioning Isabel Morrison Harrington and Isabella the slave, and the relative emotional intensity of the writing in those entries, throw Thomas's statement into doubt.

At the time of Mary Belle's birth, Thomas's journal shows her to have been far more involved emotionally with Isabella than with Isabel Morrison Harrington. The entries on Isabella the slave, before and after Mary Belle's birth, are full of affect.[104] Despite enormous affection for a black woman with whom she shared her children and her house for several years, hierarchies of race and class prevented Thomas from honoring that tie directly. On the conscious level, she could only express her attraction to Isabella the slave by reaching for someone else. Had Isabel Morrison Harrington not existed, the child could not have been named Belle. Nor, I suspect, would Thomas have sought to use the name Belle in the absence of Isabella the slave.

The turmoil of the war years revealed disparities between stereotypical women's roles and their actual lives. Thomas found herself willing not only to travel without her husband, but also to mention that she and other women held property in their own rights, even though polite usage denied women the satisfaction of calling their possessions their own.[105] The postwar section of the journal, in which Thomas faces unpleasant realities and becomes a salaried worker, favors independence of thought and action over submission to the gender hierarchy. After the war, Thomas grew less willing to rationalize her husband's shortcomings. Whereas early in her marriage, she ascribed the need to economize to Jefferson's having made a short crop and the difficulties of starting out, by 1870 she is no longer casting about for excuses. Squarely facing the facts, she cites her husband's "bad management." She writes no more of man's superior strength and woman's weakness when she is paying the bills.[106]

Thomas usually a writes about the condition of women with clarity. As in many of her comments about race, she is remarkably clear, articulating concepts that most Americans failed to frame coherently. However she did not perceive the interrelationship between her thinking about gender, race, and class. She felt keenly but did not fathom the extent to which a major trauma in her life — impending emancipation — threatened her identity as a woman.

Entries dealing with black or poor white women show that Thomas extended her definition of women across the lines of race and class. She knew that femaleness, particularly in its sexual component, united all women, and her most basic feelings and fears about gender were unbounded. When she makes judgments about given women, however, she narrows her definition. Addressing her daughter Mary Belle, she writes proudly of being "a *woman* in the *proper sense*," meaning a woman who had "suffered and grown strong," a phrase she employs twice to define true womanhood. "Woman," therefore, meant married women, not merely because young, unmarried women had not faced the ultimate tests of husband and children, but also because they were of necessity ignorant of an important aspect of womanly experience, sexual intimacy. Thomas's belief in sexual purity dictated her insistence that unmarried women should not understand (or write about) "*certain* subjects." Hence Thomas excoriates women writers such as George Sand, who broached the topic of sexuality.[107]

At one point, discussing a Civil War incident that concerns her father, Thomas confuses class and gender. After Turner Clanton had offered to sell corn at his plantation to soldiers' wives at less than the inflated market price, these poor women complained that the offer was useless to them because they lacked transportation. Thomas interprets the exchange from her class's point of view: Her father had been generous to make the offer; the poor women were ingrates for complaining that Clanton had not brought the corn within their reach. The poor women's thanklessness, she says, outrages her "womanly honor," as though the poor women lacked proper female sensibilities.[108]

Beyond these relatively straightforward observations about womanliness, Thomas records a series of intensely emotional entries that betray her anxiety over the security of her status as a wife. She expresses fear of being superseded by another woman should she die in childbirth, of mulatto women's usurping the places of white wives, and of competition between black and white women over white men. Thomas's preoccupation with the theme of replacement was deep and long standing — her observations on the interchangeability of women begin before the Civil War and continue after it.

Considering the state of medical knowledge and the real peril that confinement represented, it is not surprising that Thomas repeatedly confronts the possibility of death in childbirth. Every nineteenth-century mother would have entertained similar fears. Ordinarily Thomas takes the rhetorical high road and pretends not to be disturbed by the idea of the "future Mrs Thomas." But she returns to the theme so often that her lofty protestations ("My dear madam who ever you may prove [to be], you have my best wishes.") ring false. In the year of upheaval, she admits to being "tormented" by "jealous thoughts" as she envisions the "step mother who may be selected to take my place."[109]

But a cluster of entries on the theme in 1865, as emancipation first threatened her world and then turned it upside down, illuminates her apprehension.[110] By undermining the foundations of her identity, emancipation exacerbated her old fears about her value as an individual and as a woman, and she imagines scenes in which white wives are displaced by younger women of both races.

In Thomas's case, her imagined successor represented the competitor about whom she could write openly. But the entire issue of rivalry between women distressed her. She knew women like herself depended upon men financially, but that men held the power to choose, discard, and betray women. Recognizing men's power over women's happiness, she did not trust men to exercise that power fairly. In fact, she was certain men's weak moral fiber allowed them to seek out sex at any time. Men would not forego sex even out of respect for a wife recently deceased or absent temporarily. Wives, no matter how white or wealthy, lacked the power to curb men's hunger for sex.

With men so willing to substitute one woman for another and women unable to control them, women could only compete with one another. Thomas traced such competition within and across racial lines, but she wrote most passionately when she envisioned rivals of different ages and races and when the war had undermined the racial hierarchy from which she benefited.

### Union Generals and Mulatto Lovers

Rumors of the sexual habits of Union generals in the South reinforced Thomas's long-standing conviction that slavery had a deleterious effect on the morals of white men. As she faced the unhappy prospect of Confederate defeat, slavery's great evil became a means of exacting revenge on the North, or, more precisely, on the women of the North, the only northerners she considered within her reach. In bitter detail, she records a Union general's cohabitation with a young, beautiful mulatto woman traveling with him:

The time will come when Southern women will be avenged — Let this war cease with the abolition of slavery and I wish for the women of the North no worse fate than will befall them. Their husbands already prepare for them the bitter cup of humiliation which they will be compelled to drink to the dregs — [Union] General [Hugh Judson] Kilpatrick spent a night in Waynesboro. [H]is headquarters were at Mrs Dr Carter's. He demanded that the best bed room in the house should be prepared for himself and a good looking mulatto girl whom he had travelling with him. A seat at the table was furnished her — The officers deferential in their manner to her while thus publicly insulting Mrs Carter in her own house. Lolling indolently in a rocking chair the girl awaits the entrance of the Gen. "What not retired yet Nellie?" is his salutation. "not until your majesty returns" is her reply — Take *that scene* Mrs Kilpatrick as a reward for encouraging your husband to come amongst us.[111]

Whether Thomas writes from rumors or from her own imagination, the import of the anecdote is unmistakable. Southern life humiliates white wives, and a young black woman "usurps" the position of the general's wife in a parody of the elevation of the Negro race Thomas imagines as the abolitionists' goal.

The fantasy extends to an open letter to the wife of Gen. William T. Sherman, again playing out the drama of Negro elevation, sexual rivalry, and the revenge of Confederate women on northern women, which Thomas wrote with the intention of publishing it in her local newspaper. (She did not send it.) Thomas believes the Union Army aims "to elevate the Negro race," an aim that has been accomplished:

Be satisfied Madam your wish has been accomplished. Enquire of Gen Sherman when next you see him who has been elevated to fill your place? You doubtless read with a smile of approbation of the delightfully fragrant ball at which he made his debut in Atlanta? Did he tell you of the Mulatto girl for whose safety he was so much concerned that she was returned to Nashville when he commenced his vandal march? This girl was spoken of by the Negroes whom you are willing to trust so implicitly as "Sherman's wife." Rest satisfied Mrs Sherman and quiet the apprehension of your Northern sisters with regard to the elevation of the Negros — Your husbands are amongst a coloured race whose reputation for morality has never been of the highest order — and these gallant cavaliers are most of them provided with "a companion du voyage."[112]

Thomas's imagination inflicts upon her female enemies in the North the most fearsome punishment she can imagine: displacement from the conjugal bed.

As topsy-turvy times exposed her personal vulnerabilities, Thomas faced up to the possibility that neither education, wealth, class, nor race provided sufficient assurance that her husband would not replace her with another woman. Several oblique comments indicate that Thomas feared that a light-skinned woman of African descent had already "usurped" her place as her husband's sexual partner and had borne a boy who was about the age of Turner Thomas, born in 1853. Taking Gertrude's 1869 comments about racial competition into account, the agitation reported in the journal entries of 29 May–3 June 1855 may well concern her discovery of Jefferson Thomas's intimate relationship with another woman, a woman who is not white. There is no doubt that Thomas thought that "the serpent" had entered her home and that she had a "cross" to bear.[113]

In Thomas's particular formulation of gender relations, all women sought to bind their men to them, particularly in the crisis year of 1865. Black as well as white men were likely to wander when they could, also leaving black women vulnerable to abandonment. In May 1865, Thomas reworks the scenes in which she had imagined Union generals' infidelities, only this time she reports that the driver from the plantation in Burke County left "an ugly faithful black wife" to go off with "a good looking mulatto."[114]

In 1865 the journal is filled with evidence of extreme social trauma not replicated elsewhere. Thomas never again writes so long and intensely of women's vulnerability to displacement. But she returns to the theme of rivalry between women. Twice she mentions black men's resisting the attempts of their common-law wives to marry legally and thus stabilize their relationships.[115] Just as beautiful young mulattoes might usurp the place of white wives, so African-American women also faced rivals among themselves.

As Thomas saw it, mulattoes represented the main competition to both white and dark-skinned Negro women. A few years after emancipation, having witnessed the spread of interracial liaisons among the poor, she worries about the rivalry between white and educated mulatto women. Thomas writes that in the competition for elite white men, women of color possess one innate advantage that education will only intensify: a "tropical, passionate nature."[116] Years earlier, she had written proudly of Confederate women as "our warm hearted children of the sun."[117] A confirmed white supremacist, Thomas respects her racial hierarchy, yet as a woman she sees the similarity of all southern women's attractive qualities and their vulnerabilities to the whims of all men.

### Black People, Enslaved and Free

As a plantation mistress living in a Black Belt county, Thomas was surrounded by African Americans of both sexes and all ages. Among blacks, women figure most prominently in the journal, identified by name rather than by race. Thomas often discusses race in tandem with sexuality and, after emancipation, labor. I doubt that she separated labor relations from race relations — most Americans did not — but because she wrote so extensively of the frustrations she encountered as an economically straitened employer of household workers, I will discuss labor relations separately.

During the antebellum period, Thomas mentions blacks only occasionally, not always as workers. They appear as social beings — at weddings, funerals, church services — often under Thomas's benign regard. A black preacher has a "decidedly fine command of language," and the beau of one of her slaves is "one of the finest looking men I ever saw."[118] Her ability to see blacks as individuals, together with her keen sense of social and economic hierarchy, might seem to make Thomas more a class snob than a racist.[119] A closer look reveals that even before emancipation, she ranked people according to race and uses pronouns to mark her boundaries.

Well before establishing the use of the first-person plural for Confederates, Thomas is using the third-person plural to designate blacks, a usage that persists after the end of the war. Just as "we" and "our" refer to educated white southerners and Confederates, "they" and "their" indicate blacks, without normative connotations. Describing a church service that she finds intensely moving, Thomas writes: "How irrepressible a people they are! How easily their feelings are wrought upon!"[120] She is capable of drawing other generalizations about supposed racial traits. Retelling the story of her driver, who insists that he is a free man who had been cheated out of his freedom, Thomas uncharacteristically leaves incomplete a sentence fragment on the separation of the man's family. Without deploring a distressing act for which she undoubtedly felt responsible, she concludes the "Negro is a cheerful being."[121] Several entries exemplify an unconscious train of thought that leads from blacks directly to horses. Black people remind her of horses, whether as objects of affection or as inferior beings, and the association would serve to increase her social distance from those who served her.[122]

For all her ease in delineating racial characteristics among blacks, Thomas's thinking about race was less contradictory and less harsh than that of many other Americans. She believed that physiognomy indicated intelligence and ability or their lack, as in the case of a white amateur musician whose forehead showed talent but whose jaw was "animal." But she disagrees with the belief, common among whites of her time, that blacks are intelligent according to the proportion of their white ancestry. Even during the period when she desperately tried to convince herself of the justice of slavery, she rejects the "Ariel" doctrine of polygenesis, a view that blacks are a lower form of human life and incapable of learning. Like any other people, she says, blacks would profit from instruction. Environment, therefore, makes a difference, but in a Lamarckian way, for Thomas believes that education and refinement are inheritable. Along with such beliefs, she accepts many racist platitudes that underscore racial differences and black inferiority. Yet she tends to apply the same moral and intellectual standards to both races.[123] In sum, Gertrude Thomas believed that racial traits existed, that environment changed people's native abilities, and that blacks possessed a full measure of humanity but were presently, but not necessarily permanently, inferior to whites. Her recognition of black potential caused her much concern.

Racial designations rarely appear in the antebellum section of the journal, which covers a period when most people stayed in their distinct and separate social spheres and race did not need mentioning. However, departures from the established order did occur, and the early section of the journal includes the stories of a rumored slave revolt and a case of racial confusion in Thomas's own house. Early in 1857 and again at the end of 1858, Thomas mentions the fear of slave insurrection spreading through Tennessee and Georgia at the end of 1856. Both times her response is remarkably cool, establishing a pattern that persists throughout the journal that marks her off from both blacks and other whites. She denies a fear of blacks, even of black men, even of violent black men. While other whites run from shadows, Thomas flaunts her physical courage, which others also note. But her composure does not blind her to endangerment. Twice she evokes the image of Neapolitans going about their lives under an active volcano — the volcano here standing for the possibility of a slave uprising.[124]

Insurrection presented a frightening but recognizable departure from the racial hierarchy. On an entirely different scale of social magnitude, an incident at home illustrates the Thomases' response to a racial situation with potential for dishonor. When a man of undetermined race comes to see Jefferson Thomas, Gertrude is unsure how to deal with him. She decides to take the chance of treating a nonwhite as an equal rather than risk insulting a white man. Accepting Jefferson's invitation to eat with them, the man sits down at the table and takes off his hat. He looks, in Gertrude's words, "more suspicious than ever." When it turns out that the man is not white, Gertrude is outraged. The stranger had insulted her by sitting "at a white lady's table," something racial etiquette expressly prohibits.[125]

For Gertrude Thomas, people of mixed blood represented slavery's prime negative aspect. Ordinarily, however, her misgivings concerned mulatto women rather than mulatto men. In a very long 1859 entry on miscegenation, Thomas comments on the child of one of her mother's house slaves, the child appearing "as white as any white child."[126] Her words never hint right here that the child might be her father's. However the length of this entry and evidence elsewhere in the journal indicate that on some level, be it unconscious, Thomas's interest in the child related to the possibility it could be her half sibling.

Deploring the use of enslaved mulatto women as concubines, Thomas quotes the Swedish novelist Fredrika Bremer, then traveling in the United States, on the "white children of slavery." Thomas regrets that their very existence testifies to the prevalence of race mixing and lowers the "tone of the South" morally. Like Mary Chesnut, Thomas thought white southern women were "all at heart abolitionists" because of miscegenation, and like Mary Chesnut, Thomas restricted that thought to her journal. Thomas went even further than Chesnut; she execrated not just interracial sex, but also the hypocritical opponents of mixed marriages who tolerated interracial concubinage. To

Thomas the moral reformer, men who lived with black women without marrying them were debased twice over, through both interracial intimacy and fornication. Slavery, she concluded, "degrades the white man more than the Negro and oh exerts a most deleterious effect upon our children."[127]

Thomas disapproved of the influence of slaves and slavery upon white children. Describing the cultural interchange (in both directions) taking place when black or white children came in close contact with adults and children of the other race, she approves of whites' influence on black children but not of blacks' influence on white children. She reserves a special anguish for the moral lessons of the peculiar institution. White male miscegenators, she felt, set a terrible example for their children. To aggravate matters, the presence of mixed-race children so close to home burdened her with the awkward duty of explaining their presence to her own children.[128]

The war introduced an entirely new racial rhetoric. For the first time, inspired perhaps by the newspapers, certainly by her own intimation of loss, Thomas writes negrophobia. Suddenly her tone grows shrill and bigoted, as she descries the "vindictive passions of an inferior race." Such hysteria subsides, with the collapse of Thomas's initial burst of Confederate chauvinism. But henceforth the journal takes far more note of blacks, as a race and as individual workers. Along with money matters, they are the journal's main concern after 1864. Having heretofore seen herself at the center of a system of black and white families in which she assumed that blacks gave their labor willingly, Thomas comes to see herself within a system in which (at least) two sets of interests competed.

If the intensity of her defense mechanisms is any indication, emancipation confronted Thomas with the most traumatic situation of her entire life. A funeral's healing ritual salved the wound of her father's death. But emancipation lacked precedent and established expectations. This revolution perturbed Thomas despite her attempts at preparation.

In the fall of 1864, she apprehends the possibility of Confederate defeat and the abolition of slavery. For the first time, she thinks about slavery as a labor system, not merely as a source of moral endangerment. The process is not easy. She begins by deciding that "the Negro *as a race* is better of with us as he has been than if he were free, but I am by no means so sure that we would not gain by his having his freedom given him," for slavery imposes a heavy burden of responsibility on slaveholders. A few days later she slips into denial and describes what, had there been no war, would have been a perfectly normal scene. She paints a reassuring picture of her slaves at work around her, yet concludes that "to hold men and women in *perpetual* bondage is wrong." Shortly afterward, she repudiates this doubt.[129] Before she has reached firm conclusions, emancipation overwhelms her.

Thomas's response to Confederate defeat is denial. She says she feels "no particular emotion." But the next day her body manifests her alarm, and she nearly blacks out at her piano lesson. Professing not to know what has made her faint, she describes the swoon and, a sentence later, brings in freedom. At the end of a very long entry, she describes what had taken place that very morning. Her husband had called their slaves together to tell them they were free, which utterly delighted them. Over the succeeding days she records the departure of workers who had been with her for years and says she renounces any further interest in their welfare.[130]

The entries of May and June 1865 capture the meanings of emancipation for the white elite. With her characteristic intelligence, honesty, and sensitivity, Thomas articulates the betrayal former owners felt. Years later she sorts out her confusion: Having given credence to the appearance of contentment slaveholders demanded of slaves, she had assumed her slaves served her voluntarily—that their labor was not "extorted." She had supposed them happily enslaved. But now she must make sense of their joy at becoming free.[131]

At the moment of emancipation, Thomas tries to distance herself from a situation in which she has a great emotional investment. She douses old feelings of affection and, exasperated and angry, declares that "I do most heartily despise Yankees, Negroes and everything connected with them. The theme has been sung in my hearing until it is a perfect abomination. I positively instinctively shut my ears when I hear the hated subject mentioned and right gladly would I be willing never to place my eyes upon another as long as I live. . . . I feel no interest in them whatever and hope I never will."[132] Over the next few years, Thomas copes with the loss of household workers through rationalization: Those departing were not very good, and the new ones are much better.[133]

By the late 1860s Thomas had settled down psychologically, but black people continue to play a major role in her journal. Appearing primarily as employees, they also figure as political actors and competitors in a new social order.

During Reconstruction, Thomas's thinking about blacks ran along two distinct tracks, one leading toward a calm tolerance, the other into agitated fears of racial and sexual competition. Although by no stretch of the imagination could she be termed a supporter of Reconstruction, she responded more reasonably than leading Democrats like her husband.

She felt desperate and wrote (again) of living at the mouth of a volcano. Yet she was able to discuss the crucial Reconstruction election of November 1868 with her servants and draw an analogy between their situation and her own. She confesses to her journal that "I do not in my heart wonder that the Negroes vote the radical ticket. . . . If the women of the North once secured to me the right to vote . . . I should think twice before I voted to have it taken from me." Meanwhile, her husband fills the house with guns, leads a local military company poised to attack the Republicans, and eavesdrops from under the house on the servants' political deliberations. Thomas finds this all somewhat excessive, for the two sides (well-armed white Democrats, poorly organized black Republicans) are so ill matched. She keeps her composure but denounces her white neighbors' "exhibition of fear": panicky whites might "encourage evil passions in the Negroes."[134]

Reconstruction does alter the tenor of her remarks about blacks, for the first time allowing physical revulsion and small-minded surliness to creep into her comments about educated black men. Such observations would become more characteristic of twentieth- than nineteenth-century southern racism.[135] The threat of blacks as competitors, not merely servants, would have lent her words an edge.[136]

## Competition across the Color Line

The late 1860s confronted Thomas with two disturbing realities. First, her oldest child, Turner, instead of attending college, left school at sixteen to work for his father in the fields. The interruption of Turner's education troubled Thomas, who viewed education as a crucial attribute of elite standing. Turner had been born into wealth, but he now plowed beside a poor and uneducated black boy, or, more properly, a boy of mixed race. Thomas asks herself: "Can this white boy with the aid of hereditary antecedents accomplish more than the one beside him? What are his [the white boy's] talents for?" As in her anxieties about competition between women, Thomas sees mulattoes (not blacks) as the likely rivals.[137] She contrasts her husband's depriving her son of his education — because farm hands are scarce — with the Negro mother's sacrificing to give her mulatto son an education. In a political system in which both boys will vote and hold office, the two parents' actions jeopardize white supremacy. Thomas advocates education for white boys, in order to maintain a white supremacy further undermined by the postwar innovation of social equality.

Thomas's agitated diction discloses the second peril in this scene of the two boys plowing in a field. She reveals her anxieties about mulatto-white rivalry between women and between boys as connected and far from hypothetical. She does not identify either her husband or her son, although she has already written a good deal previously of her heartbreak over Jefferson's putting Turner to work in the fields. Also unnamed is the African-American plowboy, whom she describes, precisely, as "the mulatto boy, perhaps his father's son by a woman a shade darker than *his* mother."[138]

Thomas cannot name her husband, Jefferson, or her son, Turner, here, because to do so would shred the veil over a painful fact: the existence of her husband's outside child. She generalizes the situation into a danger for all white boys of good family who are not being educated. Without adequate education, a new, post-emancipation version of miscegenation would spread, one entailing legal marriage. Gertrude Thomas reports that educated white women almost never marry black men, but poor white women have been doing so since emancipation.[139] Her great fear, at least ostensibly, was for the men. But something else unarticulated may well have perturbed her.

If young men of the better classes do not receive the education they deserve, Thomas writes, they will sink into "degradation," the word she employs in the antebellum era when writing about miscegenation. Earlier journal comments reveal her awareness of the widespread practice of elite white men's cohabiting with black and mulatto women, presumably without withdrawing from the marriage market or creating a shortage of partners among elite women. Reconstruction, however, is a different time. The present danger is not so much miscegenation, which has been "so common as to create no surprise whatever," but "social equality," that is, marriage as among equals, which Thomas predicts will come about in her children's generation.[140] Having known of interracial sex her whole life, Thomas now worries about interracial marriage.

She foresees the possibility of newly impoverished, uneducated men from formerly elite families not knowing any better than to marry mulatto women legally. Brought together, then, the separate threads of Thomas's comments about race and interracial sex lead back to women, as well as men, of her own class and race in the fear that few suitable marriage partners will remain for her daughters. That her oldest daughter, Mary Belle, reached the advanced age of twenty-five before marrying must have reinforced her mother's fears of spinsterhood on her behalf. Mary Belle's mother and grandmother had both married as teenagers.[141] Mary Belle was eleven when Thomas expressed her fears, seven years younger than her mother had been when she married. Mary Belle married the socially prominent Frederick Laurens Ingraham in 1883.

Thomas's fears of racial competition subsided as a more familiar, and, to her, less threatening racial system began to be restored with the end of Reconstruction in Georgia in 1872. However the post-Reconstruction era brought her no greater satisfaction as an employer. With other women of her class, Thomas did more and more of her own housework, a hard reality for which her antebellum training had not prepared her.[142] Although her husband would have taken comfort from the return of the Democratic party to political power in Georgia, Thomas saw few analogous improvements in her house and yard. Post-Reconstruction race relations may have threatened her less emotionally, but labor relations continued to plague her.

## Gertrude Thomas in the World of Work

In the prewar journal entries, work is often accomplished by invisible hands, so that Gertrude *has* a fire made or Jefferson *has* piles of brush burned. Often, Thomas names the workers whose actions constitute much of the fabric of everyday life, as in two entries concerning the same versatile domestic worker: "Tamah has just got out supper," and "I have been quite busy today having the front garden spaded by Tamah."[143] As the focal point in her household and as a slaveholder,

Thomas never had gave much thought to her slaves' needs, which were automatically subordinated. Only one set of interests counted in her household: her own.[144] Emancipation abolished what she had taken as frictionless labor relations. For the first time, Thomas had to contend with employees who pursued interests of their own.

The spring of 1865 introduced Thomas to new, bilateral labor relations that were internally complex. All by itself, emancipation plunged black families into turmoil, throwing matters of power and place into question. Black men and women were not only adjusting to individual and familial autonomy, but they also were establishing and reestablishing relationships of domicile and authority within their families. Emancipation also occurred in the wake of a war that had tangled gender relations among black men and women, as among whites. Just as southern white women had begun to seize the opportunity to write, speak, and work for wages, so black women in and around Augusta were also moving into openings that had never existed before. They could withdraw from the paid work force to stay home to care for their husbands and children, or they could sell food in the streets and railroad stations or keep other women's houses and babies for money.[145] The resulting upheaval tested Thomas's limits as both employer and housekeeper.

Freedwomen's increased opportunities inside and outside the work force caused a shortage in household labor disadvantageous to Thomas. White workers seemed a natural resort to fill this gap, and in 1865 Thomas predicted the speedy displacement of black labor by white. Experience proved otherwise. An experiment with poor Irish Catholic workers convinced Thomas that whites were no improvement over blacks. In the house and in the fields, workers of either race pursued their own interests; one race proved no more selfless or reliable than the other.[146] To aggravate matters for an employer used to a permanent work force, emancipated household workers engaged to work only one month at a time.

Free labor presented Thomas with a number of frustrations, the greatest of which was workers' new mobility, both into and out of the work force and between employers. Considering that emancipation coincided with financial losses, Thomas found the second sort of mobility more trying. Chronically short of cash, she complained for years of only being able to afford the young, inexperienced, or careless workers who annoyed her within the household. Jefferson Thomas was also acutely aware of the difficulty of keeping efficient workers. But he worked less intimately with his employees. The two Thomases disagreed over the extent to which employers should make concessions over wages or working conditions. He saw the necessity for conciliating first-rate workers, but she insisted that every worker respect her standards of employee-employer etiquette.[147]

Deference proved a touchy question for both sides. Former slaves sought to separate freedom from slavery by dropping extreme forms of submission, as between an older worker and a younger member of the employer's household. On the other side, Thomas tried, as much as possible, to preserve older forms of subjection and to widen the distance between employers/whites and employees/blacks. In her scheme of labor relations, deference counted for more than efficiency: "[H]ands are scarce but respect is a quality I demand from servants even more than obedience. I can overlook neglected work but cannot tolerate disrespect."[148]

In the long run, Thomas seems to have won the battle over defer- ence, if not over wages. During the five years following emancipation, the only period in which she reports the wages she is paying, a labor shortage of farm as well as household workers drove wages steadily upward. In 1865 Thomas paid a mere twenty-five cents per week to a full-time household worker; this person seems, not surprisingly, to have departed quickly, for Thomas not only offered minuscule wages, she disregarded prompt payment. Wages quickly increased from thirty cents per day for washing to fifty cents per day for ironing and five dollars per month for a cook. By late 1868 wages had increased to seven dollars per month plus board. In 1870 Thomas paid two young girls nine dollars per month to do the work for which, in 1865, she offered one dollar per month.[149]

Thomas gradually paid better wages, but her management style never stabilized. She jawboned her employees and hinted they should leave, then was surprised when they actually quit. Others she told to leave without meaning for them to do so. She expected that workers would discern her wishes through intimation or overhearing.[150] Lack- ing the wherewithal to pay wages first-rate workers could demand and imposing an etiquette workers found demeaning, Thomas shouldered more and more of the burden of household work, work she pronounced "utterly uncongenial." Keeping the house in perfect order so wore her out she lowered her standards. Frustrated and exhausted, she began to question her use of her own energy. In the end, her decision to take up teaching grew not only from a need for money, but also from her realization that she was already performing much unpaid labor. Considering her level of education, she could make more efficient use of her time in another line of work. Thomas's actions and reactions characterized women of her background throughout the South.[151]

The conjunction of emancipation and impoverishment made Thomas a working woman; Reconstruction imposed a hitherto unimaginable burden of work, whether paid or unpaid, whether she supervised it or carried it out herself. She realized she was working more than ever and straightforwardly recorded her views. But she also recorded a great deal about events she did not understand. As though spellbound, she described labor relations she no longer controlled.

Thomas writes an exceedingly long and detailed description of a physical fight between two farm workers that breaks out repeatedly right outside the Thomases' door. Verbal commands do not hinder the combatants; only threatened recourse to armed force stops the fights, and then temporarily. The conflict enthralls Thomas because it reveals a side of life hidden during slavery: violence unmediated by white control. The two men's all-consuming fury bears no relation whatever to Thomas or any of her wishes. Before the war, however, her mere presence would have subdued the men's conduct, for as slaves, blacks did not exhibit such independence and self-absorption. Thomas finds this new self-centeredness utterly fascinating and unfathomable.[152]

Her impotence in this situation emphasizes the changes wrought by the war. Having sat securely at the top of the social and economic ladder, where she remained unconscious of workers' concerns and never had to adjust to them, Thomas fell into a less privileged rank. Now her needs competed with those of other people whose desires used not to count. Emancipation cost her the serenity of not having to think about how work got done.

## Gertrude Thomas's Secrets

Valuable as Thomas's observations are as social history, what she withholds from her journal offers priceless insights into long-standing tensions over gender and sexuality in the South and, ultimately, into the nature of nineteenth-century southern society. The journal represents a composed text, which, had Thomas succeeded completely, would have stressed the positive and omitted the negative. That it tells more than she wanted her readers to know testifies to her long-running struggle between unburdening herself of her feelings and maintaining her self-consciously crafted persona.

Beyond the representation of a southerner of a certain class at given historical junctures, the journal consists of another, veiled text that is far less timely. The hidden layer of the journal — the layer of secrets — is murky, personal, and highly gendered. The journal actually conceals two great secrets, one of which, Jeff's drinking, Gertrude did succeed in hiding. The other proved too painful to suppress entirely: the hurt she experienced as a woman — as a wife — and its great secret, too, is timeless.

Even when she is strongest and most outspoken, Thomas veils certain realities of her life she shared with large numbers of other plantation mistresses. Like them, she tries not to see. But unlike the great majority of her peers, Thomas left a huge, magnificent journal. Her writing hints — through what psychologists call "deception clues" (cues that something is being withheld) and "leakage" (inadvertent disclosure) of highly charged material — that some important truths remain obscured.[153]

Both leakage and deception clues are associated with the phenomenon of self-deception, the concealment of painful knowledge from the self. The line between Thomas's deception of her readers (her children) and self-deception is not entirely clear in the journal, for Thomas's concept of her audience varied over the many years that she wrote. At times she addresses her children, at other times her God. In the later years she speaks with remarkable candor to her journal as a confidante (herself). Drawing the line between deception and self-deception may not be an indispensable task here, for, as observers as disparate as the sociologist Erving Goffman and the poet Adrienne Rich point out, the intention to mislead others quickly becomes the misleading of the self.[154]

Thomas leaves two obvious deception clues: one in her fascination with family skeletons, the other in a favorite refrain. Thomas never addresses her husband's drinking directly, but the journal abounds in oblique references that indicate her keeping secrets. Twice, for instance,

she relates the same anecdote about closeted family skeletons. Express-
ing a desire for a female confidante in 1864, she rejects the Catholic
confessional because "these priests are *men*." She says the novelist Susan
Petigru King (the Charleston author of *Lily*, an 1854 novel about competition between women for men that fascinated Thomas) invests
every household with a skeleton:

> Dining one day with Thackeray when he visited the South, a door of
> the sideboard just behind her would remain open. Jumping up she
> fastened it by inserting a piece of paper. "Does that door contain
> your skeleton?" was his enquiry seeing her interest. "Ah" replied she,
> "that would not contain one half of my skeletons." . . . No, it is the
> writings of some sensible, practical woman, one who has "suffered
> & grown strong."[155]

Four and one-half years later, Thomas returns to family secrets:

> We all have our troubles, our thorn in the flesh but sometimes we
> are more sensitive to its piercing than others. I wonder too if there is
> not some truth in the remark that in every house there is a skeleton,
> some subject which by mutual consent it is best to avoid. . . . I try
> not to look but I cannot always help it, even to you my dear friend I
> must not confide every thought I have. I would like to.

and to the King-Thackeray anecdote:

> When Mr Thackeray was dining with Mrs. King some years ago in
> Charleston a sideboard door flew open. She rose & was shutting it
> when Mr Thackeray said to her "Does that door contain your skel-
> eton?" "Oh no" she lightly replied. "it is not large enough to contain
> one half of them" The best plan to adopt is to do as she did. Shut the
> door upon them and keep it locked — and if sometimes the door *will
> open*, don't stand to look but shut it quick.[156]

Four times between 1852 (the year in which she married) and 1870,
she cites a poem (or alludes to it by quoting the first line) by the
Georgia poet Richard Henry Wilde:

> There are some thoughts we utter not.
>     Deep treasured in our inmost heart
>         Ne'er revealed and ne'er forgot.[157]

After writing the entry for 4 November 1852, in which she explains that Jeff's illness has postponed their wedding, she quotes the first line of the poem twice in three sentences, and adds "there are some emotions too powerful for words." Thomas did not write again until 8 April 1855. On 26 June 1856 she underlines the last two words of the poem; on 10 Jan. 1870 she cites only the first line.

The intensity of portions of the writing also manifests Thomas's uneasiness over certain subjects, e.g., competition between women, the dual sexual standard, without going to the heart of her distress. The most important deception clues begin with the entry of 2 June 1855, in which Thomas writes: "[T]here are some thoughts we utter not and not even to you my journal . . . yet there are some moments when I must write — must speak or else the pent up emotions of an over-charged heart will *burst* or *break*. . . . With a heart throbbing and an agitated form. How can I write?" Thomas cites "one of the most excit-ing conversations I have ever held. A conversation which in a moment, in a flash of the eye will change the gay, thoughtless girl into a woman with all a woman's feelings" and the "chilling influence (it may be of disappointment) to wonder at the wild tumultuous throbbings of early womanhood." She says that she is troubled by something.

I have never entirely succeeded in deciphering this confusing entry, for the language is more than ambiguous; these phrases lead in two separate directions at once. Thomas's language echoes other women's private descriptions of infatuations at the same time that it represents Thomas's own language of disappointment. When she writes of "all a woman's feelings" elsewhere in the journal, she speaks of chagrin rather than fulfillment. Neither this entry nor those around it provide clues as to the cause(s) of her agitation. But she clearly manifests great anxiety over the contents of a conversation that takes place when her first child is eighteen months old. Moreover, in two other entries in the same season, she speaks of the "bitter agony" and the bitterness of "taunts and expressions" that are the lot of married women.[158]

Several years later, Thomas begins to explicate her concerns in what I call her leakage entries, in which she inadvertently reveals that certain matters are significant to her. The lengthy, intense entry of 2 Janu-ary 1859 deplores miscegenation, which she acknowledges as matter "thought best for [white] women to ignore." Thomas castigates white men of uncontrolled, animal passions who buy mulatto slave women for sex. In general, Thomas had a very low opinion of all southern white men's morals, but bachelors' actions are not uppermost in her mind.[159] Rather, she laments the effect of miscegenation on "our Southern homes." While she believes "slavery" — by which she means the miscegenation the institution effects — degrades white men more than blacks, white families are her main preoccupation.

As early as the 12 May 1856 entry, Thomas includes the following cryptic comment on men's morality: "[W]ere that faith [in her husband] dissipated by *actual experience* then would be dissolved a dream in which is constituted my hope of happiness upon earth. Of course between a husband and wife, this is (or should be) a forbidden subject but to *you* my journal I would willingly disclose many thoughts did I not think that the prying eye of curiosity might scan these lines."

A young mother worrying over slavery's pernicious effect on children, Thomas tries to point away from her own nuclear family and toward the setting in which she was herself a child: her father's household, where she finds "so many" mulatto children. But her unease brings her back to her own home, at first indirectly, through the mention of equally guilty, but unnamed "others." Thomas deplores interracial sex as a violation of the racial hierarchy but is aware that the significance of the miscegenation she has in mind exceeds simply race mixing. It is also sex outside of marriage, so that some individuals worth worrying about in her father's household and in the household of "others" had violated one of the Ten Commandments. As a devout Christian who knew that there was a heaven and a hell and that the sins of the fathers were liable to be visited upon the children, she worries "upon whom shall the accountability of their [the mulatto children's] future state depend."[160]

By 3 January 1865 the combined strains of the war, her father's death, and the impending Confederate defeat have brought Thomas's anxieties closer to the surface. She writes at length about competition between women. Finally, in the 26 June 1869 entry, she writes of her son, Turner, the mulatto plowboy, and his mother who is only slightly darker than Turner's mother.

With the 26 June 1869 entry, much of Thomas's passionate writing falls into place. Gertrude Thomas worried about competition between women because it tormented her as a daughter and a wife. Thus her long, impassioned comments on the effect of slavery on white families and on black women's usurpation of the places of white wives now appear as commentary on her own family's tragedy. She believed that her father had had children and that her husband had had a child outside their marriages. It is possible, though far from certain, that whatever unspeakable thing distressed her when her first child was a baby was the discovery that her husband was sleeping with someone else.

Pulling all these leakage entries together, I conclude that the great secret of Gertrude Thomas's journal is something that she experienced as adultery. As a devout, nineteenth-century Methodist, she was deeply concerned with matters of moral rectitude and divine retribution. At the same time, however, she reacted to her husband's sexual relations with a slave as people have traditionally responded to adultery — with jealousy, anger, and humiliation, not with the cool assurance of superiority.

This should come as no surprise, as some of the best-known observations about antebellum southern society make more or less the same point. Abolitionists — who are currently out of favor with historians as analysts of southern society — routinely pilloried slaveowners for the sexual abuse of mulatto women.[161] Female visitors to the South criticized slavery for its deleterious effect on white men's morals. In the 1830s Harriet Martineau spoke of the plantation mistress as " 'the chief slave of the harem.' " Fredrika Bremer, in the 1850s, coined the famous phrase about slaves of mixed ancestry that Thomas quotes in her journal. And Mary Chesnut wrote of the mulatto children present in every slaveholding household. Gertrude Thomas was far, very far, from alone.[162]

As of yet there is no way of knowing what number of married slaveowners slept with their slaves, only of recognizing that the phenomenon was exceedingly common and the testimony one-sided. White men passed over their extralegal involvements in silence, so that it fell to wives and blacks to point a finger.[163] White women, black women, and black men all deeply resented white men's access to black women and said so, although comments from the two sides of the color line are contradictory. Where black men and women saw gross racial and sexual exploitation, white women saw sexual competition, which carries connotations of parity between participants in the contest.

The intense hurt and anger in Thomas's entries on competition between women and sexual relations between slaveowners and slaves indicate that she experienced her husband's action as a breach in her marriage. Yet there may be an alternative and more appropriate definition of the phenomenon Thomas deplored.

The pattern of slaveowning married men's sexual relations with women to whom they were not legally married was widespread, and these nonlegal relationships sometimes endured — like marriages. Seen another way, Thomas may have been party to a social pattern she did not recognize and for which anthropologists use the term "polygyny." It may well have been that men like Jefferson Thomas, more than regularly committing adultery, were establishing something like polygynous marriages.

Gertrude does not say how long Jeff's relationship with his slave partner lasted, whether it was a fling or might qualify as some sort of a marriage. Evidence from the journal supports at least a suspicion that the relationship may have endured from 1855 to 1870, perhaps even until 1880, but it is far from conclusive. As late as 5 December 1870, Thomas draws a triangle connecting herself, Hester Prynne of *The Scarlet Letter*, and African-American women who bear mixed-race children. On 24 November 1880, Thomas writes of having her cross to bear. The stresses Gertrude reports in her marriage — Jeff's irritability, his refusal to give her moral support, his withdrawal from intimacy — could as easily represent the human cost of financial ruin as an expression of the distance between partners that accompanies extramarital relationships.

There can be no well-founded representation of the circumstances that led to the conception of Jefferson Thomas's outside child, for Thomas was keeping secrets from herself and from her readers. But other cases are clearer. James Henry Hammond, a prominent antebellum South Carolina statesman, for instance, had two slaves who were, in effect, multiple wives. Southern court records are full of litigation over which set of families might inherit from men who had had children by more than one woman.[164] Thomas's South more or less concealed slave wives as an open secret polite people pretended not to see. Secrecy, the very heart and soul of adultery, is much of what makes adultery toxic to marriages, families, and, ultimately, society. Of itself, secrecy destroys trust, stifles intimacy, and rigidifies relationships, even when partners are not so deeply religious as Gertrude Thomas.[165]

In the early nineteenth century, Harriet Martineau understood that adultery places enormous strains on families, and modern scholarship makes the same point. Adultery breaks the pact of sexual exclusivity in marriage and undermines the betrayed spouse's trust in the other. The consequences of such ruptures could not always be confined to the private sphere. James Henry Hammond believed, with good foundation, that his wife's angry reaction to his taking his second slave wife ruined his political career.[166]

Adultery also subverts the social order by weakening the most fundamental social relationship, upon which procreation and socialization depend. Adultery breeds moral and sexual ambivalence in children, who vacillate between the outraged virtue of the betrayed parent and the adulterous parent's indulgence in sin. Ultimately, adultery creates chaotic inheritance patterns, which in the antebellum South meant that fathers were liable to own, sell, or bequeath their children. Twentieth-century white southern women from two sides of political spectrum grasped the horror of this fact.

Rebeca Latimer Felton, a Georgia suffragist and white supremacist writing in the aftermath of the First World War, blamed the Confederate defeat and continuing racial violence on "violations of the moral law that made mulattoes as common as blackberries."[167] A liberal two generations younger than Felton and a perceptive twentieth-century southern observer of her region, Lillian Smith, grasped the way that secrets, miscegenation, sin, and guilt combined to endow white southerners with a terrible fear of impending disaster.[168] Women like Gertrude Thomas knew this all too well and abhorred slavery for its effect on personal and social morality. Considering the pain adultery and sexual coercion inflicted, why did wives like Thomas not keep their men at home or protect the women they owned as the ex-slave narrator Harriet Jacobs suggested?[169]

The power relations of antebellum slave society made it extraordinarily difficult for plantation mistresses to police their husbands' sexuality. In order to protect themselves from what they saw as sexual competition, women of the planter class — who could not own property, vote, or hold office — would have had somehow to make slave women less vulnerable to sexual attack, to have somehow provided female slaves with a measure of power vis-à-vis wealthy white men. Lacking political and economic power, white women could hardly begin to shield slave women from white men. Perhaps the recognition that the power dynamics were so heavily weighted against them stopped white mistresses from making common cause with their female slaves. But white women rarely entertained such notions.

Even in the privacy of their journals, plantation mistresses did not forge rhetorical solidarity with their slaves. Instead, slaveowning women usually adopted a commonplace of southern race relations: that morally degraded slave women inveigled white men into their beds. According to this line of reasoning, the blame for interracial sex fell squarely on slave women.

Gertrude Thomas, however, stops short of this conclusion. Although she deplores the morals of blacks, she nonetheless comes close to recognizing that slave women are powerless to resist slaveowners. Several times she writes of the moral depravity of (white) men and how slavery was "demoralizing" to them. Yet she resists the temptation (as Mary Chesnut did not) to cast clear blame on slave women. Thomas is unable to exculpate slave women directly; she cannot say that miscegenation is not their fault. But she can say of the children that "They are not to blame. Oh No!"[170]

The English novelist Elizabeth Gaskell's *Ruth* fascinated Gertrude Thomas. In a long discussion of *Ruth*, which deals with unmarried (but not interracial) sexuality, Thomas explores the sexual double standard. She asks herself, "Oh how many of those women are more sinned against than sinning[?]"[171] Thomas is not able to take the next step, to bring slave women into her commentary, but obviously the theme of impure women troubles her deeply.[172] I suspect she avoided spelling out her ideas about sexual purity as they applied to her own household to prevent undermining the foundation of her place in her world. She could not clarify her thinking about slavery and sex without damaging her social and religious identity. To absolve black women and wholly blame white men would have belied the supposed superiority of herself, her family, and her society. She could not close the circle of meaning that connected gender and race and class.

According to the ostensible mores of her society, Gertrude Thomas was better than nearly everyone else. She was a plantation mistress in a society dominated by the 6 percent of white families qualifying as planters by owning twenty or more slaves. She was an educated woman at a time when only elite men could take higher education for granted. And she was white in a profoundly racist culture.

These same hierarchies also permitted her husband liberties she was denied. As in any slave society, male slaveowners in the South counted sexual access to enslaved women as one of the perquisites of masterliness. Slave women had no rights or means of resisting, nor could their families (ordinarily) protect them from the sexual advances of white men. That is, enslaved people had no legal ability to prevent or redress rape.

From the other side, neither Gertrude Thomas's economic and educational attributes or her social status protected her from what felt to her like sexual competition from inferior women. From Thomas's point of view, white men saw women — whether slave or free, wealthy or impoverished, cultured or untutored, black or white — as interchangeable sex partners.[173] She and other plantation mistresses failed to elevate themselves sufficiently as women to avoid the pain of sharing their spouses with slaves. Those slaves were perfect women, from the masters' point of view (but not the slaves', of course), because they existed to fulfill their masters' wishes.

Enslaved women's sexual availability was a function of their powerlessness, which not at all ironically made them formidable competition to elite women. Thus the institution that assured plantation mistresses of their social prestige also gave them sexual nightmares. The effects of the victimization of slave women could not be contained, for (otherwise) privileged women like Gertrude Thomas felt their husbands' adultery intruding into their own as well as their slaves' families.

Beyond the calculus of sexuality lies that of class. The powerlessness that made slave women vulnerable to male slaveowners simultaneously made slaves attractive to mistresses as workers. For as workers, in theory at least, slaves had no interests of their own. They were on the job whenever they were needed and could be made to do whatever their owners ordered. Slaves could not refuse or leave work for reasons of their own. Powerless people may have made ideal workers and ideal women, but those same characteristics conflicted with the gender interests of female slaveowners like Gertrude Thomas.

In the final analysis, slaveowning women were not willing even to imagine relinquishing the labor of their slaves, even though slavery made mistresses vulnerable as women and as wives. Stripped down and phrased most starkly, documents such as Gertrude Thomas's journal indicate that slave mistresses preferred the enjoyment of unlimited class privilege to the limitation of their husbands' opportunities for adultery. Reluctant to pit their class position against their gender interests, they avoided the facts and kept their secrets.

### Conclusion

Gertrude Thomas belonged to a Deep South generation of privileged white southerners that was virtually unique, sandwiched between the settling of the frontier, when planters lived in cabins and did not bother to educate their daughters, and the post–Civil War generation of hard-scrabble elites who could no longer appeal to the Bible as an authority on the rightness of their world.

As a young woman, Gertrude Thomas was not intended to suffer losses. Even deaths—of her babies, of her father—came as a shock. She was destined, or so it seemed, to be a golden child and a golden woman, the product of wealth in a life of privilege in which superiority was taken for granted. But almost as soon as her part of the South had been settled long enough to produce gentry with pretensions, the Civil War, Confederate defeat, and emancipation turned things upside down. Debt, not wealth, became her constant companion.

Not surprisingly, the most passionate and most memorable writing in this long and thoughtful journal concerns loss: social, moral, financial, and intimate. Considering Gertrude Thomas's socialization into an automatic, censorious self-control, her journal's intense emotions mark a contradiction. Although she very nearly succeeded in keeping the most intimate, painful, and common of southern family secrets, less private adversity freed her pen. Financial loss took her out of her life's script as laid out in 1852 and drove her to honesty, even to perplexed self-revelation. Gertrude Thomas did not live the life that she had anticipated, but she survived to delineate the unexpected.

# 3

## Three Southern Women & Freud

A NON-EXCEPTIONALIST APPROACH TO RACE,

CLASS, & GENDER IN THE SLAVE SOUTH

. . .

In my work on sexuality in the nineteenth- and twentieth-century South, my mind returns often to the late Herbert Gutman's remark about Marx, but with application to Sigmund Freud: He raises some very good questions. While I have plenty of feminist company in my turn toward psychoanalysis, the Freud I am using here is not quite the Freud who has been making recent appearances.[1]

As a historian of the nineteenth- and early twentieth-century United States South trained in a history project grounded in the archives, I find Freud valuable mainly as an acute observer of nineteenth-century bourgeois society, as an analyst (pun intended) who recognized the relationship between sexuality and identity. His writing permits unusually clear views into the ways in which social, economic, and ethnic hierarchies affected households and families, for he was accustomed to dealing with people in households that encompassed more than one economic class. Such a vision enriches southern studies, which is still impoverished by an exceptionalism that cannot see commonalties between the American South and other hierarchical societies not structured along racial lines and by a tendency to see race as an opaque barrier to feminist investigation.

My subject is the family relations that affected the richest and the poorest of antebellum southern daughters. A tragically tiny number of actually or nominally free black daughters and the large cohort of white daughters who lived beyond the reach of aristocracy belonged to families able to shelter them from predatory rich men. These young women were more likely to escape the fate of the daughters under discussion here. But black and white young women living in households in which men had access to the poorest and most vulnerable — women who were enslaved — all these daughters ran gendered risks related to sexuality that did not respect barriers of class and race. The unbridled patriarchy of wealthy white men produced adultery and miserable legal marriages.

It has been no secret, then or now, that during the slavery era, owners and slaves lived on terms of physical closeness and often engaged in sexual intimacy. Yet historians have followed the lead of privileged nineteenth-century southerners like Caroline Howard Gilman who, though well aware that sex figured among the services masters demanded of slaves, pushed the matter beyond their peripheral vision. Even psychoanalysts like Abram Kardiner and Lionel Ovesey pass quickly over the repercussions of interracial sexuality on southern white families and hence on southern society generally.[2] Virtually by default, the conclusion of southern history has been that as a social phenomenon, interracial, interclass sexuality has been relegated solely to African-American history; unless paranoid, self-pitying mistresses are taken seriously, which they are not, the problem of master-slave sex belongs to the families of slaves, not to the families of the masters. This is not my view. Because intimate relations affected wealthy, white as well as poor, black families, I argue that such sexuality and its repercussions belong not to one race or the other, but reside squarely in southern history.

One needs only read the work of class- and gender-conscious historians of Great Britain and Europe to recognize the parallels between nineteenth-century European bourgeois societies and that of the United States society in a similar period.[3] Such usefulness is not limited to historians' insights. While it is very much in vogue with literary critics, Freudian psychoanalysis also offers historians thought-provoking assistance, particularly on the formation of individual identity. Specifically, Sigmund Freud's "Dora" case history raises fundamental questions about the dynamics of elite families in a hierarchical society in which the employment of servants — and here I concentrate on female servants — is routine. This essay addresses the pertinence of three pieces of Freud's writing to southern society, as reflected in the histories of three southern women: Gertrude Thomas, "Lily," and Harriet Jacobs / Linda Brent.

Gertrude Thomas (1834–1907) spent much of her life as a plantation mistress near Augusta, Georgia. Her journal, written over the better part of forty years, takes a long but self-censoring look into one privileged white woman's family. Gertrude Thomas was not a fictional character, but she tried to make the record of her everyday life into a portrait that fitted her ideals.

Lily is the title character of an 1855 novel by the Charleston writer Susan Petigru King (Bowen) (1824–1875), a daughter of the wealthy, respectable planter-lawyer Thomas Petigru. Having been educated in Charleston and New York, she returned to South Carolina to pursue her career as a socialite and writer. King's protagonist, Lily, is the quintessential young plantation mistress: hyper-white, wealthy, pure, and beautiful.

Much better known today, thanks largely to the work of Jean Fagan Yellin and other literary critics, is the character Linda Brent, who in contrast to Lily, was a slave. Brent is both the central character and the pseudonym under which the Edenton, North Carolina, fugitive slave Harriet Jacobs (1813–1897) wrote her autobiography, *Incidents in the Life of a Slave Girl*, originally published in Boston in 1861.[4]

Rich, white, and free Gertrude and Lily stood at the top of the antebellum South's economic and racial hierarchies, but poor, yellow, and enslaved Linda Brent lived near, but not at the very bottom. Linda, after all, has some free relations, and her grandmother, though nominally enslaved, lives in her own house in town. Things could have been much worse for Linda Brent.

Gertrude's, Linda's, and Lily's are stories about women and sex; taken together with Freud's "Dora" they tell us a great deal about southern family dynamics in slaveholding households. As all three of these texts are about race and sexuality, I begin with the phenomenon of master-slave sex as I discovered it in Gertrude Thomas's journal.

### Gertrude Thomas's Secret

Although historians have not begun to quantify its incidence, we know that sexual relations between male slaveowners and female slaves were exceedingly common in the antebellum South — as in any other slave society, as Orlando Patterson points out.[5] Nineteenth-century fugitive slave narratives, such as those of Frederick Douglass and Moses Roper, and the Fisk and WPA ex-slave narratives from the 1930s, are full of evidence that masters did not hesitate to sleep with their women slaves, despite the marital status of either. In her antislavery *Journal of a Residence on a Georgian Plantation* (1863), the English actress turned plantation mistress Fanny Kemble documented and condemned the viciousness of such sexuality. Although I have not had an opportunity to pursue this hunch, I suspect that about ten percent of masters also slept or wanted to sleep with their enslaved men and boys; some mistresses may also have regarded their female slaves as objects of desire.[6]

Most supporters of slavery simply closed their eyes to owner-ownee sex. Other nineteenth-century white women — southerners and observers — penned and sometimes published criticisms of the institution of slavery based on what they perceived as the demoralization of white men who engaged in adultery and/or polygyny.

I began to draw my conclusions through study of the journal of Ella Gertrude Clanton Thomas. Initially I appreciated this journal for its value as a primary source for the study of the social history of the South, for which Thomas is an excellent witness. Extraordinary as is the historical source, however, the journal works on yet another level that is characterized by the keeping of secrets, lack of candor, and self-deception that psychoanalysis is well equipped to explore. What Thomas tried to hide in her journal offers glimpses into persistent tensions over gender and sexuality in southern marriages and, ultimately, into the nature of nineteenth-century southern society.

Pulling together all of the leakage entries, I conclude that the great secret of Gertrude Thomas's journal is something that she experienced as a victim of adultery. As a devout, nineteenth-century Methodist, she was deeply concerned with matters of moral rectitude and divine retribution. At the same time, however, she reacted to her husband's sexual relations with a slave as people have traditionally responded to adultery — with jealousy, anger, and humiliation, not with the placid assurance of racial superiority.

Thomas never denounced marriage as an institution, just as written evidence of her husband's drunkenness does not appear in extant volumes. Through erasures and leakage entries, Thomas's journal reveals its author's disappointments, notably her father's and her husband's adultery and the moral monstrosity of her inheriting her siblings. As a married woman, Thomas lets go of the fantasy of the husband as a protector and comes to see misery and competition between women as necessary parts of life.

Some of the most engaging corroboration of Thomas's experiences comes from fiction, which, considering the subject, should not be surprising. Most respectable nineteenth-century people retreated — or attempted to retreat — behind the veil of privacy, rather than reveal their actual patterns of sexuality, whether in their homes, in their letters, or in their journals. The very ability to conceal the rawer aspects of the human condition, an ability that we sum up in the term privacy, served as a crucial symbol of respectability when the poor had no good place to hide. Nonetheless the topic of interracial sexuality was of enough fascination to reappear in fiction under various disguises. Taking my cue from Gertrude Thomas, who was hypersensitive about sexual competition between women, I began to pursue sexuality through the theme of competition. Tracked in that guise, southern fiction reveals some interesting manifestations.

### Lily

Sue Petigru King sounded themes that occur in the work of several white southern women writers, such as Caroline Hentz, Grace King, and Willa Cather. For example, Cather's final novel, *Sapphira and the Slave Girl* (1940), is precisely and openly about a white woman's perception of sexual competition between herself and a Negro woman. In its racial candor, *Sapphira* is exceptional. More often the competition between women is not about individuals with different racial identities, but about two white characters who are color-coded in black and white. While I realize European writers such as Walter Scott and Honoré de Balzac used light (blonde) and dark (*la belle juive*) female characters symbolically, Ann Jones, Mary Kelley, and Jane Pease, scholars familiar with southern writers, corroborate my view that nineteenth- and early twentieth-century white southern women writers were singularly fascinated by competition between light and dark women. While most publications by these women followed the usual theme of a young woman's quest for autonomy and her eventual marriage to a good man, they also echo Gertrude Thomas's fixation on female rivalry. Sue Petigru King's biographers note her lack of happy endings and contrast King's melancholy domestic narratives with the more common and triumphant themes of mid-nineteenth-century American writers.[7]

The author Sue Petigru King is no longer very well known, but she loomed large in Gertrude Thomas's literary world. With Thomas at home in and around Augusta, Georgia, just across the state line from coastal South Carolina, King and Thomas inhabited the same extended region of the low country slavocracy. As an aspiring writer and as a woman with secrets ("skeletons in the closet"), Thomas read King's books and identified with her.

King achieved a certain celebrity through her two novels, *Lily: A Novel* and *Gerald Gray's Wife* (1864) and other publications: *Busy Moments of an Idle Woman* (1854), *Sylvia's World: Crimes Which the Law Does Not Reach* (1859), and stories in leading New York literary magazines such as *Harper's*. William Thackeray, one of Britain's most celebrated authors, met her and subsequently dined at her house on a trip to the United States.[8] (She mentions Thackeray's visits in both her published novels.) King's novels stress themes of jealousy, competition between women, and the misery of southern women's married lives. Published in New York in 1855, *Lily* is better known than *Gerald Gray's Wife*, published in the Confederacy during the Civil War.

*Lily* is the story of Elizabeth Vere, whom her dying father nicknames "Lily" because she is "as white as any lily that ever grew."[9] Over the course of the narrative, Lily grows in age from seven to seventeen. Serious and morally upstanding as a child, she grows into a flawless young woman, rich and stunningly beautiful. Throughout the novel, Lily adores her childhood sweetheart, Clarence Tracy. As the novel draws to a close, Lily and Clarence are about to marry.

King describes her heroine's character and appearance in similar terms: "white," "pure," "innocent," "simple," and "lovely." At fifteen, Lily's complexion is "exquisite," her shoulders, like her dress, are white. Her bright, blonde hair, falling to her waist in "long gold ringlets," resembles "prisoned sunbeams." She shows "honest fearlessness" and has "so modest a charm" and a nature of "pure and clinging earnestness."[10]

King's descriptions of Lily praise her whiteness in myriad terms, which, taken together, actually conflict as to hue and texture. Lily's white shoulders are like "polished ivory," conveying an impression of beige-tinged opacity. At the same time that King extols this bony, dense white, she also describes Lily's skin as "pellucid," i.e., transparent or clear. The character of Clarence Tracy admires Lily in appreciative but mixed metaphors that he and his creator seem to find complimentary:

> "You look fresh as a rose-bud," said Clarence, admiringly, as he noticed the fine, transparent texture of lips, cheek, and brow. "You have such a wonderful skin! See your hands! They are like little rolls of white velvet, with a reflection of a new-born carnation thrown on the palm."

Transparent skin actually exposes the mottled red and gray blood and fat beneath it. Nonetheless, King describes transparent Lily in white cashmere as looking like something lustrous, like "a pearl in its shell." The narrator, described as Lily's neighbor and acquaintance, sums up the heroine like this: "Lily was perfect."[11]

King pairs Lily with her cousin, Angelica Purvis. Angelica is also a rich white woman of the South Carolina low country, but in Angelica's case, King focuses on the "sallowness" (i.e., a gray, greenish, yellow conveying an impression of darkness) of her skin and the blackness of her dresses and hair. Not only does yellow-skinned Angelica wear red and black dresses, her lips are red and full, and King twice describes the lower part of her face is as "heavy." Her lashes are "thick" and "black," her "intensely black" hair shines "like polished jet."[12]

At one point, King draws a direct contrast between Lily, who seems to be "made up of light and purity," and Angelica, who is "dark, designing, distracting." Angelica is fashionable, bewitching, exotic; King describes her as an "Eastern princess" and twice calls her looks "Andalusian." Whereas Lily is pure, Angelica is passionate, evil, and voluptuous. Angelica says of her attractiveness to men: "I am original sin."[13]

At seventeen Lily is on the verge of marriage to her first great love, Clarence Tracy. Tracy, a childhood friend and, like Gertrude Thomas's husband Jeff, a graduate of Princeton, is also false and vain. Like Jeff Thomas, Clarence Tracy has a weakness that alarms his sweet little fiancée: Thomas drinks too much; Tracy gambles. Each man further conceals a deeper character flaw: passion for another woman. Despite all Lily's goodness, or, rather, because of it, she cannot command Tracy's love. He is crazy for bad, married Angelica. Clarence sees Lily as "such a mere girl," "a child," "sugar and water," and "insipid." To Angelica he declares: "I love Lily, but not as I love you."[14]

On the face of it, the most obvious theme in *Lily* is competition between two white women, which the less virtuous is winning. But race hovers in the very near background. First, these ostensibly white competitors are color-coded dark and light. Then, leaving no room for doubt, King abruptly introduces a new character, Lorenza, at the very end of the novel. Lorenza is Clarence's beautiful African-American mistress, like Angelica, twice described as possessing the "Spanish" beauty Clarence admires.[15] Clarence loves Lorenza and intends to remain intimate with her after marrying Lily. He realizes, cynically, that Lorenza lacks alternatives and will simply have to accommodate herself to her subordinate position.

Though a working girl, Lorenza is no poor slave. She has given up a promising life in Europe, where her attenuated African ancestry would not have prevented her marrying an honest German workingman. But she loves Clarence and follows him back to Charleston, even though she knows they can never marry legally. Clarence's impending wedding to Lily devastates Lorenza. The night before the wedding, Lorenza poisons Lily in an act of jealous desperation, then commits suicide.

King leaves nothing to guesswork in this novel; to hammer home her message, she addresses her readers directly. Her point is the same Mary Chesnut made in her Civil War diary: that southern planter husbands repaid their wives' faithful virtue with base infidelity. Wealthy southern men married young, pure, rich, white girls like Lily, then left them for mistresses tinged by blackness, whether of descent or intimation. Like Clarence Tracy, the men are weak and treacherous; they lie and cheat with impunity.

Only partial blame lies with the Clarence Tracys of King's southern aristocracy. King lays the burden of guilt on parents who routinely fail to investigate the objects of their young, innocent daughters' infatuation. In *Lily*, as in *Gerald Gray's Wife*, young girls fall blindly in love with liars. The parents acquiesce to the silly girls' wishes, without investigating the character or personal history of the men in question:

A young girl, brought up with every care, educated in every refinement, tutored by nature and by association in delicacy of sentiment
and taste, becomes the victim of a possible brute, without her family
or friends troubling themselves farther than to know that he has a
roof to shelter her — often that but a temporary one.

He may have debts, he may have mistresses, he may have associates that will ever after cloud her future. Who knows it? Who asks
about it?[16]

Lily, says King, was "sacrificed," like "so many" others like her.
Southerners may even be more at fault in this respect than northerners:
"we sell a 'slave' with more hesitation to a new owner than we give our
girls in marriage."

Art imitates life in King's fiction, where marriage is southern white
women's "prison house."[17] Tracing King's marriage and those of her
sisters, her biographers dedicate an entire chapter to the topic of "Surviving Miserable Marriages." The turn-of-the-twentieth-century white
supremacist, woman suffragist, Rebeca Latimer Felton echoed King's
sentiments. Felton repeatedly berated white southerners for putting
more investigation into real estate, livestock, and seed transactions
than into their daughter's marital partners. Felton, like King, linked
the habit of "haphazard" marrying for money with the prevalence of
wretched marriages.[18]

King sums up Mary Chesnut's conviction and Gertrude Thomas's
fears: "It is not the woman most worthy to be loved who is the most
loved."[19] This conclusion echoes in the writing of Sigmund Freud.

In 1912 Freud discussed precisely this phenomenon in his second contribution to the *Psychology of Love*: "On the Universal Tendency to Debasement in the Sphere of Love." Freud appraised the practical results
of "civilized morality" and the sexual double standard from the stand-
point of middle- and upper-class men susceptible to psychosomatic
impotence with women of their own class. According to Freud, well-
brought-up women are taught that sex is distasteful. They reject their
sexuality and tend to be inexperienced, inhibited, and frigid in marriage. This means that their husbands, who also regard the sex act as
polluting, relate to their wives more as judges than as joyous physical

partners. Hence only sex partners, "love objects," who seem to these men to be debased — prostitutes, women of the lower class — can inspire in them full sensual feelings and a high degree of pleasure. This phenomenon explains why such men keep lower-class mistresses. Freud said, making King's point: "Where such men love they have no desire and where they desire they cannot love."[20]

In *Lily*, the pure, young, rich, white daughter loses most dramatically in the southern sex game. In this interpretation of southern sexuality, the motif is competition between women, and the losers — the victims — are wealthy white women. A writer from the other side of the color line painted a disturbingly similar, yet differently shaded portrait.

### Harriet Jacobs's Linda Brent

Many ex-slave narrators touch on master-slave sexuality, but the most extended commentary comes from Harriet Jacobs, who, writing under the pseudonym Linda Brent, tells of being harassed by her master for sex from the time she was thirteen. Her character, Linda, becomes the literal embodiment of the slave as sexual prey in the testimony of slaves.

Harriet Jacobs grew up in Edenton, North Carolina, on the northern edge of Sue Petigru King's South Carolina low country and in the same eastern North Carolina plantation neighborhood as the North Carolina (Pettigrew) branch of King's family. Although legally enslaved, Jacobs lived with her own family during her childhood. Throughout all her years in Edenton, she benefited from the protection of her grandmother Molly Horniblow, an enterprising caterer and relative of one of the town's leading families.[21]

As the possession of a child, Harriet Jacobs became the de facto slave of Dr. James Norcom, a prominent citizen who tried to force himself upon Harriet from the time she entered her teens. To elude Norcom's grasp, Harriet entered a sexual relationship with another privileged white man, Samuel Tredwell Sawyer, the unmarried son of Norcom's medical partner. She bore Sawyer two children, who survived into adulthood. Ultimately motherhood did not put Jacobs beyond Norcom's reach. To elude him, she hid for nearly seven years in her grandmother's attic. Finally escaping to New York in 1842, Jacobs became an abolitionist.

Jacobs intended her revelation of slaveowners' abuses of those they

owned as a woman's own blow against slavery. Since the 1830s, abolitionists had railed against the rape of slave women in general terms. On
the urging of her Rochester friend Amy Post, Jacobs came forward with
direct testimony in the form of a first-person narrative. Due to the
sensitive nature of her subject matter, she published her autobiography
under the pseudonym Linda Brent.

Jacobs's narrative presents a counterpoint to the non-fiction journal of Gertrude Thomas and the novels of Sue Petigru King. Speaking
as the figure Thomas and King can only mention obliquely — the figure
with whom they see themselves and their peers in competition —
Jacobs unveils the figure of the slave mistress. As someone owned
outright by her tormenter, Jacobs's Linda Brent understands but does
not share owning women's interpretation of the balance of power between women in different situations. Jacobs denies owning women's
fantasy, in which their husband's sexual partners are gorgeous mulattoes and quadroons whose beauty seduces white men.

In *Incidents in the Life of a Slave Girl*, Jacobs calls slavery a "deep, and
dark, and foul . . . pit of abominations."[22] She indicts the institution on
several grounds: its use of physical torture to force obedience; its debasement of family attachments among white as well as black; its cor-
ruption of southern white religion; its forcing young women into pros-
titution. This last charge becomes Jacobs's hallmark, for she confronts
the sexual component of servitude straightforwardly — as a matter of
power rather than seduction or romance.

Puberty opens a "sad epoch in the life of a slave girl." As Linda Brent
becomes nubile, her master begins to whisper "foul words in my ear,"
precisely the sort of act we now term sexual harassment and whose
consequences Freud comprehended. Jacobs generalizes Linda's predicament to note that color does not provide protection: "whether the
slave girl be black as ebony or as fair as her mistress" — she, the slave
girl, is sexually vulnerable. Nor can personal ethics, innocence, purity,
religion, or family honor adequately protect her:

> No pen can give an adequate description of the all-pervading cor-
> ruption produced by slavery. The slave girl is reared in an atmo-
> sphere of licentiousness and fear. The lash and the foul talk of her
> master and his sons are her teachers. When she is fourteen or fifteen,
> her owner, or his sons, or the overseer, of perhaps all of them, begin

to bribe her with presents. If these fail to accomplish their purpose, she is whipped or starved into submission to their will.[23]

Hearing "foul words" from her master and angry and jealous outbreaks from her mistress, the slave girl, in Jacob's phrase, becomes "prematurely knowing in evil things." The more beautiful she is, the more speedy her despoliation. Beauty, for Linda Brent and young women like her, carries no blessings: "If God has bestowed beauty upon her, it will prove her greatest curse."[24] Linda's beauty, like Lily's serves no good purpose toward furthering a woman's life's chances.

Jacobs recognizes, too, that women who were slaves and women who were owners interpreted the situation quite differently. She dedicates an entire chapter of *Incidents* to "The Jealous Mistress." Here and elsewhere, Jacobs laments that mistresses whose husbands betrayed them felt no solidarity whatever with their slaves. Writing as Linda Brent, Jacobs supplies a key word, "victim," and sees it as a matter of contention between slave and mistress. Looking back upon herself as a teenaged slave pursued by her owner, Jacobs understandably sees herself as his victim. Like other ex-slave narrators, Jacobs could ascertain the view of slaveowning women but emphatically did not share their conclusion that they, not their husbands' enslaved prey, deserved the true status of victim.

Years later, Jacobs understands the mistresses' agony, for wealth and whiteness did not cut the pain of intimate betrayal: "Slaveholders' wives," says Linda Brent, "feel as other women would under similar circumstances." As her husband James Norcom was chasing after Linda, his wife suffered:

> She felt that her marriage vows were desecrated, her dignity insulted; but she had no compassion for the poor victim of her husband's perfidy. She pitied herself as a martyr; but she was incapable of feeling for the condition of shame and misery in which her unfortunate, helpless slave was placed.[25]

White women, black women, and black men all resented deeply white men's access to black women. But comments from the two sides of the color line clash: where white women saw sexual competition—with connotations of equality—black men and women saw a rank exploitation stemming from grossly disparate levels of power. Moses Roper, his master's child, relates the story of his near-murder, shortly after his birth, by his father's jealous wife. Frederick Douglass also wrote of slaveowning women's distress when faced with the bodily proof of their husband's adulteries. Fanny Kemble described the white overseer's wife's flogging and exiling enslaved women who bore her husband's children.[26]

For Jacobs as for other ex-slave narrators the prime victim was the slave woman, not the slaveowning woman, no matter how slaveowning women perceived the situation. So far as slaves were concerned, slaveowners' sexual relations with their women slaves constituted one of several varieties of victimization of slaves by men whose power over their slaves was absolute. Slaves of both sexes were oppressed by class and by race, and women slaves suffered a third, additional form of oppression stemming from their gender. Slaves were victims several times over, and extorted sex was part of a larger pattern of oppression embedded in the institution of slavery.

This is not to say that Jacobs saw the enslaved as the unique victims of slavery. So great an imbalance of physical, racial, and gendered power corrupted everyone involved, not just those most at risk. Along with Gertrude Thomas and Sue Petigru King, Jacobs grasped the ways in which slavery ruined lives at both ends of wealth's spectrum. But unlike women in Thomas's and King's position, Jacobs did not benefit from slave labor. Calling slave society "that cage of obscene birds," Jacobs had nothing to lose:

> Slavery is a curse to the whites as well as to the blacks. It makes the white fathers cruel and sensual; the sons violent and licentious; it contaminates the daughters, and makes the wives wretched. And as for the colored race, it needs an abler pen than mine to describe the extremity of their sufferings, the depth of their degradation.[27]

Jacobs rooted the evils of slavery in a society built upon extortion, while Thomas and King focused more on individual faults and weaknesses. All three agreed that adultery ruined the lives of women and that in their world, slavery allowed men the run of women of both races.

Located in very different places within the complicated families of slavery, these three southern women can be seen as Freudians *avant la lettre*. Half a century later, Sigmund Freud, in his analysis of "Dora," recognized the damage the father's adultery inflicted upon the daughter in a world ruled by the sexual double standard.

## Freud's "Dora"

In the "Dora" case, Herr K had made sexual advances toward "Dora," Ida Bauer, who had overheard Herr K's propositioning a servant woman in exactly the same phrases that he used with Bauer. Entangled emotionally with several women, Bauer identified (at the least) with Frau K, her father's mistress, and with the servant. She also felt like a pawn in an adulterous game between her father and the Ks. When Ida Bauer's father took her to Freud in October 1900, after she had tried to commit suicide, Freud was already anxious to try out his ideas.[28]

Freud had been thinking about hysteria for several years and had worked out his notions in letters to his close friend and regular correspondent, Wilhelm Fliess. These comments are exceedingly helpful to me, particularly in observations that Freud enclosed with a letter dated 2 May 1897. Here Freud notes that children, even very young babies, hear things that later become the raw material for fantasies and neuroses. Accompanying this letter was "Draft L," which includes a paragraph on "The Part Played by Servant Girls."

In Draft L, Freud echoes his society's assumption that the poor young women working in bourgeois households were "people of low morals" because they were likely to become sexually involved with the men and boys of the household. Here Freud was echoing the commonest of common knowledge about black people in the South. But whereas Freud identified moral stature with class standing, white southerners saw low morals as a racial characteristic of African Americans. For my purposes, however, this comment about morals is not the crucial point of Freud's failed analysis of Ida Bauer.

Freud's most relevant observation relates to the critical importance of servants in the psychological and hence social dynamics of the families in which they work. Although Freud thought mainly of the ramifications of the situation on the family of the employers, servants, too, as we saw with Linda Brent, felt the effects of adulterous — should I add incestuous? — family dynamics.

Freud wrote to Fliess that in households in which servant women are sexually intimate with their employers, the children — and here I believe he means the female children — develop an array of hysterical fantasies: fear of being on the street alone, fear of becoming a prostitute, fear of a man hidden under the bed. In sum, says Freud, "There is tragic justice in the circumstance that the family's head's stooping to a maidservant is atoned for by his daughter's self-abasement."[29]

Freud underscores the degree to which women in a household are emotionally intertwined, for he observed that "Dora" identified with the servant whom her would-be lover had tried to seduce. Observing situations in which race was not a factor, Freud understood that the very structure containing class and gender power dynamics is virtually Foucauldian in its leakiness. No class of women remained exempt from a degradation that aimed at the least of them. Just as Gertrude Thomas saw that her adulterous father and husband treated rich and poor and black and white women as interchangeable sexually, Freud saw there was a "part played by servant girls" and an object connection between "Dora" and her father's mistress. The Freud scholar Hannah Decker put her finger on the phenomenon that poisoned young women's lives in Freud's Vienna and that also characterized the nineteenth-century South: the careless sexual abuse of *das süsse Mädel* — the sweet young thing.[30] Sue King used other words, but she, too, objected to men's free exploitation of unprotected, young women.

Freud's letters to Fliess, "On the Universal Tendency to Debasement in the Sphere of Love," and especially the "Dora" case analysis, show that "Dora's" predicament is reflected in both *Lily* and *Incidents in the Life of a Slave Girl*, but in somewhat different ways. Linda Brent is more directly comparable with "Dora," for she is the object of unwanted sexual advances, as was young Ida Bauer. The case of Lily Vere is less obvious, for she is the daughter of "Draft L," of "The Part Played by Servant Girls." Lily is the daughter whose affective value is lowered by the existence of the sexually vulnerable servant class and the allure of enticing dark/Negro women like Angelica and Lorenza. While Linda Brent is a clear victim of her society's hierarchies of race and gender, Lily, unloved by her fiancé and murdered by his servant lover, is victimized as well. Her fiancé, Clarence, is the very figure of the Freud patient suffering from psychically-induced impotence.[31] Attracted to two dark, sexually active women, Angelica and Lorenza, Clarence feels no passion for the pure, white, young Lily to whom he is engaged.

## Historians

Listening to these southern women's stories and taking Freud to heart leads to two conclusions: First, that historians of the United States South have sheltered too long in southern exceptionalism and let an intellectual color bar obstruct their grasp of the complexity of gender roles within economically heterogeneous households. Lily and Linda Brent, two examples of a spoliation of young women that is no respecter of race or class — underscore both the sexual vulnerabilities and the psychological interrelatedness of southern daughters. Second, Freud points the way toward an understanding of Gertrude Thomas's problem: that families and societies cannot designate and thereby set apart one category of women as victims. The victimization spreads, in different ways and to different degrees. But where historians have been prone to construe southern family relations within watertight racial categories, the stories of Gertrude Thomas, Lily, and Linda Brent pose complicated new questions whose answers do not stop at the color line.

Historians have wanted to teach a single conclusion that would characterize the relationship between slaveowning and slave women in the antebellum South: *Either* slave women were at the bottom of a hierarchical society, as the exslave narrators testify, *or* all southern women were, finally, at the mercy of rich white men. The relationship between black and white women through white men deserves to be named, for slavery often made women of different races and classes into co-mothers and co-wives as well as owners and suppliers of labor. The question is whether there should be one name or, corresponding to the number of races involved, more than one.

So far the history of southern women has neglected investigation of the meanings of interracial sexuality and the gender relations flowing from it. But the work is coming along. The older, full-length studies of race and gender in the antebellum South by Deborah Gray White, Catherine Clinton, and Elizabeth Fox-Genovese and the more recent work building upon them all tend toward use of one concept to characterize relations within extended southern households: oppression. Deborah Gray White, in *Ar'n't I a Woman*, stresses the "helplessness" and "powerlessness" of slave women vis-à-vis slaveowners and in American society in general. Conceding that white women and black men may have envied black women, White nonetheless views black women at the bottom of a malevolent system that disempowered all women, even those who were rich and white. She places slave women at the negative end of a continuum of power, on which white women also occupied positions of relative powerlessness and exploitation.[32]

Viewing matters from the other side of the class/race divide, Catherine Clinton, in *The Plantation Mistress*, also acknowledges a "parallel oppression of women, both white and black." But where Deborah White cites instances of aggression on the part of white women against black, Clinton stresses plantation mistresses' roles as nurturers, mediators, and nurses. Clinton speaks of a patriarchy, in which rich white men possessed slaves of both sexes as they possessed their own wives. In *The Plantation Mistress*, slaveowning women do not appear in hierarchical relationships with slave women. Rather than portray slaveowning women as rulers of their workers, Clinton sees white male masters as the font of all power and all evil.[33]

In *Within the Plantation Household*, Elizabeth Fox-Genovese departs from the view of black and white women's parallel exploitation that White and Clinton evoke. Stressing the spacial and emotional intimacy in which many slave and slaveholding women lived in plantation households, Fox-Genovese softens the domination of the master. She prefers the term "paternalism" to Clinton's "patriarchy," because paternalism carries an air of "legitimate domination," which was how slaveholding men viewed their role. (Let us not quibble about whether slaveowners should be allowed to choose the words we historians use to characterize them more than a century and a half later.)

Fox-Genovese stiffens the authority of slaveowning women over their female slaves, providing theoretical and empirical arguments for a somewhat ambiguous but clearly hierarchical relationship between women of different races and classes. Rather than see masters as the proximate wielders of power, Fox-Genovese shows that slaveholding women and slave women were cognizant of who held the power between them and who could inflict the greatest violence with impunity. To make her point, Fox-Genovese enumerates instances of violence and minimizes slaveholding women's abolitionist leanings. For her, slaveholding women who saw themselves as victims of the kind of adultery that the slave system allowed were simply mistaken.[34]

Clinton's later essays reveal the pathologies of planter families in which rape and adultery distorted descent and parental attachment.

While her essay "Caught in the Web of the Big House" glimpses the ways in which owner-slave rape affected mistresses, the emphasis still falls mainly on the tragedy of the direct victim of assault: the slave woman. In "Southern Dishonor," Clinton's spiked critique of both southern historiography and slavery's brutal system of reproduction, she announces themes and works-in-progress in the study of sexuality and slavery.[35]

Three works from the 1990s further enrich the historical literature through investigation of the complexities of southern sexuality. Mary Frances Berry's 1991 presidential address to the Organization of American Historians encourages historians to pay attention to neglected themes, including sexuality. Martha Hodes's *White Women, Black Men: Illicit Sex in the Nineteenth-Century South* concentrates on relationships previously considered virtually impossible, between black men and white women, without delving into the far more common sexual dynamics of slave-holding households. Hodes also edited a collection of promising essays: *Sex, Love, Race: Crossing Boundaries in North American History.*[36]

So far, this work, though intriguing, stops short of completing the investigation of the relationship between southern families, society, and history. If feminist history has taught us anything in the last two decades, it is that important private matters become important historical matters. One great example makes the point: the South Carolina fire-eater, James Henry Hammond. Hammond's wife deserted him when he took a second slave wife. His subsequent emotional turmoil so incapacitated him psychologically that he missed an important secessionist meeting that would have bolstered his sagging political career.

Hammond's loss of influence among secessionists serves as a reminder that Gertrude Thomas's preoccupation — competition — needs to reenter historiographical reckoning. Otherwise historians risk overlooking much of the psychodrama of southern history. Focusing principally on the political economy, only one part of the picture (even though more it represents the part most compatible with present-day understandings of relations of power), flattens out the inherent complexity of southern history. If historians do not acknowledge that wealthy white women saw themselves as victims, as the losers in a competition with women who though black and poor and powerless

seemed somehow more attractive, we miss a vital dimension of southern history. This historical dimension helps explain the thorniness of
women's contacts across the color line across the entire twentieth century. We must acknowledge the existence of two ways of seeing, even
while we keep our eyes on fundamental differentials of power.

What my approach means for southern history is a renunciation of a
single "The South" way of thinking. For me there is seldom a "The
South," for simple characterizations eliminate the reality of sharp conflicts over just about everything in southern culture, slavery most of all.
Saying that "The South" was pro-slavery (or, later, pro-segregation)
equates the region with its rulers and annihilates the position of at least
one-third of its inhabitants. As a labor historian with a keen sense of the
historical importance of all groups of people within a society (not
simply the prestigious, published, and politically powerful) I insist on
going beyond neglectful characterization in the singular. Recognizing
the complex and self-contradictory nature of southern society, I can re-
phrase my conclusions about the study of southern history succinctly:
Southern history demands the recognition of complexity and contradiction, starting with family life, and therefore requires the use of plu-
rals. Southern history must take race very seriously, but southern history must not stop with race.

# 4

## "Social Equality" & "Rape" in the Fin-de-Siècle South

. . .

### "Social Equality"

At the turn of the twentieth century, "Social equality" worked as a symbol containing two notions: race and equality. It meant people of two races, usually including black men, sitting down together at table or on a train, sharing a smoke at a club, or belonging to the same organization on a footing of equality. Even though slavery entailed the complete integration of wealthy white people's lives, such interracial intimacy contained no hint of social equality. For when a slave slept in the same room with his or her owner, that was the farthest thing in the world from "social equality." When a servant sat on a train with his or her employer, that, too, was not "social equality."

"Social equality" meant associating as equals, which, according to the logic of the slogan, would lead inexorably to black men's marrying white women. The North Carolina Democrat who became Woodrow Wilson's Secretary of the Navy, Josephus Daniels, led a howling campaign against what he and many other white southerners saw as President Theodore Roosevelt's "insult" to the South: the president's sharing a meal at the White House with Booker T. Washington. Yet no one, not even Daniels, cited as evidence any case when a black dinner guest walked off with a daughter of the host on his arm.

"Social equality" existed only in the negative. Yet so potent was it a symbol that whites and blacks of all persuasions united against it. To be for "social equality" was to favor race mixing, which no one could support. Denouncing "social equality" was as necessary for southern

whites as denouncing communism became in the 1950s (and for similar social and political reasons). As in red-baiting, the burden of proof
fell on the accused, and no one pressed Josephus Daniels to present his
proof. In a highly charged, white supremacist atmosphere, simple neu-
trality would not suffice, at least not in public. *Not* to deplore "social
equality" and race mixing was tantamount to confessing to a lack of
race pride. On both sides of the color line, race pride was the equal of
patriotism in time of war and anticommunism in cold war.

The rhetoric of "social equality" spoke in racial terms, but its deeper
meaning was packed with class distinctions rooted in slavery. Slavery
had made races into classes, with black people as the South's basic and
symbolic labor force. Class consciousness was not nearly so acute as race
consciousness, in rhetoric, at least. Many southern whites worked and
were poor, of course, but the concepts of race in the antebellum South
contained the inherent assumption that whites = planters, blacks =
slaves, assumptions that emancipation sharpened considerably.

Although the word *class* almost never appeared in turn-of-the-
century writing about the South, the hierarchy of racism expressed a
clear ranking of classes, in which the word *white*, unless modified, indicated a member of the upper class, and *black*, unless modified, equaled
impoverished worker. So deeply embedded in racial categories were
assumptions about class that deviation from these assumptions required the use of adjectives: *poor* white, *middle-class* black. The obscu-
rity of class and the salience of race have produced either/or thinking
among concerned Americans, who ask whether class *or* race was more
important in twentieth-century southern history. This choice need not
be made, for the confounding of the two produced not only gross
inequities of wealth according to race, but also a racial ideology based
on power, including the power to inflict hurt and humiliate.

## Class Oppression after Reconstruction

The regime of class oppression set in place at the turn of the century
had several aspects that are perhaps familiar, but let me underline how
multifaceted the controls were. Vagrancy laws pressured all blacks to
remain employed (though hard times created black as well as white
tramps throughout the region). Convictions for petty crimes that poor
people were likely to commit, such as selling cotton after dark or stealing livestock, led to the chain gang, and convicts were likely to be leased

to planters or industrialists. Contracts that ran for twelve months kept workers from switching jobs in pursuit of better wages. Crop lien laws tied agricultural workers to their employers or suppliers through debt and bound them into the cash-crop economy. Tenancy laws lodged control of shared crops in the hands of landowners, from seeding to marketing, so that sharecroppers were in practice wage workers rather than joint proprietors of a crop.[1]

On top of controls on laborers' mobility and freedom to change employers laid down in law, black workers faced other difficulties as employees. Night-riding and other forms of violence made planters into protectors, providing further means of dominating workers, whose lack of education kept them too uninformed and too lacking in self-assurance to challenge planters' authority. Low wages made saving next to impossible while hard work increased the attraction of liquor and other ways of spending what little was on hand. Finally, the southern tradition of deference that was both racist and paternalist made it dangerous for employees to dispute their employers' words. All this together meant that mobility, except downward, was extraordinary.

Poor whites were also subject to the debilitating economic effect of this "Prussian road" toward development. They, like blacks, became increasingly enmeshed in the web of farm labor, as the proportion of tenants and sharecroppers of both races increased in the South. But given the racism of the society as well as everyday class oppression masquerading as racial hierarchy, poor blacks found themselves at a greater economic disadvantage than poor whites. Through laws and racist traditions, well-off whites were able to increase their economic power at the cost of poor blacks and poor whites, but the harder hit were the blacks, particularly rural laborers.

Disfranchisement also increased the political power of well-off whites vis-à-vis the poor, black and white. The radical decline in ballots cast by poor men meant that office holding reverted to the well-to-do, who furthered their own ends. Even legislators elected by the Farmers' Alliances in the late 1880s, who had as candidates measured up to the "Alliance yardstick," failed to perform in office in ways that would help modest farmers — for instance, by passing any version of the subtreasury plan. Perhaps large numbers of southern farmers would have lost their land or never have been able to afford to buy without the narrowing of the franchise. But clearly legislatures dominated by the better-off

did little to ease the plight of the poor and everything to assure employers ample supplies of docile labor at low wages. Summing up labor
relations in the late nineteenth-century South, Pete Daniel sees the law
as the central point of compulsion.[2]

Tenancy and disfranchisement crippled all the poor in the South, but
they affected black southerners more harshly than white. Poll taxes and
secret ballots disfranchised many poor whites, but Democratic pol-
iticos continued to appeal to them at election time, and their voting
was not likely to be resisted with nearly the same vigor as blacks'. Poor
whites benefited from the money wages and relative mobility of textile
employment. In cities like Birmingham, moreover, white workers held
jobs classified differently from "Negro jobs," the latter being harder,
dirtier, and less remunerative. Even though blacks and whites might be
doing the same tasks, the highest-paid blacks would make about the
same as the lowest-paid whites.

Poor whites thought they had something to lose by being treated
equally with blacks, because they *did* have something to lose — political
standing and wages, not to mention other little perquisites of whiteness such as knowing there is someone who is considered your inferior.
The shibboleth of "social equality" worked at the bottom, even though
working-class whites profited less from white-skin privileges than the
wealthy. Poor whites who banded together with rich whites against
blacks were not simply victims of a false consciousness, at least not in
the short run. Obviously, race mattered.

*Race Matters*

One need not agree with the whole work of U. B. Phillips to see that
Americans — southern and otherwise — have long been fascinated by
the racism that he called the central theme of southern history. Race
means many things to Americans, but so long as it continues to flourish
as a way for Americans to define one another it will cast its spell. In this
essay about racism, sex, and power I will start with an insight of my
former colleague at the University of North Carolina at Chapel Hill,
Joel Williamson, who observes that "ultimately, there is no race problem in the South, or in America, that we, both black and white, do not
make in our minds."[3]

The mind problems — values, mores, ideologies — are precisely what
characterize societies and provide the subject matter that anthropolo-

gists, sociologists, and some historians study, seeking to delineate the ways in which people arrange themselves within their worlds. Williamson rightly accords mentalities a good deal of attention, as I will, examining black as well as white views of miscegenation and white supremacy. Like Williamson, I discuss rhetoric as well as events, subjective as well as objective realities, noting the many silences in the dialogues that occurred between whites and whites, blacks and blacks, and blacks and whites.

While respecting the importance of the subjectivities surrounding race, I also stress what I see as the fundamental point (though not the single fundamental manifestation) of racism, the economic and political domination of the poorest part of the southern working class. Reconstruction after the Civil War did not usher in socialism or communism — far from it. But Reconstruction's policies, from the Freedmen's Bureau to the abolition of the whipping post, to the creation of schools for former slaves, and, above all, the enfranchisement of black male workers, reoriented southern politics away from the interests of planters and toward those of workers.[4] Money and laws express mentalities, but they also create solid, material conditions.

In the American South the seizure, maintenance, and cession of power have long been expressed in racial terms, as though race were a real, not a social, category whose fundamental function has been to rank people and keep them in place. As Edmund Morgan has shown, it is no accident that racism hardened as masses of southern workers were sealed into hereditary servitude.[5] After Bacon's rebellion of 1676, individuals of a variety of shades of skin color and textures of hair — some physically indistinguishable from "whites," others mixed with Native Americans — were called Negroes. The main identity of "Negroes" was that of an enslaved working class. Out of the infinite variety of human physiognomy the makers of southern laws created two categories, two "races." This scheme — which simplified empirical realities considerably — benefited the majority by oppressing the minority and outlived slavery by more than a century. An early twentieth-century white supremacist, Myrta Lockett Avary, summed up the enduring relationship between racial identity and economic function: "The white man does not need the negro as *litterateur*, statesman, ornament to society. . . . What he needs is agricultural labour."[6] Avary pointed to the basis of white supremacy in economic domination. But as I show later

in this essay, another dimension—the sexual, therefore the psychological—counted fully as much.[7]

### Turn-of-the-Twentieth-Century White Supremacy

The men and incidents that I use to embody white supremacy date
from the turn of the twentieth century: Josephus Daniels and the North
Carolina white-supremacy campaign of 1898, the writings of Thomas
Dixon, and the Atlanta race riot of 1906. If this era did not necessarily
produce more racial violence than had earlier times, it assuredly did
circulate an enormous amount of rhetorically violent propaganda.[8]
White-supremacist rhetoric had existed during the antebellum period,
but the addition of politics into the mixture came with black enfranchisement in the 1860s. Enfranchisement undermined—or seemed to
undermine—the politics of deference that planters enforced. Although
the rhetoric against blacks attacked their unfitness for citizenship on
racial grounds, class-based issues counted heavily. In terms of issues
and style, large numbers of black voters shook the political plum tree
during Reconstruction by voting and influencing public policy in the
interests of the poor.[9]

White-supremacy campaigns, speaking of race, not class, were aimed
at taking the masses of black workers out of politics and realigning
politics along lines that political elites considered favorable. By stressing race, white supremacists reinterpreted the opposition against the
working-class masses (which black men represented in subjective and
objective realities) as political actors. In the 1870s men like General
Martin Gary of South Carolina spoke lines that became commonplace
later on. Democratic power in the South seemed to require black disfranchisement, which in turn demanded an extraordinary mobilization
of the white electorate. Democrats had discovered in the early 1870s that
ordinary political campaigns failed to bring large numbers of white
voters to the polls, never mind into the streets armed.

Sex was the whip that white supremacists used to reinforce white
solidarity, probably the only whip that would cut deeply enough to
keep poor whites in line. Political slogans that spoke straightforwardly
of property or wealth (which not all whites held) had failed to rally
whites en masse. However, nearly all white men could claim to hold a
certain sort of property, in wives, sisters, and daughters. When women
were reduced to things, they became property that all white men could

own.[10] White women also discovered they could raise themselves to the status of ladies in their own and in white men's eyes by joining the outcry against black men.[11] The sexually charged rhetoric of "social equality" issued two invitations: to all white men to protect their property in women and to all white women to be recognized as worthy of protection. White supremacist racial discourse became a sort of machine for white upward mobility. Now all whites could share in the maintenance of all sorts of power, including the economic and political, which disproportionately benefited the better-off, in the name of protecting the sexuality of white womanhood.

### Sex and Rape

The most emotional issue of southern race relations that grew out of slavery was sex.[12] Even so enthusiastic a lyncher as Rebeca Latimer Felton recognized that slavery made "mulattoes as common as blackberries."[13] Sex was a kind of human property that slavery transferred involuntarily from slaves to masters. Like labor, it was a stolen thing. Sex, even — or particularly — when stolen, is no simple thing. It is *the* thing underlying post-war white sexual hysteria.

In the American South, the theft of sex occurred in a society dominated by evangelical Protestantism. As personal morality had become more important with the growth of the Baptist, Methodist, and Scotch-Irish Presbyterian churches, extramarital sex had become identified with sin in a more tortured way than in more formalist religion. By the late eighteenth century, what Lillian Smith summed up as the "race-sex-sin spiral" in which "guilt, shame, fear, lust spiraled each other" already existed.[14] This association of sex and race spiced with sin endured into the turn of the twentieth century, when white supremacists put it to political purposes. The resulting argument was rickety at best, but few examined it closely at the time. In fact, the combination was so piquant that Thomas Dixon's version enjoyed popularity as a novel, *The Clansman* (1905); a play, *The Clansman* (1906–7); and as a film, *Birth of a Nation* (1915), that continues to be shown. In successful lecture tours of the whole United States, Benjamin "Pitchfork" Tillman of South Carolina replayed the same themes.[15]

Identifying the figure of the white woman with civilization, Josephus Daniels, Tom Watson, Benjamin Tillman, and Thomas Dixon drew on dualities established before the Civil War. The slave South, like all other slave societies, cloistered women of the master class, elevating the mistress/virgin and simultaneously debasing the slave/whore. Drawing on these conventions at the turn of the twentieth century, white supremacists predicted that the ultimate outcome of black voting would be what they called "social equality" or race mixing, which would entail the downfall of civilization. White supremacists did not carefully define what they meant by civilization, but they assigned to themselves the favorite qualities of chauvinists throughout the Western world. Whether they are sexists, racists, anti-Semites, or pornographers, chauvinists divide the world into two, assigning to women/blacks/Jews the sphere associated with nature: savagery, emotions, lack of control, sexuality. The stereotypical notions that incited mob violence in the South — the bleeding female victim and the black beast rapist — united two aspects of otherness, blacks and women, through sex. No other conjunction could seem so seriously to threaten civilization. This emphasis on the sexuality of women who belonged to men and the division of mankind into two utterly dissimilar parts are characteristics of what Susan Griffin has called the pornographic mind. I will return to this concept later in this essay.

While white-supremacist rhetoric never let the fear of women as a force of nature percolate up to the conscious level, the obsessive concern over white women's sexuality hints at an identification with disorder. (White) women's sexuality, exploited by black men, could ruin "the South."

Seeking in the late 1890s to overthrow the biracial fusionist regime in North Carolina, Josephus Daniels heated up the rhetoric of disfranchisers, joined sex and race, and warned that black voting endangered "the sanctity of [white] women."[16] The virulent white-supremacist campaign culminated in the downfall of the fusionists and the death of eleven black men in what came to be known as the Wilmington riot.

In Georgia would-be disfranchisers like former Populist Tom Watson studied the North Carolina model and embellished the same line: "[The Negro] grows more bumptious on the street. More impudent in his dealings with white men; and then, when he cannot achieve social equality as he wishes, with the instinct of the barbarian to destroy what he cannot attain to, he lies in wait . . . and assaults the fair young girlhood of the south. . . . It is time for those who know the perils of the negro problem to stand together with deep resolve that political power shall never give the negro encouragement in his foul dreams of a mixture of races."[17]

In Atlanta in the summer of 1906 the overt themes of sex, race, and politics resonated with fears other than the political. An evangelist had recently awakened familiar American fears (indeed, Western fears) of what strong drink might do to the lower class — in the South identified as blacks — while temperance agitation reinforced apprehensions stirred by the performance of the play *The Clansman*, which made much of the figure of the black-beast-rapist. Finally, the summer witnessed continual agitation in the newspapers about rapes of white women by black men. Extra editions announcing rape after rape within a matter of hours set off a white mob that attacked the roughest and the most refined black sections of the city. By the time the Atlanta riot ended, some twenty-five blacks and one white had died, and the white supremacists had won the election. In both Wilmington and Atlanta the three provocative concepts of sex, race, and political power combined with a potency that is difficult to imagine today.

The issue of crime, defined primarily as black on white rape, appears repeatedly in white-supremacist writing, but without assumptions that figure in discussions of criminality today: that poor people commit most of what our society defines as crimes; that crime rates increase during economic hard times; and that sentences vary according to the class and race of both victim and offender (that is, white offenders from the better-off classes are punished less harshly, and defendants whose victims are whites are punished more harshly than defendants convicted of assaulting blacks). Feminists stress further that rapists and wife-beaters come from all classes and races.

When it comes to actual crimes — real rapes — at the turn of the twentieth century, the record is full of silences. There seems not to have been any investigation into the alleged crime wave in eastern North Carolina at the end of the nineteenth century, even though supposed black crime furnished the rationale for a bloody attack on blacks in Wilmington and for subsequent black disfranchisement. In Atlanta in 1906 Ray Stannard Baker found no attempt to discern the number of actual rapes. He investigated the twelve rapes and attempted rapes that black men were said to have committed before the riot. He found two rapes, three attempts, and all the other attacks imaginary or unfounded. Baker also discovered three rapes of white women by white men, which had attracted little or no attention in the newspapers, even though one assault was especially grisly. Baker either did not think to check rapes of black women by black or white men or such crimes were not in police records. Whichever was the case, Baker did not mention black women as victims in his discussion of rape in Atlanta.[18] His silence regarding black women typifies turn-of-the-twentieth-century discourse.

According to commonplace assumptions of the time, rape was a crime whose only victims were white women.[19] Every reason in the world exists to suspect that a great deal of crime, including what we call rape (sexual intercourse with a woman of any class or race against her will through the use or threat of force), existed in turn-of-the-century Atlanta, perhaps also in Wilmington and surrounding rural eastern North Carolina, for the city of Wilmington was probably not an exception to the southern rule of inadequate police forces. Southern society seems generally to have been poorly served by law enforcement, and observers noted with horror the ferocity of black criminals and the blood lust of white mobs, but not as though they were manifestations of the same angry culture.[20] Well into the twentieth century, native southerners like Lillian Smith, Richard Wright, and Maya Angelou spoke of the fear pervasive in the region.[21] In 1898 the United States was just emerging from a long and deep depression, which was accompanied by a crime wave in the South.

In 1906 Atlanta was a fast-growing city that had an unusually high crime rate, even in comparison with cities with larger total populations and larger black populations. The city struck Ray Stannard Baker as ill-policed, and he noted that the mob freely looted stores, whether owned by blacks or whites, in the pursuit of black victims. Under such conditions, one would expect a good deal of crime of all sorts, but whether this would have been interracial crime is another matter.

Homicide (in the nineteenth- and twentieth-century South) and rape (in the twentieth century) followed similar patterns. Most murders involved a black assailant and a black victim. Less frequent were murders involving white assailants and white victims, then white assailants and black victims, then, rarely, black assailants and white victims. I have been unable to find any statistics on rape in the nineteenth or early twentieth century, but according to mid-twentieth-century statistics, far and away the most common rape cases brought to trial involved black assailants and black victims, then white assailants and white victims. In much smaller numbers were rape cases with black assailants and white victims and rare instances of trials of white assailants and black victims.[22] In short, if actual crimes of violence had been occurring with increased frequency in Wilmington or Atlanta at the turn of the twentieth century, the largest number would most likely have involved black attackers and black victims, then white attackers and white victims.

Actual incidence of crime was not at issue. The anger that incited the mob in Atlanta was not connected to actual crimes, and no indictments or convictions of alleged rapists followed the riot. According to the businessmen's committee of inquiry, none of the victims was a "vagrant," the class from which rapists reputedly came. Instead the riot victims were reported as "honest, industrious and law-abiding citizens and useful members of society," though modest members of the working class.[23] Attacking blacks indiscriminately, the mob seems to have been completely indifferent to the identity of actual rapists.

On the black side of the color line the specific question of black rape of white women met silence. Two black journalists, Alex Manley, who was in the midst of events in Wilmington, and Ida B. Wells, tried to explain black-on-white rape away or to disprove it as not the main cause of lynching. After the riot in Atlanta, northern black newspapers blamed the riot on the rhetoric of the political campaign — which did, in fact, incite the violence. Northern black newspapers circumvented the charge of rape; they made little attempt directly to refute the white-supremacist accusation that black men raped white women. I suspect that as educated, middle-class people susceptible to class prejudice against the poor, black journalists secretly feared that the black lower classes might actually be capable of such attacks. Ida B. Wells hints at such apprehensions before embarking upon her crusade to expose the relevant circumstances after the lynching of her friends, who were successful businessmen, not criminals.[24] Better, perhaps, to concentrate on obviously hysterical white supremacists than to pose questions unlikely to find honest or satisfactory answers.

Reading evidence backwards is a risky matter, and I hesitate to conclude that because an Eldridge Cleaver in the 1960s said he took revenge on white men by raping white women — having practiced up, he said, on black women — that black men of similar mentality existed in the nineteenth or early twentieth centuries. It is certain, however, that if more than a tiny handful of black men of Cleaver's viciousness had acted, we would know their reputations through infamy. They would have turned up in the historical record and in folklore, probably as mythologized bandits and lynch victims. Instead, no evidence of either sort exists to show that black men were especially prone to raping white women. More to the point, those leveling the charge that black men raped white women undermined their credibility through their total unconcern about actual guilt—their willingness to murder suspects and suspects' relatives or associates on flimsy evidence. Wells found that although rape supposedly explained lynching, only about one-third of 728 black lynch victims in the late nineteenth century had even been charged with rape. Using 1903 figures, Baker found that only 21 of 104 lynch victims had been suspected of rape or attempted rape.[25]

Today it is not possible to discover how many and what sort of rapes occurred, because what actually happened seemed relatively unimportant at the time. There simply is no good evidence to show much of anything about real rape, only that it was a matter of high emotional salience. Rather than a type of behavior, rape functioned as a symbol related to other symbols of southern society, one of which was "social equality."

The ideals of "social equality" grew out of slavery and its enforced deference and submission. Southern slaves were overwhelmingly agricultural workers, and from them their masters expected not only labor but also the deference associated with the rural working class in areas shaped by British custom: hats off before masters, avoidance of looking masters in the eye, humility manifested as uncertainty. White supremacists were exceedingly touchy about infractions of this code of employer-employee patterned deference, and contempt in employees, often called "impudence," was occasionally a capital offense in the postwar South. "Impudence" threatened the employer-employee aspect of race relations and seemed to hint that the employee (actual or symbolic) was independent of the employer (actual or symbolic).

White supremacy in the South after the Civil War further embedded class relations into the etiquette of race relations. Blacks—all blacks—were supposed to act like servants with all whites. Segregation codified the relationship between people of the better class, which was one racial group (whites), and people of the lower class, which was another racial group (blacks). "Social equality" seemed ludicrous to whites who conflated race with class. A fantasy exemplifies this point.

In the 1870s Charles Manigault, a Charleston aristocrat, was looking back on the events of 1865 and philosophizing about the future. First he wrote about blacks, then he intended to speak about whites. White people did not engage his attention, so he drifted back to blacks. Manigault said he pitied blacks, whose hopes for freedom were so misguided that they believed they would become the social equals of whites. By "whites" Manigault meant people like himself, very rich planters with long years of formal education, gentlemanly status, and considerable real property. Manigault imagined the people he had formerly owned would spin as elaborate a daydream of social equality as did he himself: He envisioned " 'Cuffy' (the Beau of Ebony Belles) will be seen *Dancing with the Governors Daughter*, when Old Mauma 'Sucky,' so highly esteemed by her Coler'd Brethren for the fine *pan-cakes* she made, will in *their opinion*, not only be received in the best society, but courted & flattered, by distinguished *White Gentlemen*."[26]

The mismatch of classes makes Manigault's fantasy absurd: a gardener dancing with debutantes, gentlemen courting a cook. This horror of the mixing of the classes, an unacknowledged aspect of "social equality," was rooted in the unremunerated labor that masters extorted from slaves as well as in the masters' sensitivity to gradations in the social hierarchy. For Manigault and many of his peers, the merging of class and race seemed completely natural, as utterly natural as the fact that white people owned black people, and black people worked for white people. This notion outlasted the institution upon which it was based.

Thomas Dixon's early twentieth-century stories of the Ku Klux Klan were flagrantly racist, and like Charles Manigault and most American writing about race, he confounded race and class. The most important people in his work were whites, all of whom functioned as aristocrats. Dixon's *The Clansman* (unlike some of Thomas Nelson Page's work) did not include poor white villains. In Dixon's work all whites display the attributes of power, not only wealth and education (formal or informal), but also height, slenderness, and refinement.[27] These are the natural rulers of Dixon's made-up society, in which whites unfitted for leadership do not exist.

Below whites/aristocrats in Dixon's scheme are mulattoes, middling people, middling in refinement, middling in beauty, middling in intelligence. They are interested in attaining the accouterments of whiteness—political influence and white mates—but they are not prepared to use anything more efficient than cunning. Dixon associates his mulattoes closely with sex, and it is they who introduce the issue of "social equality." In *The Clansman*, the Silas Lynch character proposes to a white woman.

The linking of mulattoes and sex occurs in other contemporary southern white writing.[28] Myrta Avary thought of mulatto women as inherently impure, mostly because she assumed that they were the products of race mixing parents. She overlooked the possibility that light-skinned blacks could be the descendants of light-skinned blacks. For Avary, consequently, only black black women might be morally honest (that is, engage in sex only in marriage); race mixers and the products of race mixing could not be.[29] Walter Hines Page, who lived in New York and was as moderate a white southerner as could be imagined, fell into similar habits of thought. His autobiographical novel *The Southerner* (1901) includes a scene in which a young woman of mixed blood seduces the protagonist.

In the early twentieth century, Alfred Holt Stone, a sociologist who was also a Mississippi planter, was widely considered an expert on race relations. Stone weighed the purported qualities of African-American men of mixed blood and pure blood, to the disadvantage of mixed bloods, whose "white blood" supposedly made them restlessly ambitious. Stone considered men of pure "black blood" more patient and respectful toward whites. Stone's "mixed blood" example was W. E. B. Du Bois, the picture of impatience, and his paragon of blackness (although in reality a brown, not a black man) was Booker T. Washington.[30] For Stone and others of his ilk, vilifying Du Bois outweighed a careful investigation of Washington's lineage. Most white writers tried to avoid this sort of discussion because it contained some thorny contradictions. One unavoidable contradiction concerned the abilities of men of mixed race. Whites who deplored race mixing ran up against the fact that blacks who displayed qualities that Americans prized, such as education and wealth, more likely than not had white ancestry.

No matter how much blacks and whites denounced "social equality," the actual existence of a body of people in the South of obviously mixed race put many in a quandary. For the most part, whites tended not to bring up the obvious unless pressed, but prominent blacks flung the

facts in their faces repeatedly. Whenever someone like Benjamin Tillman began a tirade defending lynching as the punishment for the unspeakable crime of black-on-white rape, a black person in the audience
or in the columns of a newspaper would remind him that white men,
not black, were the South's premier race mixers.

Self-appointed spokesmen for "the South" would then concede that
in the antebellum days a few masters might have dallied in the slave
quarters, but that the whites who mixed races, in general, were the
"vicious," that is, they belonged to the lower class. Here the handy
conventions of white supremacy (white = upper class, black = lower
class) served well, for by portraying white miscegenators as the poor
and the criminal, white supremacists read them out of the white race
entirely. White race mixers, by this logic, were not *real* whites. They
could not be, because (real) whites possessed an inherent passion for
racial purity. An attenuation of this line survives in the work of late
twentieth-century historians.[31]

### An Egalitarian Consensus

In a system that classified anyone of African descent, however attenuated, as black, whites could fairly easily sweep under the rug the actual
race mixing that occurred between white men and black women. Black
people could not. Yellows and browns were as much Negroes as blacks,
so African Americans had to tussle with matters of miscegenation.

An egalitarian consensus among blacks grew out of their denial
of racist tenets. Without much public discussion African Americans
downplayed the significance of different shades of color among blacks.
Most whites believed and said so out loud that one's worth depended
on the color of one's "blood," one's physical inheritance, which was supposedly unalterable or, at least, not very susceptible to change through
manipulations such as education and increased income. But black people traced individual attainment to favorable circumstances. Denying
that race predicted one's abilities, blacks insisted that given the proper
advantages, any man — black, brown, or yellow — could become a gentleman, any woman a lady. If some blacks prospered and others suffered, the difference was not to be sought in the "blood." Taunting
white supremacists, however, blacks unfailingly yielded to temptation.
They pointed out that "the best blood of the South" flowed in the veins
of people classed as Negroes and that white aristocrats, not white low-

life, had fathered the South's mixed bloods. Even so, blacks would not concede that the descendants of planters were superior to the descendants of slaves on both sides.

This refusal to link achievement to color is remarkably consistent in black nonfiction writing, in which every black person is the potential equal of the other, from Mrs. Booker T. Washington to the mother of the poorest and least-educated sharecropping family in Mississippi. Blacks censored themselves in nonfiction, which almost never judges intraracial distinctions of complexion.

In black fiction, in contrast, the quandaries abound. How to deal with the obvious fact that most of the leaders of the race — the wealthy, the educated, the published — were men and women of mixed blood? How to face the fact that blacks as well as whites equated light complexions with feminine beauty? How to explain that brown and yellow people often discriminated against black people socially, as though the latter belonged to a lower class? Like Americans generally, blacks who wrote on such themes described individual attributes rather than the advantages or injuries of class. And, like other Americans, black fiction writers produced characters in which relative whiteness symbolized refinement and blackness embodied coarseness. Charles Chesnutt followed these unspoken rules, so that his Reena Walden character in *The House Behind the Cedars* (1900), so fair that she can pass for white, speaks standard English and is naturally refined even before attending school. White ancestry may make Reena Walden a natural aristocrat, but whiteness alone does not elevate Chesnutt's characters. In *The Marrow of Tradition* (1901) they include a crude, poor white politician and an uneducated but astute black black man, as though to demonstrate that virtue does not invariably accord with color.

Still, black fiction writers often accepted the conventions of white supremacy unconsciously, and the confusion of values remained in black fiction at the turn of the century; for the most part yellows stood for the Negro elite in a way parallel to the white supremacists' appropriation of aristocracy for the white race. There existed an articulate exception. A black novelist from Memphis, Sutton Griggs, wrote creatively about mixed and pure blood. His solution was to balance his characters carefully by sex and shade. His yellow men marry black women, his black men marry yellow women, and all of them are genteel. Griggs's future Negro race would finally emerge a uniform, medium brown. Like most other black writers of the late nineteenth and early twentieth centuries, Griggs created characters, especially women, of relentless refinement and long, naturally flowing hair.

One minor character in the white-supremacist mythology never appears in black fiction: the dissolute black woman who seduces white men (Wilbur Cash's "complaisant" Negro woman), on whom white supremacists placed the blame for miscegenation. Most whites—and some blacks—agreed that black women's morals were so deplorable that they welcomed the advances of white men. This stereotype of black women was rooted in slavery and in low class status after slavery. As Susan Brownmiller points out, women of subject or conquered populations and women who belong to groups susceptible to abuse, such as European Jews and American blacks, have long been considered especially seductive by men of more powerful groups.[32] Many disparate groups of women have been set outside prevailing moral systems and thereby provided men an excuse for rape. Men have turned the vulnerability to sexual assault of groups of women into a reputation for sensuality.

### Black Women

As slaves and as members of a despised racial minority, black women belonged to categories labeled "libertine." As working women, too, they were vulnerable to the abuses of employers and fellow workers and likely also to be misunderstood by people of the better-off classes. Kathy Peiss notes that at the turn of the century working-class culture in the North horrified middle-class social workers with its sexual explicitness, free use of liquor, and moral flexibility.[33] In the South, black women (most of whom worked in agriculture or as domestic servants) became the targets of stereotypes of working-class hyper-sexuality that prevail throughout the Western world. White supremacists claimed the working women at hand—black women—had no morals. By extension, there could be no such thing as the rape of a black woman.

While whites saw black women's sexual availability as an inherent trait, blacks either denied it or ascribed it to conditions: poverty, lack of education, and the corrupting influence of slavery. Blacks emphasized further black women's long-standing powerlessness before white men. "Oh, if there is any one thing under the wide canopy of heaven horrible enough to stir a man's soul, and to make his very blood boil," wrote William Craft in his slave narrative, "it is the thought of his dear wife, his unprotected sister, or his young and virtuous daughters, struggling to save themselves from falling a prey to such demons!"[34]

This anger, prevalent in the writing of black men, interprets attacks on the bodies of black women as an insult to black men, as though the mistreatment of women served as a proxy in a struggle between black and white men. This view echoes an approach to women as old as the Bible and seemingly common in the South: that women are the property of men and that raping a woman is an attack on the man who owns her. Black men, like white men, were not immune to this interpretation of relations between the sexes.

Black women's writings, like the narratives of white women who had been in Indian captivity, betray little of this anger over sexual exploitation, as Frances Foster demonstrates. Female autobiographers such as Harriet Jacobs (Linda Brent) and Elizabeth Keckley mention sexual abuse, but as briefly and obscurely as possible. They see themselves as powerless victims whose loss of virtue was not their own fault. In this their approach resembles that of black male narrators. But more important, female narrators do not stress their identity as victims, as male narrators do.

Women seem to wish to suppress unfortunate occurrences in order to demonstrate that they succeeded in transcending oppression to achieve something praiseworthy, which they interpret also as a service to their race. Female narrators had not initiated sexual relations with white men and were not indifferent to sexual exploitation, but they do not define themselves in terms of sexual victimization. These women, showing that even the humblest American could become autonomous and contribute to her society, chose not to emphasize the aspect of their experience that involved rape, the ultimate victimization, the extreme proof of powerlessness.

Black women's reticence about sexual victimization was not unique. In the most famous "rape" case of the twentieth century, the Scottsboro case, the two alleged victims seem to have been intimidated into claiming that they had been assaulted by the young black men, and one of the women recanted later and joined the Scottsboro defense. In that same decade, a group of white southern women, led by Jessie Daniel Ames, worked to halt the practice of lynching, claiming that it was an insult to white women. As Jacquelyn Hall explains, the Association of Southern Women for the Prevention of Lynching realized that lynching terrorized white women as well as blacks, furthering the goals of both sexual and racial control.[35] Whether the women victims of rape were black or white, they were far less bent on publicity and revenge than their men. The struggle over "social equality," race mixing, and violence was fundamentally economic and political, thereby an affair of men.

This is not to say that the panoply of laws and traditions designed to immobilize and weaken blacks as workers and to humiliate them as individuals did not apply to women. It most certainly did. But with women disfranchised and with men as the usual heads of household and therefore as the main political and economic persons in their families, the emotional nexus of power connected black and white men; black women's victimization was virtually incidental to white supremacy. White supremacists intended black women to remain vulnerable as workers and available as sex objects, but the main targets of violent, collective, emotionally charged racism at the turn of the century were men, poor black men, the foundation of the southern working class. Educated and well-to-do black men also fell victim to racism, of course, as in the politically charged burning to death of a black postmaster in South Carolina in 1898. But as in the case of black women, the victimization of prosperous black men, who were few in number, was almost incidental to the immobilization of millions of black workers.

### White Supremacy's Pornographic Power

White supremacists of various stations fashioned a series of controls over blacks that has often been summed up in the word "segregation." Borrowing a term from Susan Griffin, I want now to stress its "pornographic" aspect. Griffin describes what she calls the "pornographic mind," which is the same as the "chauvinist mind," and which, objectifying what it hates—whether women, blacks, or Jews—seeks to injure and humiliate the object. She links pornography to sadism, stressing the pornographer's obsession with rituals of hurting and humiliating.[36] Chauvinists like Adolph Hitler and Thomas Dixon both played out the fantasy of the dark man raping the fair woman, but for Hitler the man must be a Jew; for Dixon, a black. And for both the proper response was violence that punishes everyone within the symbolic category of the other. Whether on the mundane or catastrophic level, the essence of pornographic power is degradation.

The system of segregation was an obvious display of pornographic power, relegating blacks to inferior public services and treating them all like servants (for example, making any black person enter buildings through the back or service door, refusing any black person the titles Mr., Mrs., Miss, and calling any black person by a first name). The formula of "separate but equal," like "social equality," was never meant to materialize. In a white-supremacist society, "separate but equal" was nonsensical, for segregation was intended to insult blacks and to remind them at every turn of their lower status. Segregation was the everyday aspect of racial degradation that corresponded to symbolic class roles for the races.

Just as the effective end of black political power in the late nineteenth century did not reassure white politicians who continued to fear — or at least say they feared — the possibility of "Negro domination," so segregation and other humiliations did not sufficiently reassure white supremacists of their pornographic power. It was not by chance that they seized on the cry of "rape" to incite violence that was often blind, for the very word resonates with the pornographic symbols of degradation and sexuality. Here the real or imagined violation of a woman served as a pretext for another kind of rape.

Rapes of a sort did occur when Ku Klux Klansmen administered beatings, white supremacists of North Carolina and Georgia incited riots, and nameless whites joined lynch mobs. But these lynchings, symbolic rapes were by white men against black men. Symbolic rapes, like actual rape against women, were rituals of power and degradation, as white men burned, whipped, and murdered in an attempt to close the circle of their power over black men. Aping the forms of legal executions, these symbolic rapes constituted the bodily aspect of the maintenance of white men's physical power over black men.

Viewed in an anthropological light, the rituals of riots and lynchings may be interpreted as reaffirmations of community values, as one historian describing the culture of the southern "deme" has done.[37] But the values in question upheld the oppression of the poorest people in the society and today appear obscene. White-supremacist riots and lynchings were rituals whose analogues are more nearly fraternity gang-bangs than rites of passage. Racial violence, so much out of place in a democracy priding itself on the rule of law, was another aspect of the maintenance of a multifaceted power that had both enormous class import and deep psychological resonance. There was both oppression that was racial, for the oppression of a race of people was the obvious point of segregation and other forms of racial humiliation, from the virulent to the niggling. But there was also another large, deep meaning of white supremacy: the creation and maintenance of a powerless working class that was as vulnerable to the whim of employers as possible and as unfitted as could be for competition with working-class whites. The psychic need for one kind of supremacy did not obviate the need for the other.

It is true that the need for pornographic power existed only in the "mind" of southern society, or, more to the point, in the "mind" of a portion of the South. It is also probably true that the exercise of pornographic power indicates that the symbolic rapists of black men felt insufficiently powerful. But what must also be remembered is something that the Association of Southern Women for the Prevention of Lynching knew in the 1930s: that lynching was the product of white supremacy and that the very notion that one group ought to hold power over another was at fault. More than that, the need for pornographic power reinforced and was reinforced by the realities of other kinds of domination, economic and political.

### Change

Not until 1940 could the Association of Southern Women for the Prevention of Lynching proclaim the passage of the first year without a lynching, which means that the practice continued for a very long time.[38] What ended the regular exercise of pornographic power was not the assurance that blacks had been sufficiently intimidated to stay in their place.[39] Change came through phenomena that were both global and national.

The senseless carnage of the First World War dealt white supremacy a tremendous blow. True, the slaughter of some thirteen million soldiers did not end the conceit that white people held the genius of civilization. But the irrational lengths to which Europeans took the war diminished the relative standing of the white race and made possible the emergence of jazz and the figure of non-white peoples as emblems of authenticity and vigor. In the 1930s and 1940s the German Nazi movement and the Holocaust also served greatly to undermine the respectability of racism.

In the United States, blacks served in the American armed forces. They also migrated out of areas where lynchings and riots occurred and employers lost their work force. Riots ruined the business climate of cities in which they took place, so that white employers and businessmen came to discourage racial violence out of sheer business sense.

The undermining of white supremacy nationally and internationally brought change. Blacks gained moral and political standing in American society, and black power, attenuated as it was in the early twentieth century, challenged white supremacy bit by bit, in organizations such as the Niagara Movement, the Negro Business League, and the National Association for the Advancement of Colored People. It is not by chance that the worst of white supremacist mouthings ended between 1915 and 1945, for these were the years when blacks began to make themselves felt as workers, political actors, and intellectuals in the North. An articulate handful of individuals (most noticed in Harlem) demonstrated that blacks were also writers and social scientists. Their white allies — social workers, publishers, and anthropologists — also publicized facts that challenged white supremacy. By the second quarter of the twentieth century, Congress was considering antilynching legislation and several southern states had passed statutes that opposed the practice in name, at least. White supremacy's loss of legitimacy was largely the result of a struggle that went back to Frederick Douglass and William Lloyd Garrison and extended right through the twentieth century. Without this campaign against the notion that racial domination is legitimate, the exercise of pornographic power — like the exercise of other kinds of power — would have continued as an acceptable means of maintaining the southern version of the right of the privileged to exploit the poor. And white southerners would not have begun freeing themselves of the need to placate their own racial demons through offerings of violence.

# 5

## *Hosea Hudson*

### THE LIFE & TIMES OF A

### BLACK COMMUNIST

• • •

My favorite photos of Hosea Hudson are the ones I took in Atlantic City in August 1978, just after we ate lunch on the boardwalk and shared a second bottle of champagne. We were celebrating the completion of our taped interviews, or so we thought — the taping continued on into the fall. After lunch Hudson stood before the chain-link fence that protects his neighbor's vegetable garden from dogs and children.

I snapped several photos of him as he told me what a fine book this would be if they printed it like we wrote it. He was in good spirits, and it showed. When the photos were developed, I saw they were better than any I had seen of Hudson before.

The pictures I had taken in 1976 resemble the portrait on the cover of his first autobiography, where, smiling under a collage saying "Free Angela and All Political Prisoners!" he looks too young, too ingenuous, and too open for a man who has lived his life. Another photo I don't like was taken in 1973. There he looks too old, sick, and angry. But in the 1978 photos, Hudson looks like the crusty and knowing man who speaks in his narrative.

Partly it's that by then I knew Hudson well enough to capture him on film. He talked to me instead of posing. But it was also that he changed. The previous two years of severe weather and his brother's death took their toll on him physically. When he was seventy-eight years old, he looked sixty-five. When he was eighty, he looked about seventy. The idea of death made him seem older than before, but it also encouraged him to drop his guard.

During much of our long conversation Hudson spoke as if his life divided into forty-six years in the Communist Party and thirty-three years of groping toward it. Later, however, he began speaking of his youth as a time that was interesting because it was *his* youth. He put on record events that in the past he refused to let me tape, much less print. His youth was no longer simply an object lesson in the persecution of black people under capitalism; it was also the time when he learned to gamble. I heard it as a youth of want, instability, unremitting hard work, and fear, but also of bravery, family effort, piety, and occasional joys.

## *Family*

Hudson was born on 12 April 1898 in Wilkes County, Georgia, a cotton county near the South Carolina border. His mother, Laura Camella Smith Hudson, was eighteen when he was born; his father, Thomas Hudson, twenty-seven. Two years later, his brother Eddie was born. The parents were quarrelsome, and they chopped up their marriage with many short separations. After three years, Mrs. Hudson left her husband for good, taking her two babies to her parents in Oglethorpe County, four or five miles to the west. With these three new members, the family consisted of Hosea's grandfather George Smith, his grandmother Julia Smith, his uncle Ned, and his aunt Georgia Mae. George Smith had been born a slave and had failed to improve his fortunes very much over the years. In 1901 the family owned one mule named Bailey and sharecropped on Tom Glen's plantation. Like other poor sharecropping families, the Smith family moved often and owned very little.

Among Hudson's earlier memories is his grandfather's preaching to the trees behind the cow barn. An illiterate who never was pastor of a church, George Smith was only a jackleg preacher, but he solemnly considered himself a Methodist minister. Behind his back, the older members of the family laughed at his preaching to the pines but, for five-year-old Hosie, Smith's sermonizing was no laughing matter. At noontime, Hosie would have to go call his grandfather to dinner, terrified always that he would see a snake in the woods. That fear ended

only when George Smith left home after Ned's difficulties with the law supplied a pretext for a quarrel.

Hosea's uncle Ned attended church regularly with the rest of the family, but somehow that young man always attracted trouble. One Sunday in 1903 when he was seventeen, several white men, including his grandmother's half-brother, waylaid him, stripped him, and beat him badly, forcing him to flee Oglethorpe County without going home. That night the whole family worried. Julia Smith stayed up, peering down the dirt road and calling her son's name. As soon as it got light

> She went down that farm road through the forest and cow pastures until she got to the gate at the other side of the pasture near the church and near the pasture gate. She found his top dress coat, his vest, and his white shirt with blood stains on all of the clothing, and she cried out that Ned had been murdered. . . .
>
> It was a bright and sunny day about September. I can remember how I heard the old people there talking and planning to search the forest and drag Long Creek for my uncle's body.[1]

A few weeks later, Ned turned up thirty miles away. He was sent back to Oglethorpe County and charged with jumping the bond his land-lord had posted to get him out of difficulties earlier in the summer.

As Ned awaited trial, George Smith grew testy and refused to take clothes to the boy in jail, as his wife asked. George and Julia Smith were "already at the breaking point" because of Laura's return and the strain she and her two sons imposed on the family. Swearing he would not support them all, Smith left home for good. Hudson remembers his departure as a minor loss. Even before then, Julia Smith had headed the household in all but name. Smith had begun "running around in his late years," Hudson says. "I don't know whether to say he wont no man or what."[2]

Ned spent twelve months in 1903 and 1904 on the county prison farm. The rest of the family moved to Dave Arm's place to sharecrop without him. After his release, Ned farmed near them and sometimes helped them out with the work. In 1906 the family moved to the Jones place, then to Burl Sill's place in Wilkes County. The main plowhand in these years was Georgia Mae, Hudson's hardworking aunt, ten years older than he. When she ran away and got married in the fall of 1908, ten-year-old Hosea inherited her job and plowed full-time.

What remained of the family—Hosea, his grandmother, his mother, and his brother—moved to Dr. Rail's place in Oglethorpe County in 1909. Crops were so bad that year that Ned left farming entirely to work as a porter on the railroad, depriving the family of women and boys of valuable assistance. They moved to Jim Allgood's place in 1910 and suffered a loss Hudson regretted keenly. Laura Hudson had mortgaged two cows to buy a sewing machine for $40 but was never able to pay off the debt. Allgood foreclosed, appropriating "two *fine* jersey cows." In 1911 the family lost even occasional assistance from Ned when he moved to New Jersey.

Hudson's mother married again in 1911. Her new husband, Bill Blackburn, added to the family's working hands and moved them to a promising situation, farming with a well-to-do friend of his, a black man named Willie Pollion. Soon Blackburn's friendship with Pollion soured for the rest of the family, although Hudson never understood exactly what took place. Bill left Laura, moved in with Willie Pollion's brothers, then lived with one of Pollion's female relatives. After Blackburn left them to farm alone, the family rarely got enough to eat:

> We was trying to pick out some cotton where we'd be able to sell some seed and get some food, cause we practically working without food. Eating roast ear, what you find from late corn planting in the corn fields, roast ear and apples, late apples, peanuts out of the peanut patch. Nothing to eat.
>
> My grandmother got some roasting ears was too hard to make roasting ear corn out of. She took a piece of wire, a piece of tin, and put holes in it with a nail and bent it around, put it on a piece of plank and grated that corn and made something like grits and we had that for bread.

Before they were able to pick a single bale of cotton, Willie Pollion seized their crops, garden, and livestock. In court Laura Hudson lost the crops and garden but won the right to keep the cow and pig and to leave Pollion free of any further debt to him.

A black neighbor, Man Wallace, invited the family to live with him and pick his cotton in exchange for shelter and food. The food was still scanty. When Wallace's cotton was all in, they picked cotton for a white man named Bell, making 50 cents per hundred pounds.

One day as they were picking in Bell's field, "Willie Pollion came down there on his horse Sally," Hudson recalls. Pollion claimed that Laura still owed him money. Demanding payment roughly, he threatened to hit her:

> My mother told him she wont paying no debt. He looked like a white man. You couldn't tell him from a white man. And when he started talking big talk at my mother, I told him—I wont but fourteen years old—I got mad, I told him, "God damn your white soul! You done took all we made up yonder on your place, now you come down here trying take what little we got down here!" I said, "I'll kill you with a rock." I said, "You hit her, I'll . . . I'll kill you with a rock!"
>
> I was crying, I was so mad. He done took all we had made, we's hungry, and I just got mad.

Hudson had raised his voice to speak sharply to an adult for the first time. Willie Pollion left the family alone, but the hard times continued.

In January 1913 Hudson's family moved back to Dave Arm's, where Laura cooked for the hands at the sawmill and Hosie carried water and chopped firewood. They earned no wages for their work, only room and board—"fried meat and clear grease and biscuit. I think we had white meat [fatback] sometimes and some peas. My mother cooked peas sometimes. No money. Didn't know nothing about money."

Hudson's first accident at work occurred one cold morning. "All they's firing the engine with was green slab, pine slabs," and Dave Arm sent Hudson into the woods to cut some "fat pine" to kindle the fire. Splitting a piece of wood, Hudson struck his foot with the ax and cut three toes badly. "The toe next to my big toe, it like to unjointed it." He drove back to the sawmill, "Oh, it was long, about two miles, I guess, down in the woods, cold in the morning, frosty." From the sawmill he limped home with his shoe full of blood.

His grandmother bathed the foot and applied soot and turpentine. Dave Arm allowed the boy a few days convalescence, then ordered him back to hard work. Hudson's grandmother refused to let the injured boy work before his foot healed, and she sent him to stay with his aunt Georgia Mae. Then the family moved to Bob Johnson's.

Back on his feet, Hudson worked at Johnson's sawmill six days a week. They agreed on 50 cents a day in wages, but the wages turned out to be only food for the family. "The most stuff they fed my grandmother and them with was from the table and from his garden. He had a large turnip patch, and he just give her a bunch of those turnips ever so often, give her a piece of hog jowls or something, or some cornmeal. That's the way we made it, until we got able to start the crop, where she could open a account where we could buy some food on the crop to make the crop. Oh, it was rough."

Laura Hudson Blackburn made a lasting marriage to John Henry Blakely in 1913, leaving behind a family of Hosea, his grandmother, and his brother. At fifteen, Hosea headed the household and "traded" with landlord Jones Collins on the family's behalf:

> I come in, say, "I hear them say you got a extra farm that you want to let out for sharecropping. I come to see could I get it."
>
> Old man Collins say, "How old are you?" I was so young till he wanted to know "who did you have to work a farm with?" I told him me and my grandmother and brother. He want to know how old my brother. My brother then was about thirteen or something.
>
> "Do you think you can work a farm?" I told him I *been* working.
>
> "You reckon your grandmother mind you trading with me?"
>
> "No, she don't mind me trading. I always do the trading anyhow for the farm." And that's the way I traded with them.

Hudson traded with Collins for three years, until the family moved to Taylor Hall's in 1917. That spring Hudson courted Sophie Scroggs (a pseudonym), and they decided to marry at the end of the year. After he sold the cotton early in December, his grandmother divided everything they owned into three equal parts. Hudson took his third and married Sophie on 31 December 1917. They remained with Hall, sharecropping until the end of 1922. Hosea and Sophie made good crops until 1921, paid their debts, cleared a little money, "nothing much."[3]

Boll weevils appeared in Wilkes County in 1921 and ruined Hudson's 1922 crop. He made less than two bales of cotton and very little corn — the bud worms got in the corn. Working on halves, he broke even. That was Hudson's last year of sharecropping. For the next seven months he hired out with Tom Jackson for $10 a month, intending to stay out of debt and save a little something to get started in the city. He planned to quit farming in the summer and leave Wilkes County.

But by May Hudson still had saved nothing and owed Jackson 50 cents. Then he got an idea:

I began to go and find out who was it among the farmers that had peanuts left over after planting their peanut crop. I bought them at $2 a bushel [on consignment] . . . I took the peanuts home and removed the rack from my little four-eyed wood cooking stove and made a hot wood fire in my cooking stove. I would put a peck of the peanuts in the stove at a time until I parch a bushel of peanuts. . . .

I took a salmon can and shined it up very nice. I had a strap that I put on each end of the bag of peanuts. I would go out to Mr. Jackson's grocery store on Saturdays . . . where the Negroes would hang out . . . and sell a salmon can of parch peanuts, 5 cents a can.

I went to the church on Sunday and took a stand down to the spring where the people would come to get a fresh drink of spring water. There I would sell my peanuts.[4]

But at 5 cents a can, roasted peanuts netted little profit. Hudson had another idea: "I got me a pipe and a barrel and went out there in the fields and got some of that old syrup, what you mix with arsenic to kill boll weevils, and I buy me some meal and made me a barrel of mash, made me some whisky." Peanuts and whisky brought him $40. "That's the way I left the country," he says. "I come out of there and I didn't go back for nineteen years."

### Leaving Wilkes County

When Hudson speaks of leaving Wilkes County, he lists his gambling, bad company, difficulties with his relatives, run-ins at Jackson's store on Saturdays. The city offered both an escape from personal tensions and well-paid work. He focuses on the personal side where his own actions counted for something. Unmentioned are the evils he could not affect, the boll weevil or the iniquitous system of sharecropping.

Little wonder that Hudson did not return to Wilkes County for so many years. He had grown up materially and emotionally impoverished and spent his youth in unending hard work. School had been no fun either, but a place of high anxiety. Before he was old enough to be a regular pupil, he went along to Professor Hardiman's school at Rocky Branch Church with Georgia Mae. His grandmother had sent the five-year-old "just to learn the rules and regulations of the school." He remembers only that his grandmother had made him a little calico shirt, a "waist," with buttons around the bottom to fasten to his pants. "I used to go, set up in school, and I'd eat the sleeves of that calico, of that waist. I'd just bite it and nibble on it, just bit it. When I go home, I done had bit holes all in my waist sleeve." Julia Smith sent word to Professor Hardiman to whip him when he chewed his sleeves, and that broke the habit.

Even after Hudson began school in earnest in 1904, the whole experience remained disagreeable. Of these years he says that "it was just really a horrible frightening life for me." Rocky Branch Church was two or three miles from home, and he had to cross woods and pastures to get there. "I was always scared to death of seeing a snake or a mad dog. People always talking about mad dogs." He remembers vividly his return home from school one afternoon:

> I was going home in the spring of the year, and a dark cloud was back in the East. The sun was shining here, and it was thunder back over here. You could just stand and look at the drops of water through the sky, and they was shining. And I just stood there, afraid to move. I just looked at it. I could see them drops ashining, falling against that black cloud here. I was just scared to death.

As he got bigger, plowing took Hosie out of school by late February or early March. He attended school in spells until 1912, but for all his years in the classroom, he only learned to read haltingly, spelling out each word before he could pronounce it. To explain his lack of facility, he usually says even now that he only had a few months of schooling as a child. His brother Eddie was a very different case.

Hosea's brother became a preacher and was obviously a better-educated man. Eddie was the favorite child of their grandmother and mother. Hosie was the hard-working older son, the "thick head," while Eddie was the baby, the pet. All the family and friends predicted that Eddie would become a preacher. He was the good boy who could "talk like a mockingbird," but he also tattled on Hosie whenever Hosie did something wrong. Hosie prepared the fields, mended fences, and cleared ditches while Eddie attended school every year from beginning to end—Christmas to Easter. "It was always something between me and him," Hudson says, and even as adults the brothers often verged on trading blows. Yet they never lost sight of one another. Hosea went to Atlanta to nurse Eddie during his terminal illness in 1977.

Of his mother and grandmother, Hudson remembers their "contempt" for him, which still puzzles him. They would hit him on the head with a piece of stove wood "when they got mad around the house." He says that his mother gave him away to his grandmother when she left his father, because Julia Smith often told him he "belonged" to her. When Laura married for the third time in 1913, she moved away with her husband and left the boys with her mother. When Hosea married, his grandmother and brother went to live with Laura and John Henry Blakley.

Despite his parents' early separation, Hudson recalls his father Thomas Hudson "ever since I can remember anybody." His father was a handsome man, outgoing, and a bit of a show-off. He sang and spoke in a fine bass voice and was a favorite for singing during collection or selling dinners at church. Hudson can still recapture his father's scent: "He always carried that good perfume on his shave and on his clothes, like men used to carry, 'Heart's Home.' I can smell it now."

The day Hosie and Eddie learned that their father was working on the Elberton Seaboard Railroad, they searched the line for him. To their pleasure, they found he was the boss of a gang laying pipe. He stood in the ditch with his overalls rolled up, ordering the other black men about in his rich deep voice, making a fine show of directing them. On the job and at church, Tom Hudson stood out.

> He was kind of showish, all right. He'd have all the women, especially, at the church. He'd set his hat to one side, and he'd always have something to say.
>
> People always admired Tom Hudson. "Tom Hudson! Tom Hudson!" He was known everywhere.

Church service at Winn's Chapel on the first Sunday of June 1907 gave Hudson special delight. His father was there in the choir, and he sang with him. "I was so small that he would stand up in front of the bench, and I was standing on the bench, standing beside him," Hudson recalls. The boy glowed with pride when the other men kidded Tom Hudson. "What you doing with that boy?! You know that boy can't sing!" Tom Hudson laughed back at them, "Yes, he can sing!"

His father's visits always pleased young Hosea, and he especially remembers one of them in 1906:

Poor man, I bet you he walked fifteen miles, walking, and these was swamps then, woods forest. But he came over there one night to see us, and he brought a can, a baking powder can full of sugar for us, and he brought some canned goods.

He had me sitting on his knee, and he was letting me eat all the candy I want. And my grandmother said, "Thomas, don't be giving that boy all that candy. You make him sick."

"Oh, let him eat it," he said, "I brought it for him to eat." And he stayed there that night and he left, I don't know what time, going back, walking those fifteen miles back through the swamps and woods.

And the next morning I got up looking for some of that candy and them canned goods, and I haven't seen them yet. My grandmother took them and wouldn't let us have them. I asked about the candy.

"Shut up your mouth! Your daddy will spoil your guts out! You go around here and just eat everything he bring here!" She never did give me any more of that candy.

Hudson thinks that his grandmother's meddling caused his parents' divorce. Julia Smith didn't like Tom Hudson and never spoke kindly of him. Often she told Hosie, "Your daddy no good. He don't give you nothing." Eddie shared his grandmother's views and felt little affection for his father. Eddie "didn't care anything about him," Hudson says, but "I didn't feel that way against him. I always had a feeling I always wanted for a daddy." He feels that warmth in spite of ambivalent memories of his father.

One Sunday in the summer of 1913 Hilly Mount Zion Church held a fair where barbeque dinners were on sale. Tom Hudson smiled and winked and called to all the people to come buy barbeque. His oldest son stood off to one side, certain his father could see him:

I wanted some, but I didn't have no money to buy it. And my daddy didn't give me none, didn't offer me none. I don't remember how I felt, I didn't get mad, but I remember it very well how bad I wanted some of that fresh meat. I was *so* hungry. I wanted some of that food *so* bad.

Hudson says he was "kind of shy in them days" and probably did not ask his father for food. But he cannot remember his feelings that day and offers no good explanation for the incident. In the end, however, he sums up his father as "a great man. He was a good man."

## Church

Until 1932, Hudson attended church regularly. His family were all believers, and no one ever missed a Sunday at church. Meeting Sundays came only once a month, but there were several churches in the vicinity with different meeting days: first Sundays were meeting Sundays at Winn's Chapel, second Sundays at Rocky Branch, third Sundays at Jordan Chapel, fourth Sundays at Lionsville. Some of the churches were Missionary Baptist, like Hudson's family, others were Methodist, but many of the same people attended them all.

For several of his churchgoing years, Hudson wanted to be a preacher, but something was missing. "I tried to get the feeling like other people, but I never could get that feeling. I went to church regular. In them years there was nowhere else to go." What he enjoyed most about church was singing. On meeting Sundays a minister would conduct services and preach, leaving little time for singing. But on other Sundays when there was only Sunday school, the program would include five or six songs.

Hudson's family all sang: his mother soprano, his father bass, Ned tenor, and Georgia Mae alto. "My mother and them used to sing when I was a kid, way back there in 19 aught 1 and 2 . . . They was singing shape-notes then, and they had a song I never will forget. I know that song yet. I learnt to sing notes off of it." I asked Hudson to sing the song, and he sang it twice for me, first: "As do mi, mi re do, do ce la, do la as, mi, mi da mi, mi re do." Then in words:

There the sun never sets
And the leaves never fade
In the beau-ti-ful city of gold.

That's the way it went. I used to listen at them sing, and I was a small kid, and I learnt how to sing notes on that old songbook.

When Hudson says "sing notes," he means shape-notes, a method of singing that takes its name from the variously shaped notes used in a score. Each shape has a name and corresponds to a relative pitch.

Singers can read a melody by the shaped notes, without contending with absolute pitch or different keys.

Shape-note singing (stemming from the British fasola system) originated in New England, where William Little and William Smith published the first shape-note songbook, *The Easy Instructor*, in 1802. This simple system of notation did not last in musically sophisticated New England. But it flourished in the frontier regions of the South and West. In the early nineteenth century, several types of shape-notation existed. Seven-shape notation, which Hudson uses, appeared in 1832. Jesse B. Aiken introduced the system of seven-shape notation that is standard today in the South in *The Christian Minstrel*, published in Philadelphia in 1846. Here is the kind of seven-shape notation used in Hudson's own *Golden Hours* songbook.[5]

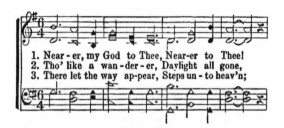

Shape-note singing did not become popular in southern black churches until the late nineteenth century. Spirituals and lined-out hymns had dominated black religious singing until then. According to Hudson, John Tiller, a preacher from South Carolina, introduced shape-note singing to Wilkes County before Hudson was born. It was popular in Wilkes County in 1902, when he heard his family sing. But in Oglethorpe, the next county to the west, there was no shape-note singing until after the First World War. A Wilkes County preacher named Tate, who lived in a place called Golden Star, introduced it.[6]

Georgia Mae preferred ballad singing to shape-note. Shape-note singing stressed the melody and printed score, but ballad sheets listed only the words:

> It used to be ministers come out there — this was 19 aught 4 and 5 and 6 and 7. Preachers would come out, had what you call ballads. You have a song wrote out, verses and choruses, on a long sheet. They sell that to poor folks out in the country, 5 and 10 cents a sheet.

My aunt got very popular singing them songs. Taking up a collection, sing a song, everybody called on Sister Georgia Mae. She was about sixteen to seventeen years old then.

Didn't have no piano then. Nothing like that in the church then. And one of the songs she used to sing — I just about forgot it now — but

My name is written, oh my Lord,
My name is written, oh my Lord,
My name is written, oh my Lord,
My name is written on the cornerstone.
If my mother asks for me, tell them I'm gone on to Galilee.
My name is written on the cornerstone.
And the whole church would be singing
My name is written, oh my lord . . .

That was the kind of singing people had, see.

And in a community where gambling and drinking were sins, singing was the only kind of amusement good boys had.

Until his grandmother and brother moved out in 1917, Hudson was an obedient child. He attended church and sang and prayed and never stayed out after 9:30 at night. He had learned to keep out of trouble, partly through the negative example of his uncle Ned. He was "a good worker," with a powerful temper he seldom showed. "I didn't bother nobody," Hudson says. "I didn't want nobody to bother me. I'd treat people nice. I'd be quiet and mannerable, you know, tip my hat." But in the month of freedom before his wedding, Hudson discovered drinking and gambling. He drank "some" and "gambled a whole lot" until he went to Atlanta in 1923.

### Into the Communist Party

In Atlanta Hudson started a new life. "When I got in the city," he says, "I wouldn't associate with nobody, gamble, or drink. That's why I stayed out of trouble." He didn't even sing. He wanted steady work as a machinist's helper in the railroad roundhouse, since helpers made nearly $5 a day. (He couldn't be a machinist, they were all white.) Failing to get the job, he moved on to Birmingham, where friends swore a man could earn $5 a day regularly. In Birmingham he became an iron molder at the Stockham foundry, but he seldom earned $5 a day for a full week, even in the 1920s. After the 1929 crash, weeks of one or two days' work were usual, if there was work. Hudson was a good worker, proud of his skill. He held his job until early 1932 when his life began to change.

He was disturbed to learn of nine young black men sentenced to death in Scottsboro, Alabama, for raping two white women on a train. It was to him a flagrant act of southern racial injustice. He wanted to act, but there seemed little he could do or say about the outrage — he was only one poorly educated, working-class Negro with a talent for gospel singing. His minister was in a position to protest the Scottsboro conviction, thought Hudson, but he would not. Faced with pressure from his congregation, the minister recommended only that the law should take its course, that "God going to take care of this thing." But one of Hudson's former co-workers, a black man named Al Murphy, offered some compelling answers.

Al Murphy had been a Communist since the summer of 1930, when the Communist Party first became active in Birmingham. His background was not vastly different from Hudson's, although Murphy was ten years younger. Born on a plantation in McRae, Georgia (about seventy miles southeast of Macon), Murphy attended elementary school for four years. He moved to Birmingham in search of work in the mid-1920s and lived with his aunt and uncle. Before the Depression hit and things got worse, Murphy attended night school.

One of Murphy's neighbors in Birmingham was Frank Williams. Williams's wife was blind, and Murphy describes them as being very poor. "I saw Frank walk along the street picking up cigarette butts. He would unwrap the tobacco and put it in an empty cigar box from which he took small amounts and gave it to his wife who smoked a pipe. He then would take some for himself and roll cigarettes."

One Sunday in 1930 Murphy found a Communist leaflet on his porch. He read it and liked it, but he mentioned it to no one. In the middle of the week, Williams asked him casually, "Say, Mr. Murphy, did you get one of them papers?" Williams said he himself couldn't read, but he wanted Murphy to see it. Murphy replied that he agreed with it. "A conversation began which was to seal our friendship and last as long as I stayed in Birmingham," Murphy said. He wrote to the New

York address on the leaflet and received pamphlets and copies of the *Daily Worker* by return mail.

Frank Williams took him to a meeting of the CP, "held in a standing room only smoke-filled room somewhere not far from the [Stockham] shop," where a white Communist led a discussion about unemployment, political rights for Negroes, self-determination for the Black Belt, and the Depression. Murphy joined the Party that night. Later he joined the Young Communist League and attended Marxist-Leninist classes. Then he looked around the shop for other likely recruits.

> Hosea Hudson . . . had worked at Stockham for many years. He knew the workers and about their conditions. Hosea was a large hunk of somebody, about six feet tall or more, his complexion was medium brown. He was popular in the black community because he was well-known as a fine singer and music group leader.
>
> I was cautiously optimistic about recruiting Hosea. He was too valuable to the Birmingham working-class struggles to miss him. I was determined to reach him.[7]

Murphy led the discussion at the meeting Hudson joined. In turn, Hudson recruited people such as Henry O. Mayfield, a co-worker on the city relief-work project.

Frank Williams, Al Murphy, Hosea Hudson, Henry O. Mayfield, and all but four of five of the Communists Hudson worked with in Birmingham in the 1930s were black, poor, and formally uneducated. They had been born on the plantations of Georgia and Alabama and grew up in the cotton fields. In search of work, they had migrated to the foundries, mills, and mines of Jefferson County. When there was work, they worked hard and made less than whites. Many of them resented their condition as blacks and as workmen.

Before the Communist Party came south in 1929, black steelworkers and miners lacked access to any protest organization, although members of what Hudson calls "the better class of Negroes" might join the National Association for the Advancement of Colored People or the Interracial Commission. The NAACP extended membership to all, but the organization's activities made it offensive to Alabama whites, and its membership made it uncomfortable for working-class blacks. Class lines in the black community were unwritten but clear, and men like

Hudson did not associate with educated or well-off black people until the united-front period of the late 1930s.

"The better class of Negroes" numbered only a few among Birmingham's 100,000 blacks in the 1930s. (The total population was about 260,000.) Hudson says they were "teachers, preachers, little homeowners, big deacons of the churches," and they lived in a different world. The city's housing pattern drew the distinctions. Workers lived next to the mines and foundries—like Stockham Pipe and Fittings, which owned little neighborhoods—or near the whites they served. Blacks of the better class owned their own houses and lived where they pleased, within the acceptable areas in a racially segregated community. But Hudson has never owned his own home. In the Depression years, when he was out of work most of the time, his family moved every few months in the same poor neighborhoods.

In its appeal to radical black workers in the 1930s, the CP was occupying virgin territory. In Birmingham there were virtually no unions, no Socialist Party, no leftist parties other than the CPUSA, not even the Universal Negro Improvement Association. (Murphy said that he had read about the Garvey movement and heard that a chapter of the UNIA existed in Birmingham, but he was never able to find it.)[8] Between 1930, when the CP began to organize seriously in the South, and 1936, when the CIO entered the field, the CP had no competition on the left. Jim Crow and hard times had created a radical black constituency in Alabama of men like Murphy and Hudson who did not find political sufficiency in church or lodge. They joined the CP gladly, at their very first meetings. "It look like the thing I had been looking for," says Hudson. When hundreds of Williamses, Murphys, Hudsons, and Mayfields became Communists, they also made the Party their own. In Alabama in the 1930s, the CP was a southern, working-class black organization, as Hudson's narrative clearly shows.

The Scottsboro defense, jobs, relief, and civil rights were the Party's short-term concerns. The long-range aim was self-determination for the Black Belt, a goal worked out in Moscow in 1928. The theory held that the Negroes of the Black Belt counties of the Deep South constituted an oppressed nation, according to Stalin's terse and comprehensive definition.[9]

In books and pamphlets in the 1930s, the historian James Allen explained that the Black Belt was the weakest link in the chain of American capitalism. If the CP could educate and awaken the black and white peasant masses, a democratic revolution might occur. Allen foresaw a revolutionary struggle that would create "councils of Soviets of peasants and workers seizing power at first on a local scale, extending their sphere, consolidating a number of areas and establishing the hegemony of the new revolutionary governmental power as the democratic revolution spreads." Only then would blacks obtain their civil rights in the South. They would confiscate the plantations and redistribute the land as collective farms.[10]

The policy of self-determination focused attention on racial oppression as part of a wider economic system that victimized both black and white working classes in the South. It presented a "scientific" explanation for the pervasive racial discrimination that otherwise seemed to defy understanding. CP periodicals presented black life as a whole national culture endowed with full dignity, not merely a flawed and comic mimicking of whites. The CP's introduction of the self-determination slogan signaled a concentration on the South and on black people that had not occurred in a national political organization since the middle of the nineteenth century.

Translated into immediate goals like welfare and voting rights, the self-determination theory was clear and attractive to Hudson. However, the theory's tortured logic and the shadow world of revolution presented problems. It proved difficult for working-class Communists to interpret the theory without reciting it like a catechism. Making sense of self-determination became particularly awkward in Birmingham, where the generalizations about the plantation economy broke down.

One day Hudson tried to explain to me the substance of discussions he and his comrades had in the early 1930s on the application of the self-determination slogan to Birmingham:

We used to discuss quite at length about the places like Birmingham—was in the Black Belt—an industrial, a coal mine. What we going do about that? Well, we had a lot of discussion, and I can tell you the truth, I don't know how we come to, what conclusion we reached.

But we said, it meant putting it maybe in that particular area, like the industrials for the mines, the ownership of mines and mills, it might have to be after the workers take power before the Negro people would be able to enjoy they full right in a place where these industrial is at.

These big industrials is owned by the North, northern capitalists, and they wasn't going give them up so easy without a real battle. And that's, that's what, we also discussed all that.

Out in the rural areas, you know, the rural area of the Black Belt, where the Negro farmers was in the majority, we felt that there, many places that the Negro would be able to get, enjoy the land, the land would be, you know, the rights of the land, before socialism.

But then they, we know that they going have a big struggle in the big industrial towns like Bessemer Alabama, Birmingham, Gadsden Alabama. All these places was in the Black Belt. It's a question of what was to do there. It just wasn't the farming area.

Really, what it meant, it meant the right of self-determination in the Black Belt, meant confiscating the land from the big landlords. It also meant confiscating the industrials from the big industrials, which was going to be a pulling of a eye tooth, but that was the correct slogan at that time, see?

It is not that Hudson is less articulate than other working-class communists in Birmingham — the theory was inappropriate. It depended on the Comintern's misapplication of Russian history to the American situation.

I doubt that anyone ever joined the Communist Party on the strength of the self-determination theory alone. It was the Party's more pragmatic activities that succeeded in attracting (if not holding) large numbers of southern blacks during the 1930s. Whereas fewer than 200 blacks belonged to the CP in 1929, over 20 percent of the new members in 1930 were Negroes — 1300 of the 6000 recruits. In the Birmingham district, the CP enrolled significant, but not massive, numbers. In the late 1930s, between 1000 and 1500 people were "in contact with the Communist leadership" either in Party-related organizations (the ILD or the Young Communist League) or in the Party itself, which numbered some 250, nearly all blacks. In 1931, blacks accounted for a little over 7 percent of the national membership; in 1932, nearly 10 percent; and in 1935, 11 percent. In 1939 the number of black Communists was 5005. The Party continued to attract black people in the 1940s, with membership hovering between 7000 and 8000 — 14 percent of the total — in the mid-1940s. The black membership has had a very high rate of turnover, however, among the rank and file. Among the leaders, blacks were more likely than whites to stay in the Party.[11]

Hudson's experience both corroborates and disputes this attraction and loss of black recruits. Hudson's forty-seven years in the CP made perfect sense for him, in terms of both his ideals and his self-interest. He said that his friends had been every bit as constant in their loyalty as he. Among his close friends, only two dropped out, Joe Howard, in an incident he recounts in Chapter 12, and John Beidel, who gave church activities first claim on his time after the Party sent him back to church in the late 1930s. The rest of Hudson's friends stayed in the Party until they died or left Alabama.

In a visit to Birmingham in the 1970s, Hudson rediscovered an octogenarian comrade and his older sister who still thought of themselves as Communists. "Archie is just as strong — he ain't active — but he just as strong in his belief as he ever was, and also his sister. On the question of people leaving the Party . . . the Party people back yonder in them rough day that I talk about . . . practically all them people dead." The people from the early 1930s didn't leave the Party, Hudson said, the Party left the people. Well after the 1950s, when the CP went underground, blacks in Tallapoosa County still considered themselves Communists or members of the Sharecroppers Union. But the organizers, unable to "make contact" with large numbers of Party people, could not keep them together in groups.

Hudson surmised that difficult conditions in Alabama bred a tough kind of Communist who did not appear in other places, or even in Birmingham in easier times. In "those rough days," as Hudson fondly termed the early 1930s, the Party in Birmingham was a tightly organized unit. Even on the national level, the workers were the center of the organization. For Hudson, the *Daily Worker* was at its best in those years, when it frequently printed workers' letters about conditions on the shop floor.

Hudson's own comrades in the South went to their graves as Communists, but that was not the common thing. Only in the Deep South was the Party overwhelmingly black. In the North and West, whites held the majority in Party units, and the CP had difficulty in holding blacks. Hudson explained that Party people, black and white, tended to push black recruits into organizational activities before they were mature ideologically. This effort, he said, "Has a tendency to swell that individual's head." Other Party members "pushing him and pushing him . . . but they don't take time to study that individual, to see what his level of understanding is. And by not taking that into account, they pushes these people too fast and too far. They push them clean up through the Party and out the Party." In his own case, Hudson said, he resisted the pushing. "If I had allowed the white comrades — and Negro comrades too — to push me like that, I would have been pushed the same way. But I always was like a mule going down a hill. I would always hold on brakes, proclaim I didn't know, act a little bashful. I took advantage of my not being able to read and write. And by that I learnt quite a bit."

Hudson's second explanation for high black attrition in the CP points to the "white chauvinism" (racial prejudice) of white Communists:

> That's another thing that cause a lot of Negroes, to my thinking, to leave the Party. Because when they come in the Party, they think they coming where everything hunky-dory, but you have to fight in there. You got the filth of capitalism, racism, and what-not, expressing itself one way or the other, in the Party, like it is out . . . just because people in the Party, don't you think that they been regenerated and born again. You got to battle them things and get that junk out of them, see. The only thing is, in the Party, you got a chance to fight.

Hudson found fault with blacks who left the Party over racist incidents, without fighting back. The Party opposed racism, Hudson said, but individual comrades were not innocent of "white chauvinism."

Anti-communist writing on the CP stresses the Party's failure in regard to blacks and places great emphasis on high turnover as proof of that failure. The argument says that Communists wanted to embarrass the United States by courting the most oppressed people in the country; but Negroes, downtrodden as they were, loved America too much to become Communists; hence the CP failed in the United States. Now that the Cold War is decades in the past, it is possible to conclude that the Communist Party never attracted masses of Americans, even in the depths of the Depression, but also to see that among the small minority of the population that is radically inclined, blacks joined the CP in numbers proportionate to their share of the population.

The racial climate of the United States in the 1930s and 1940s, rather than a strategic failure on the part of the CP, provides much of the explanation for why blacks left the Party. American life was so thoroughly segregated that, until recently, few whites and blacks were likely to have personal contact with members of the other race, most certainly not as equals or co-workers. But in the CP, whites and blacks attempted to collaborate on a basis of equality. It should come as no surprise that they experienced difficulties working together comfortably or that black Communists were annoyed by manifestations of insensitivity and "white chauvinism."

No matter how patient the blacks or well-meaning the whites, cooperating interracially in a segregated world that assumed black inferiority imposed strain on both sides. For blacks, working with whites usually meant enduring slights or insults, something to be kept to a minimum in life, not to be sought out. In the CP, blacks voluntarily associated with whites who tried — not always with complete success — to improve on American race relations.[12] In attempting to organize interracially, the Party anticipated desegregation by decades. Herbert Aptheker, Eugene Genovese, and Jessica Mitford have all observed that white Communists were conspicuous in the 1940s and 50s because, unlike other whites, they associated with black people.[13]

Black people felt out of place in the Party for other than racial reasons. During the 1930s, 40s, and 50s, the CP was strongest in the big cities of the North and West. It drew few members from the South and many from New York and, as time went on, more from the middle class and more intellectuals. Working-class Party members included a large proportion of northerners in heavy industry who had foreign parents. During these years, blacks were almost entirely working-class, but comparatively few worked in industry. Blacks were native Americans of southern, rural background and upbringing. They shared an uneasiness with organized radicalism characteristic of most native Americans and southerners.

In Hudson's narrative, one of the most potent forces in keeping blacks away from the Communist Party was fear. They were usually poor and vulnerable to employers' reprisals against radicals. Time and again Hudson quotes his co-workers warning their peers, "Don't mess with that stuff, you lose you job."

The warnings were right, of course. Only visionaries were so foolish to take the risk, because Communists did lose their jobs. Political and economic repression — usually expressed in racial terms — was so extensive and so severe in Alabama that most blacks and black institutions tended to guard their own survival. They carefully shunned even the appearance of militancy. Considering the formidable pressures against being both black and Communist in the South, it's a wonder that any blacks at all joined the Communist Party in Alabama.

Hudson heard it said often that the CP only wanted to use Negroes to further Soviet ends, a charge he dismissed as class-biased fabrication:

> I heard that, I heard it up all the way through from the early years, when I first got acquainted with the Party. That was in the papers, especially these better class of Negroes was using that slang.
>
> Now you can see from what I say, from what kind of people *we* were, what kind of people was joining the Party and was active in these unemployed block committees and in the ILD. It wont none of these little people that got they hand in the pie, thinking they going get a dollar from their good white friends. It was the people out there who knowed they didn't have nothing but they chains of slavery to lose.
>
> So any guy that say the Party was using Negro people is just lying, that's all. Because the Party is a working class, political party, and it takes in all workers, and the Negroes happen to be part of that working class. How they going use them? I mean, when these people raise the question about they "using" us, how they going use us when we're part of this working class? We play our part as the workers.

Despite Hudson's interpretation, the CP unquestionably used Negroes, as have the Democrats and Republicans over the years. What is important here is that blacks like Hudson were able to use the Communist Party in their turn. The Party supplied Hudson with a satisfying explanation for the oppression of blacks in America. It broadened his perspective by putting him in touch with Communists across the nation and the world, people who often had far more formal education and social standing than Hudson and his friends. It is clear that his membership in the Party gave him educational advantages he would never have had in other circumstances.[14] Most important, the CP gave Hudson self-confidence:

> What the Party was doing was taking this lower class like myself and making people out of them, took the time and they didn't laugh at you if you made a mistake. In other words, it made this lower class feel at home when they sit down in a meeting. If he got up and tried to talk and he couldn't express hisself, nobody liable to laugh at him. They tried to help them and tell them, "you'll learn." There was always something to bring you forward, to give you courage.
>
> Every time Reverend [Jesse] Jackson comes on television, say "I am somebody," I thinks about it. The party made me know that I was somebody.

Hudson was a leader in the Birmingham CP from the beginning. The eight others who joined with him elected him unit organizer, the equivalent of chairman of the group. When District 17 was reorganized and a political bureau set up in the spring of 1932, Hudson was appointed to the "pol buro" as one of twelve policymakers for Alabama. In the early 1930s, Hudson was responsible for the unemployed councils among all the Negroes in Birmingham, with several subordinates reporting to him. The Party practice of rehearsing procedures beforehand made Hudson more confident in public—for instance, in meetings of the Workers Alliance. The Party even helped him conquer his feelings of inferiority among the educated.

### Why Sticking with the Party Made Sense to Hudson

When the CP sent its people into liberal organizations in the united-front period, Hudson could not speak comfortably before middle-class blacks. He recalled his fear and the impact his presence made:

> You know how you feel—shame I reckon. That's the way I felt, but I just fought against it, went on in there. I just break myself in there. I just would go. Other Negroes scared to go there, go there and pull off they hat there, act like they lost.
>
> And you know one thing, tell you the truth, me and Mayfield,

just to be working type of people, me and Mayfield was the ones that woked them so-called better class of Negroes up that the lower-class Negroes had some sense.

They was shocked, they was surprised to hear what we had to say. They wonder, "where did that fellow Hudson come from? I didn't know we had people like that!"

That was the kind of miration they made. We'd get up and talk, and they'd just sit there with they mouth open. They didn't know what to say, cause they hadn't been used to something like that.

Hudson was right in his conviction that given the time, place, and his class and race, only the Communist Party would have provided him the patient encouragement he needed to master public speaking. In addition, painstaking tutoring from Jim Gray (a pseudonym), an Appalachian white minister who remained his friend, led Hudson to read and write with ease when he was thirty-six years old. During the 1940s Hudson stood out in the Alabama CIO, thanks to more than a decade of coaching and inspiriting from black and white Communists.

A retired official of the United Steelworkers of America in Birmingham insisted to me in 1978 that, if Hudson had not been irrevocably attached to the CP, he could have made a career in the union. I asked Hudson about that, and he thought back to the black union officials he knew in Birmingham, then contrasted his own life. Although he was poor, Hudson had published a book and met people from all over the world. His name and his life are known in countries he had never seen. He said it could not have happened outside the Communist Party:

> Would the steel union white officials taken such pains to show me that I still could be somebody, at the age of thirty-six years old [and] could not read and write [?] I say they would not. I could have become their servant or yes-man. I would have been a great union Negro leader in their eyesight in and around Birmingham Alabama, just like Eb Cox who had a leaning, and many other Negro leaders in the unions.
>
> Most of them has gone and the only record that is left of them is their names and a hump in the ground.[15]

The union men may have it good for a while, "the big time, nice home, nice car, and every woman I see I want, be out with her — that's the way they carry on, I know the life of them" — but Hudson was satisfied that he worked for a greater good, "to see things better for everybody," and had some permanence in the printed record.

Hudson's joining the Communist Party in the early 1930s made perfect sense in terms of the CPUSA's chronology, and it also fit into Hudson's own personal and cultural history. Although he had attended church since childhood and joined a Missionary Baptist church at eleven, he never underwent the religious experience and conversion that should precede baptism. He simply followed a girlfriend to the mourners' bench, to baptism, and to church membership. He watched people getting happy in church but never felt like shouting. He says, "I wondered how did people get that feeling, what did it feel like. I never did discover it." Nor did he understand God and preachers: "I'd wonder why did God always talk with the preachers, didn't talk to other people."

Impervious to any religious calling, Hudson nevertheless for several years wanted to be a preacher. He went to church and prayed. Better yet, he said, "I had a voice. Still got a preacher's voice. A lot of people still think I'm a minister if I don't tell them different." But Hudson's interpretation of the Bible placed another obstacle in his way to the ministry:

> I had a discussion [with] old man Spellman, a old man, every day he used to come down the house — that was when I had my leg broke. That was way back there in 1930. We discussing the Bible, and I was discussing about James. It look like it was First James or Second James. (I'm going get the Bible and read that chapter.) It says something about "servants obey your masters." And that, just reading that, I disagreed with that, cause I seed that, even up to that day, I seed that as the people have to serve the masters (was the rich), and the people was serving and wont getting nowhere.[16]

When Hudson joined the Communist Party, he said, "I began to drift off, and I lost sight of that preaching, I lost sight of the Bible."

Hudson said that the Party seemed to be a sort of alternate church at first, with restraints on worldly activity as strict as the Baptists':

> We all thought, "Well, now, this is the real religion," cause they said that Party members shouldn't mess around with another Party mem-

ber's wife or his daughter, and all like that, and live a clean life, get out and meet the public, people look upon you as a leader. So that was what we came up in the party in, and not drinking no whiskey, not being half-drunk. (And tell you the truth, I didn't know that Party members drink until 1950, the month of December 1950, when I first come to understand that top Party people drink whiskey . . . My first time seeing Party people drink was at a Christmas Party.)

The parallel between the Party and the Baptist church ran even deeper than Hudson admitted. He grew up in the Southern Baptist tradition that allows young men a period of wild youth between churchgoing childhood and churchgoing maturity. It is not unusual for adults to get baptized and join a church after having married and passed through a crisis. Hudson remembered that an adult named Merton Huff joined the church at the time of his own youthful and insincere conversion. Joining the church as an adult is the public profession of one's settling down and pledging one's life to God and to a congregation. It marks a willingness to make a commitment to a community of believers.

Even though Hudson was never able to flesh out his religious commitment or experience conversion, his life divided into periods that were recognized by Southern Baptists. He had his wild period, drinking and gambling in the years between 1918 and 1923 — and committed occasional transgressions until September 1931. When he joined the Communist Party, he pledged himself to what was the equivalent of a congregation (his comrades in Birmingham) and a religion (communism). This conversion bound him through faith to the Party in the early years, before he began to realize fully the advantages to be gained from membership. When he explained his commitment to the CP, he drew a baptismal analogy:

> When I started in, it's like you got water a foot deep here, and you don't know way out yonder the water's deep. The further you go in the water, the deeper in the water you get, the more you get out there, the more you learn out there.
>
> So finally you get out in the real deep water. So then, it's best while you out there to stay out there.

A docile Party member who never raised questions prematurely, Hudson survived all the crises of the CPUSA. Like other black members, he had not been enough distressed by events in Europe to leave the Party.[17] Hudson easily explained away the Hitler-Stalin pact and argued the need to open a second front after Germany attacked the USSR. In 1944 he voted with everyone else in the CP to transform the Communist Party into the Communist Political Association. In 1945 he turned around and repudiated Earl Browder along with all the rest. He did not have to weather the white-chauvinism campaign that battered the Party in the North in 1949–50 because there were not enough white Communists in Alabama, and because by mid-1950 the CP in Birmingham was underground. Hudson was on the Soviet side of the Hungarian uprising of 1956. But he did have some difficult moments after Nikita Khrushchev disclosed Stalin's mass butchery. Those revelations in 1956 divided the American CP on the related issues of subservience to Moscow and denunciation of Stalin. A faction led by *Daily Worker* editor John Gates repudiated Stalin and questioned the Soviet Party's hegemony in the international Communist community.

Hudson held back his criticism, remembering that the Negro Commission that had mandated the Party's move into the South in 1930 had met under Stalin's chairmanship. Without the Negro Commission, Hudson would never even have heard of the CP. In the way most Americans attribute whatever happens during a President's term in office to the President, Hudson gave Stalin credit for the Comintern position on the Negro question:

> Stalin had done more than anybody else for the rights of the Negro in the South, cause Stalin, way back there at the early stages of the Party, along about in the late 20s, first of the 30s, he called a conference of some of the Negro American comrades, and out from that, they discussed the Negro question in America. You know, how can we approach it. And they came out with the slogan of the right of self-determination . . . Stalin did something that nobody else hadn't done, to make it possible for us to be able to struggle.

On his death bed Edward Strong, a long-time friend of Hudson's, agreed with him about the anti-Stalin resolution:

> "Hosie," [Strong] said, "I'm not going against Stalin." Some of them [in the Party] wanted to come out, make a big public statement condemning Stalin. He said he wasn't going to do it. He took

the same position that I took, that regardless of what they have to say about Stalin, Stalin had made it possible for the Negro in America to liberate himself, where none of the rest of them hadn't done. . . . He wanted to be no part of going against Stalin.[18]

The resolution did not pass, But Stalin remained an awkward subject for Hudson. He disassociated himself from Stalin's activities in the Soviet Union and thought of him solely in terms of the initiatives of the CPUSA in Alabama.

Hudson also considered the infamous "third period" of CP history its best. According to the Comintern theory devised in 1928 at the sixth conference, the third period followed a first period of revolutionary upsurge in the late 1910s and very early 1920s and a second period of capitalism's temporary stabilization in the 1920s. The Comintern had designated the third period as the crisis of capitalism before the Great Depression came, and it thereby earned a brief reputation for good economic forecasting.

The third period was also said to be marked by a danger of "imperialist war," in which troubled capitalist states would gang up against their socialist enemy, the USSR. The third period was to have been followed by socialist revolution, but the Third Reich came instead. The united front of the late 30s (the popular front in Europe) was a reaction to Nazism, and because events in Germany broke the sequence, the united front was not called the fourth period.

Hudson did not use the phrase "united front," however. When he spoke of the 1935–1946 decade, he called it the "New Deal period." The first two years of Roosevelt's presidency, what some historians call the first New Deal, were a "reactionary period," said Hudson. Only what is sometimes called the second New Deal merits Hudson's use of the name. He extended that period through the war, to include the whole time that Communists were active in liberal organizations and when he worked in the union. Similarly, he did not mention the third period by name. He called the early 30s "those rough days."

The third period appears in modern writing as a belligerent phase of ultra-left sectarianism, when Communists labeled all noncommunist liberals "social fascists" and refused to cooperate with them.[19] The Party's southern salient is generally overlooked in such analyses. In Alabama, exclusiveness was not explicit Party policy, but the tone of the

CP in the early 1930s militated against a dedicated Communist's belonging to nonrevolutionary organizations. During this time, Hudson
dropped out of his gospel quartet and left his church.

In Birmingham, where a city ordinance outlawed the CP, Party
meetings were likely to be raided by the police in the early 30s, so
Communists went to great lengths to protect themselves. The Party,
ILD, and unemployed councils were organized into carefully meshed
committees and subcommittees. All prospective members were scrutinized before they attended their first unit meetings. Hudson boasts
that, in perfect secrecy, he could cover the whole city of Birmingham
with leaflets in one evening; the organization was just that tight.

For Hudson, the Party's preoccupation with the Negro question
and self-determination were appropriate for the 1930s. During the
1940s, when he was absorbed in the union, he lost sight of the self-
determination slogan. Although it was not formally rescinded, the
Negro nationality question slipped away from the forefront of the
Party's concerns. Self-determination came up again in 1956, when
Hudson's friend James Jackson presented a thesis on the right of self-
determination for the Black Belt. (Jackson was the National Educational Director of the CPUSA in the 1970s.)

"Jackson's position," says Hudson, "was that you had to fight for the
rights of Negroes, jobs for Negroes, and fight for the unions to bring
the Negroes into jobs on equal basis. That was a economic fight, along
with the question of rights to vote, of political rights for the Negro
people, which they had never got." Hudson agreed with Jackson that
the old slogan for self-determination no longer applied. "Them houses
is growed up, them plantations is briar patches, you know, and the
Negroes is all in the towns." When Jackson's resolution passed, several
black Communists who opposed the change left the Party, including
the well-known leader, Harry Haywood. That was the first instance
Hudson knows of when many blacks quit the Party on theoretical
grounds.[20]

The next great Party crisis occurred in 1968–69, but for Hudson the
issue was not the Soviet Union's intervention in Czechoslovakia. It was
black power and, in particular, a resolution before the 1969 Party convention supporting black people's right to armed self-defense. In the
bitter and confusing debate, many older Communists foundered as
black comrades argued opposite sides of the question. Hudson and

Jackson together opposed the resolution on the grounds that putting the Party on record for armed self-defense would play into the hands of enemies who accused Communists of advocating violence. "You ain't have to worry about the Negroes down South defending theyself, they going defend theyself," said Hudson of the Louisiana Deacons of Defense who were already armed to protect civil rights activists. For Hudson, the Party's duty was to reassume its role of the early 1930s, when the CP and ILD championed the Scottsboro boys and Angelo Herndon. "What you do," said Hudson to the convention, "let's organize to defend them when they do get in prison. . . . That's the self-defense." Hudson's position prevailed, But several blacks he knew placed racial allegiance before their commitment to the CP and left the Party.

At the same time, Hudson was fiercely opposed to the whole concept of black power and nationalist separatism of any kind. He saw black power as the evil corresponding to white chauvinism. Without citing the slogan, "black and white, unite and fight," he insisted that the working classes must unite to combat their mutual enemy, capitalism. Black separatism could only lead up a blind alley, he said, and he had no time for African names and clothing. In the late 1970s, however, his position had softened in practice, if not in rhetoric. He was collaborating with a minister of the Nation of Islam in Atlantic City to combat the resurgence of the Ku Klux Klan in southern New Jersey.

White Communists left the Party at various times, often because of issues of policy that turned on foreign events. Hudson said that blacks felt more strongly about what happened in this country. Like blacks outside the CP, black Communists cared most about domestic questions that related directly to black interests. They were not likely to become deeply involved with European issues.

Hudson saw his longevity as a vindication of the course his life had taken. He looked back at what happened to those who let him down, crossed him up, or betrayed him and said, "All them dead now, and I'm still here to tell it." He said that often. Only two aspects of his life still visibly disturbed him in 1978: the breakup of his marriage in 1946 and the loss of his union local and his job in 1947–48.

Hudson's first marriage lasted nearly thirty years. But in retrospect, Hudson remembered aggravations in the 1930s. Even before he joined the Party, he said in the 1970s, his marriage had tensions. Sophie complained that he spent too much time away from home singing with his quartet. "She was just as bad about the singing as she was about the Party," he said. Hudson's nightly Party meetings were not the actual reason for her making trouble, he was convinced. "That might of been her excuse. It was just a part of her."

When we first began taping our interviews, Hudson spoke even more harshly of his former wife than he does in the narrative now. He blamed her entirely for the breakdown of the marriage, finding nothing in his own conduct that might have weakened the bond. During our conversations, however, I came to sympathize with Sophie Hudson. But as she did not wish to speak about the past or give her side of a painful story, we have here only Hudson's half. Under my questioning, at least, he admitted that his absorption in the CP and his spending night after night in Party activities strained his marriage. Although he said he suspected that his wife was seeing another man in 1936, he also said that he continued to give his attention to the Party.

But all his and my reasoning about the issue thirty years later cannot blunt the surprise he felt when his marriage collapsed in 1946. He was enraged, and the rage lasted for two years. Hudson was beside himself with hurt and threatened at crosswalks and bus stops to kill his wife and the man she later married. He felt then and felt in 1978 the shame and anger of a betrayed husband.

The broken marriage was a casualty of ambitions that were Hudson's well before the CP supplied the broader ideals and the means to realize his aims. He had hoped in the days of enthusiastic quartet singing to make records and become famous. Later on he succeeded, making his mark in the Party and the union. His wife, however, did not share his aspirations. She saw only the daily hardships and his absences from home.

I spoke to Hudson's former wife and only son in Birmingham in 1976. The son was almost sixty, tall, slender, attractive, but worn-looking. He had no strong political convictions, and yet he held no brief against the Communist Party. He criticized his father for caring more for the movement — which merely happened to be communism — than for his family. He was more communicative and less bitter than Hudson's former wife. Sophie Lester spoke with me only briefly, insisting — understandably — that she didn't want to review "all that mess." She blamed Hudson for willful neglect, but she was not particularly angry with the CP. In her eyes, the Party had only furnished Hudson with a pretext for leaving his family to shift for themselves in especially hard times. It is clear that all three of them, Hudson, Sophie, and their son, still felt keenly the anguish they inflicted on one another in the 1930s and 1940s.

Hudson's other painful memory dated from the Cold War era, when the career he had gradually built as a labor leader in Birmingham collapsed, crushing aspirations he had nurtured for decades. Even before he joined the CP, the welfare of blacks had concerned him. In the 1920s and 30s he heard frequently that Negroes lacked leaders of courage who would not sell out. By the 1940s Hudson had the self-confidence to try for prominence:

> I'd study. I'd maneuver and train myself to be the spokesman. And I got to be the spokesman at practically all the meetings. I see what need to be said—they all wallowing around—I get up and speak. After I found out I could be somebody around there in Birmingham, I set out to be a leader among the Negro people.

He succeeded by monopolizing the leadership of his local. He was the president and the chairman of the grievance committee and a delegate to the Birmingham Industrial Union Council and delegate to the state CIO and national Steel convention. Judging from his power and determination in 1979, I would guess that he did not absorb differing opinions very well. Thirty years later he didn't admit that his domination of the local might have cost him some support.

In late 1947 he was expelled from the Birmingham Industrial Union Council for being a Communist. In the council meeting that voted to oust him, Hudson had the support of most of the black delegates, but all the whites and a handful of the blacks voted against him. Hudson lost, and he remembered those few Negroes very well.

Following his expulsion from the council, Jackson Industries fired him from his molding job. His local then called a special meeting to decide whether or not to appeal his dismissal through the grievance procedure, a meeting that more white members attended than had ever before turned out. They came with the express purpose of voting against Hudson, whose leadership they had long resented. As in the council, the great majority of the blacks voted for Hudson. The vote was very close in the local, but Hudson won.

When his support from blacks in the council and the local proved to be less than unanimous, Hudson was shocked and disappointed. He considered retiring from political life entirely:

> I liked to throwed up hands. I went to some of the comrades, I told Lou Burnham, "Lou," I said, "I think I'll just give up this fight, won't try to push it through."
>
> He said, "Hosie, you can't do that. You'd be letting too many people down. People is looking to you and depending on you. You'd let the people down."

He fought the appeal for his job but lost it as well as membership in the union. The Negroes, he said, let him down by "voting along with the white delegates, even when it came to voting me out the union itself." The whites, whom Hudson's leadership had offended for so long and who had taken advantage of the Cold War climate to ground him, he barely mentioned. He never expected anything from them.

Summing up his experiences in the late 1940s and early 50s, Hudson speak evenly and thoughtfully of FBI harassment, Bull Connor and the Birmingham police, and the myriad dangers of living underground. These were the risks a Communist ran in those years, and he took a certain satisfaction from having outsmarted the authorities. The historic Cold War, he knew, was a national thing, engineered by powerful whites outside the South. As an individual, Hudson could not affect it. But in 1978 he still railed against the Negroes in the Birmingham Industrial Union Council and in his local who caused him to lose his seat and his job. Unlike the Cold War, a handful of Negroes presented a problem of human proportions. Their treachery, as Hudson saw it, very nearly destroyed his life.

Recounting his disappointment, Hudson wondered why he still fought for the rights of black people at all. "I said many times, I shouldn't do *nothing*. Sometime I look back, I gets very bitter. I shouldn't do *nothing*." For Hudson, the heartfelt meaning of the Cold War was his betrayal by black people.

## Underground and After

Thanks to the encouragement of his comrades, Hudson did not give up organizing in the late 1940s. He worked in the Progressive Party campaign in 1948 and formed a United Political Action Committee in

1950. In mid-1950 he had suddenly to go underground in Birmingham and then move to Atlanta. There he served as a liaison among scattered Communists in the South until the Party brought him to New York early in 1954. By that time he imagined every white man in a suit, white shirt, and two-toned shoes to be an FBI agent. He had trouble sleeping and was unfit to work for two years. In 1956 he took a job as a janitor in a New York restaurant. Working at night, he attended Party meetings by day when he could. But the combination of long, abstruse discussions and fatigue proved deadening. He retained little of the substance of those important debates, beyond the questions of censuring Stalin and rephrasing the position on self-determination for the Black Belt.

Hudson married the widow of a New Jersey timber merchant in 1962. Virginia Larue Marson was a small, dark-skinned woman, spunky and devoted to Hudson, as he was to her. To fulfill her lifelong wish to live near the boardwalk, they moved to Atlantic City, where she died before the publication of *Black Worker in the Deep South*, dedicated to her memory.

Hudson had begun writing his autobiography in the early 1950s, while still underground. Sitting well back on the porch of friends in New Orleans, he first put pencil to paper. But the manuscript that formed the basis of the book dates mostly from the 1960s. The publishing process began when Hudson attended Ben Davis's funeral in New York in 1964 and ran into a black Party member he had not seen since Birmingham days. Eugene Gordon was a writer and told Hudson he wanted to do a book on the South and needed his help. Hudson replied, "I already wrote the book. I need somebody to edit it for me." They agreed that Gordon would edit Hudson's handwritten manuscript.

Hudson gave the manuscript to him, but Gordon did nothing. Hudson's friends would ask about the book's progress; Hudson would see Gordon and ask him; Gordon would stall. There was a falling out and Hudson took his manuscript back. Two high-ranking black Communists, Henry Winston and William L. Patterson, stepped in and encouraged the project by sending Gordon $100 a month to edit Hudson's book. In fifteen months, Gordon finished his work. By then, says Hudson, it was 1968 and the book still was not ready to go to press.

[Gordon] turned it over to a Jewish woman writer, and she got it. You couldn't make out all the words, the way he had left it. It wasn't typed, it was handwritten. He done changed it, and I had to change some of it back. So this Jewish woman, the Party had her on it for about three months. She was an elderly woman and she could understand my writing better than Gordon could.

After this writer revised Gordon's version of Hudson's manuscript, she turned it over to James Allen, editor of International Publishers, the CP-related press. International held the manuscript for several months and then rejected it. Finally Henry Winston pressured the house to publish the book. A young black teacher from St. Louis made the last revisions in February 1972 while Hudson nodded beside him. In July 1972, *Black Worker in the Deep South* appeared.

The book reads like nothing Hudson said or wrote. Here is a section of the book as Hudson wrote it in 1965 and then as it appears in print. Hudson's manuscript goes like this:

> the land lords Would furnish My Mother and grandMother pore land Which Was Meny times pore soild. Rockey. Washes cross the fields of little ditches that had to be filled with green pine Bush to catch some of the soil and stop some of the flore of Warter from Heavy Rain falls. the land lord Would take What cotton and cotton seeds that We did make that year for depts.
>
> these Depts Would be for the futlizes that we use in tryin to Make that crop.

In *Black Worker in the Deep South*:

> The way it was with sharecropping was this: First the landlord would furnish us families with the most run-down, poorest land with rocky soil and ditches cut crisscross every which way by rain water rushing from the high ground. Before we could begin to work the land, we had to lay branches of pine sapplings in the ditches. In time, this acted like a brake on the flooding waters, and the heavy rainfalls would then partly fill the ditches with soil. But though all this work helped to keep the soil from being washed away, it didn't make it any richer. It still needed fertilizer, and that cost money. (p. 9)

Hudson always carried copies of the paperback version of *Black Worker in the Deep South* with him to sell. When he addressed my

University of Pennsylvania students, they remarked on the irony of a
Communist's selling books. But they also understood that, for Hudson, selling his book was not only a way to make a little money and an
act of modest self-promotion, but also a vehicle for spreading his truth.
"I done made my day, you know," he said in 1977.

> When you get up to seventy-nine, you near about done made your
> time. Why I want this thing to be told, because I know how hard
> that the other people, my co-workers and members in the Party with
> me struggled to try to live to see this day. Most of them has been
> long gone, and I'm still here. So you know I have a right to talk.

Without the Communists in the 1930s and 1940s, he was convinced,
the civil rights movement of the 1950s and 60s couldn't have succeeded.
He overlooked the important achievements of liberal groups like the
Southern Conference for Human Welfare, the Interracial Commission,
the Southern Regional Council, and the NAACP, which also helped to
change the South in his time. For Hudson, it was the CP and only the
CP that took tough positions in the bad old days.

The publication of his book marked a step in his personal growth,
although he was seventy-four years old when it came out. In the past,
he "wasn't exactly independent on my thinking and speaking." But
now, "I'm a little bit more independent than I used to be. If I'm
wrong, I'm wrong. I say it now." During our two years of taping interviews, Hudson also revised his estimate of the role the CP played in his
development.

Earlier in our work, Hudson gave the Communist Party credit for
changing an ordinary, illiterate industrial worker into a national, even
international, figure. He wrote me a letter saying that "The Party Made
To Be Come To Be What I Am What Eaver It is."[21] He spoke of his
need to tell the story of Communists in Birmingham. If he was exceptional because he happened to be a survivor, he was no more than what
the Party could make of any man.

At the end of one of our last interviews, I asked him if there was
something special in him as a person that made his life turn out as it
has — or was he Everyman whom the Communist Party had fashioned
into a leader? He said that the Party certainly helped him become who
he was in 1979, but he felt he had always been a strong individual. "I
don't know, but I always had people to respect me. It look like they just

single me out." Then he told two anecdotes that displayed his natural leadership ability, long before he became a Communist. In 1917 he led a gang of black workers older than he away from a job cutting lumber when the quitting bell did not ring. In the second, he led molders from the Stockham foundry to the Alabama Stove Foundry where they hoped to find better-paying work.

Hudson read his horoscope recently and it confirmed his estimation of himself. "According to my horoscope, I have a very strong mind and whenever I set myself to do something, it's hard to turn me around." Hudson did not believe in horoscopes, but he thought it described him perfectly. The lesson was not that horoscopes are right, but that here the greatness was in the individual man, not in the organization. The organization only provided the necessary tools.

In 1979 Hudson was still organizing people. In Atlantic City, he worked with low-income people — of whom he was one — to protect their housing in the era of casino gambling and soaring property values. From 1973 through the mid-1980s he attended the conventions of the Coalition of Black Trade Unionists. But his consuming interest was the building of a nonpartisan voters' movement that would make government more responsive to ordinary citizens, especially in the area of jobs. He spoke of this movement in his own introduction.

Hudson's health failed in the mid-1980s, but while he was able, he worked in the public arena to improve conditions for all the people, "Negro and poor white, regardless to whoever, but particular for the Negro." He was not optimistic about Negroes, however. While everybody else could stick together, he said, "our people's all wandering." He wondered, "why is our people so far behind *everybody*?" and feared blacks might not be ready for progress. They're always "digging at each other" instead of concentrating on what needs to be done.

Maoists were Hudson's *bête noire*. Instead of organizing the working class, they passed the time "tearing apart" and criticizing the CPUSA and the Soviet Union.

They ought to try and be uniting people and work together. Now they may not agree with Gus Hall and them, but everybody is facing this high cost of living. Don't everybody benefit if they get together, fight against the high cost of living?

Everybody benefit.

But still they out here fighting . . . and they ain't doing nothing for people. That's why I call them counter-revolutionists. What
they're doing, actually, they giving the enemy of the working class a
greater chance to take a greater hold.

Agents of division on the left or squabbling and divided blacks, the
foes were at least familiar: the forces of disunity. Luckily, for every one
of them there exist ten good people who need only to be educated.
Hudson preached to anyone who would listen to him (Maoists don't
listen), confident that if he talked to enough people, he would organize
his movement. His model was the broad-based Scottsboro defense
coalition of the Depression years. He could organize this movement
among the people, he said, because "I know they respects what I have
to say."

## The Narrative of Hosea Hudson *and Afterward*

Trade publishers turned down *The Narrative of Hosea Hudson*. After
meeting Hudson, my own editor found fault with Hudson's persona
for not "tugging at your heart strings." This flinty character of Hudson's was one of the things I liked best about him: He was by no means
a loveable Negro. He demanded respect, because he knew better than
you about politics. Harvard University Press first published *The Narrative of Hosea Hudson* in the spring of 1979 and feted us with a party at
the Harvard Club in New York City. Hudson attended with an entou-
rage of supporters from Atlantic City, where he had been living since
1965 and had become a familiar figure in local politics. He also brought
Clarence Norris, the last surviving "Scottsboro Boy," who aggravated
Hudson by surreptitiously selling copies of his own book in the corner
of our party, at the same time that we, abiding by Harvard Club rules
against commercial exchange, were prevented from selling the object of
the celebration. To us, family, friends, supporters, this was a minor
irritant, for we were cheering what Hudson said would be a "great
book," if they "printed it like we wrote it," which they did. After that,
Hudson carried copies of his book to sell to those who wanted to know
more about him, as did everyone who met this intense, organic intellectual, in Antonio Gramsci's phrase for a person who has educated himself out of the thrall of conventional thinking.

Revolutions political and personal have occurred in the world since our book first appeared. Until the mid-1980s, Hudson's old age satisfied him. An inveterate politico, he remained engaged in politics, reading the papers, always the cpusa's *Daily Worker/Daily World* in addition to the non-left press. He loathed the politics of the 1980s and called Ronald Reagan my president. I had not voted for Reagan, but for Hudson he was my president because I had not voted for the Communist candidate, whom Hudson saw as the only real alternative to the Republicans and Democrats, whom he lumped together as the same crowd that had gotten us into this fix in the first place. Politics for Hudson was not merely a matter of parties, and his support of working people's organizations was unwavering. He attended every political meeting in Atlantic City and the annual meetings of the Coalition of Black Trade Unionists, where he was respected as a forerunner in the cause.

When the weather warmed up enough for him to resume interstate bus travel, Hudson would make the rounds of his old friends and colleagues on the Left and visit college campuses where students were reading his books. He spoke to my students at the University of Pennsylvania and at the University of North Carolina, and I recall going to see him when he had been invited to speak to electricians in Winston-Salem, North Carolina. After his speech, we visited the well-marked grave of Moranda Smith, a leading member of the Food and Tobacco Workers Union in the 1940s who had died in her prime. In 1985 we met when he was at Columbia University. By then his eyesight was dimming, but his touch was acute enough to pick up my having gained a few pounds, which he commented upon.

Hudson and I stayed in touch by letter and by telephone until he died at age ninety in Gainesville, Florida, in October 1988. I had spoken to him last in the early summer of 1988, as I was leaving North Carolina definitively. After I had written Hudson of my plans — a year at the Center for Advanced Study in the Behavioral Sciences and a new position at Princeton University — he called to corroborate what had been read to him in my letter and to wish me luck. A few days later he called again, disoriented. He had forgotten much of what we had said, and that distressed him greatly. His phenomenal memory had been a great source of pride to him, and now it was failing. He faltered in a way I had never seen and, for the first time, seemed old.

As far as I knew, Hudson's extraordinary strength of recall was the last of his forces to abandon him. Two or three years earlier, his eyesight and emphysema had worsened, to the point that the combination of near-blindness and acute shortness of breath made travel hazardous, as he discovered after being mugged in Washington, D.C. I can't imagine how anyone would dare mug Hosea Hudson, but someone with no sense of respect did so. The mugging left Hudson feeling vulnerable, not a familiar sensation to him since he had outgrown his black working-class timidity in the 1930s and 40s. Hudson never had much money and so never carried very much. But the money he carried was needed, and the mugging was a financial disaster.

The mugger also got away with one of Hudson's most prized possessions, a key to the city of Birmingham on a red, white, and blue ribbon, which had been awarded to him in 1980, when Mayor Richard Arrington proclaimed 26 February Hosea Hudson Day in the city that Hudson still considered home. Hudson's leadership of the Right to Vote Club in the 1930s had earned him this honor as a civil rights pioneer in the city that was then the most segregated in the entire United States.

The key to the city and Hudson's return to Birmingham to accept it had prompted some rewriting of local history, in which Hudson and his brutal arch-enemy, Police Commissioner Eugene (Bull) Connor, emerged as men whom accidents of history had made antagonists but who, despite their opposition, had been able on some level to transcend race and respect each other's manhood and ability. This sort of sentimentalizing of Birmingham's bloody, racist past Hudson perpetually repudiated. He never stopped to make peace with his adversaries and always wanted more for the working people, particularly black people of that city, the other places where he lived, and the whole United States.

Were Hudson commenting on these remarks, he would make me add the working people of the world, because despite his concentration on the southern United States and what he called the Negro people, his orientation was ultimately international. He would be dismayed by the revolutions in the former Soviet Union and Eastern Europe and would doubtless see them as counter-revolutions that have betrayed the interests of the workers. Looking at the bloodshed in the former Yugoslavia, he would be appalled — for the slaughter and the rape, for the excesses of a creed that he never had very much time for: nationalism. Even in the high days of black nationalism in the United States, Hudson had resisted the claims of race to stay on what he saw as the side of all workers.

For all intents and purposes, that side no longer exists, at least not in lively form, for the Communist Party of the United States, the organization in which Hosea Hudson found his niche for life in 1931, fell victim to the upheaval in Eastern Europe and the former Soviet Union and to internal racial tensions that had long been building.

The Communist Party of the United States still exists and still publishes a newspaper, no longer a daily, the *People's Weekly World*. But when the most vital members walked out of the twenty-fifth convention in Cleveland in December 1991, they left little that was vigorous. The issues of reform, democracy, and black civil rights had been brewing since the 1960s and fusing since the late 1980s, in the wake of the CPUSA leadership's trivialization of the Jesse Jackson presidential campaign of 1988 and Mikhail Gorbachev's stirring *perestroika* campaign. In the United States, as in the Soviet Union, the old-time Party hierarchy seemed stuck in outmoded visions and unable to adapt to change.

African-American Communists had been growing steadily more self-confident, and in December 1991 they argued that the functional equivalent of revolution had been taking place in the United States, even under a bourgeois, capitalist regime. But, rigidly fixated on the promise of a Russian-style (and implicitly white-led) revolution, the longtime leadership of CPUSA downplayed reforms that could occur democratically and declined to press for the consolidation of the American civil rights revolution.

When the leadership failed to accept the importance of black initiative on civil rights and the necessity of revisioning the American workforce as racially and ethnically diverse, a score of black and white CPUSA leaders formed a Committee of Correspondence (the phrase was coined by the historian Herbert Aptheker) that is still less than a political party but includes many whom Hosea Hudson knew and admired, including James E. Jackson, Angela Davis, Charlene Mitchell, the late John Pittman, James Steele, and Maurice Jackson. Considering that they were calling for some of the reforms that he had championed before his death, notably organizations for democratic reform at the grass roots level, especially among people of color, it is very likely that he would have joined them in the Committee of Correspondence, even though he had weathered so many other Party crises over the years. But this is to write Hudson's biography beyond the grave, to imagine what Hudson would have done had he lived to an even more advanced age.

My own situation has changed, though not as drastically as Hudson's. When *The Narrative of Hosea Hudson* first appeared, I called it a collaboration between an old radical and a young historian: I no longer fit my description. With a quarter century of experience under my belt and a title on my chair, I now belong to the ranks of senior historians. Still writing and teaching, trying to use my power in the historical profession responsibly, I have worked hard and have had the good fortune of being rewarded for my work, which has taken me out of my former regional and chronological fields.

I have had the good luck to enjoy writing each of my books and of liking them after they left my hands. Yet after more than twenty years, I still feel that *The Narrative of Hosea Hudson* is my favorite. I wrote it as a labor of love; at the time the work began, I was an assistant professor, whose most trusted advisors said the project would retard my career. Hudson was too far left, too southern, too working class, and too alive to make for productive (in the sense of professional advancement) history.

Perhaps a nineteenth-century figure, long dead, less left, better schooled, and, if left-leaning, martyred, would have gained me more professional standing. Be that as it may — or, as Hudson would have said, howbeitsoever — I have no complaints about my career. And I am still delighted to have had the opportunity of working closely with this thoughtful, pungent radical who did not "tug at one's heartstrings." Thank heaven that Hudson, though finally an engaging man, was too strong, too opinionated, too convinced of his own rightness to be lovable in the way that so many Americans want to love black people. He demanded to be heard and respected, and I am honored to have had the opportunity of learning about his life and knowing him personally for twelve years.

# 6

## *Sexuality & Power in*
## The Mind of the South

. . .

The cultural landscape of the American South, like other cultural land-scapes, is profoundly sculpted by polyvalent relations of power, includ-ing politics, which, in turn, affect personal relations that are shaped according to conventions of race, class, and gender. Because the recent past of this region of the United States includes a cultural, political, and relational watershed—the civil rights movement—Cash's South be-longs, in many regards, to an era far removed from our own. To the degree that the figurative landscape that he surveyed between 1929 and 1940 differs significantly from the present-day South, the maps that he drew of his society and those that we take for granted do not coincide. The last part of *The Mind of the South* shows that Cash could glimpse a changing landscape and the advent of a different time. But he did not (could not? would not?) discern the approach of a civil rights move-ment and could not imagine the social revolution that would result. This revolution ultimately recast literate southern culture, influenced readings of his book, and permitted the enunciation of this essay.

Just as Cash did not foresee the changes that have occurred since the original publication of *The Mind of the South*, he could not have imag-ined my existence as a critic. Not only am I able to speak as an equal, I can deploy part of his theoretical conceptualization—that based on Freudian psychoanalysis—to read his work against the grain, but not without a certain sense of irony.

As a mind and a body, I personify the changes that have undermined the pertinence of so much of what Cash had to say; hence my comment represents an odd clash of generations that emphasizes change more dramatic than merely generational. I do not ignore the awkwardness of our historical coexistence, which is due to the continued interest in his book as history and historiography. As a current historian of his region, I can analyze Cash's South and Cash's southerners; yet it is extremely doubtful that he, who in this sense wrote and died too soon, ever supposed that he would be confronted by a critic who is educated, black, female, and feminist.

I also belong to a different world of scholarship from Cash's own. I view the Freudian concepts that he employed through lenses of feminist theories, which in the 1970s and 1980s reoriented psychoanalysis away from the popular, antifeminist manifestations of Cash's time. Cash would be astonished to behold what has become of both southern studies and psychoanalytic theory. Looking around in the 1930s, Cash described a South without women who could be other than "his women" or "complaisant" sexually and without black men who might have a capacity to reason independently and as full-fledged southerners. He is being reread in a world bristling with people saying and doing unfamiliar things.

As was the case with so many of his peers, it seems not to have occurred to Cash that black people (beyond, perhaps, the problematic Walter White) could or would read — never mind write — books. Cash spoke to an audience of people who more or less resembled himself, though some were not southerners. Addressing fellow white North Carolinians, educated white southerners, and northern book buyers, Cash never conceived of any but the most informal black or female critics. Nor, despite his acquaintance with Lillian Smith and Paula Snelling and the acquisition of his book by a woman publisher, Blanche Knopf, did Cash imagine that female persons would ever gain enough intellectual prestige or initiative to formulate and publish gendered analyses of his work. Like so much that emanated from the American intellectual tradition before the civil rights revolution, black studies, and feminism, *The Mind of the South* was not intended for eyes like mine.

My apparent unfitness as a critic of Cash is not simply a matter of Cash's personal, regional shortsightedness; changes in the marketing and reviewing of books are also implicated. In the 1930s Cash's New York publishers, Blanche and Alfred A. Knopf, acquired his books after having read his 1929 essay "The Mind of the South," which contains phrases that would have offended people like me at the time, such as my parents and grandparents. My family might have grumbled to themselves, but they lacked the ability to publish their critique in out-lets that reached a national readership and that the Knopfs would have heeded. Hence Cash's language did not give the Knopfs pause when it came to assessments of audience, market, and critical reception at the time.[1] That *The Mind of the South* is still in print would probably have surprised Cash and the Knopfs, for Alfred A. Knopf evidently had to be persuaded to reprint the book in the early 1960s.[2] But even then, it is unlikely that he and the ghosts of Blanche Knopf and Wilbur Cash would have imagined that a black feminist would influence the way in which the book is perceived. My views on Cash contrast sharply with previous appraisals, even those of recent vintage.

Cash was thoroughly criticized in the 1970s and 1980s, notably by C. Vann Woodward, Michael O'Brien, and Eugene Genovese, who yet preserve a qualified fondness for the author. Until 1990, all published Cash commentary came from white men who identify themselves, by origin or field of study, with the South.[3] Some white woman or person of color may be discovered who reads *The Mind of the South* with affection; yet I doubt that a feminist or race-conscious reader could go so far as to add, as did one of his most biting critics, C. Vann Wood-ward: "Peace to his troubled spirit."

I respect this book's persuasiveness for masses of readers and have assigned it in my southern history courses. However, I have never been susceptible to what some of my colleagues see as its magnetism. I cannot agree with Richard King that this book "improves with reread-ing," or that it is "exciting" and "audacious" and compelling, or that "at times Cash edged toward a vague, hazy sort of racism, especially when discussing black women."[4] I have always had to dissent from such analyses.

When I first encountered *The Mind of the South* as an undergraduate in the 1960s, I found it thoroughly racist. To my graduate student eyes, rereading it in the 1970s, the book seemed to be deeply sexist. Reread-ing it as a teacher in the 1980s, I noticed Cash's contempt for the poor of both races, particularly as manifested in his inability to see poor women of either race as much more than sexualized subject beings. I was struck by Cash's blindness to the ways in which slavery and racism had distorted relations of power, whether in politics or the household.

I see as narrow-minded Cash's characterization of the slave South — a society in which one-third of the men did not even own themselves, never mind vote, and no women, no matter how wealthy or educated, enjoyed the rights of citizens — as a region in which there existed an "old basic feeling of democracy."[5]

*The Mind of the South* may be more clear-eyed than many on white southerners. But as Cash's contemporary Lillian Smith realized, the analysis is superficial.[6] Cash wrote out of a conservative "common sense" (in the Gramscian meaning of the term) that reflects the conventional racism, sexism, and class prejudice of middle-class white southerners of his generation. Given all our differences, I may be an unseemly critic, but this book, because it is still in print, remains fair game. I begin at the beginning, by asking what Cash was writing about.

### What Is "the Mind" of the South?: Freud and Cash

The central character in *The Mind of the South* is "the South," an anthropomorphic construction synonymous with the "Southern psychology" and its mind.[7] Only in the last section, in which so many of the patterns that typify the preceding chapters of the book break down, does the "body" of the South make an appearance.[8] Without his having pulled them together in so many words, Cash leaves the distinct impression that "the South," "the mind of the South," and "the Southerner" are all the same thing. His verbal constructions reinforce this conclusion.

Cash's anthropomorphism is striking in a book that presents itself as a history of the South in the nineteenth and early twentieth centuries. In the "Preview to Understanding," Cash says that the mind of the South "has actually always marched away . . . from the present toward the past."[9] He contends that "the South" has always been "natively more extravagant" and "more simple and less analytical" than the rest of the country. It has "horse-trading instincts" and a "trigger-quick dander," and it believes only what it wants to believe.[10] Can such language be employed when the subject at hand is a society? Can collectives, as opposed to individuals, be said to have "*a*" mind? Hardly. "The South/the Southerner" has a personal identity, which wavers as the identity of the narrator fluctuates. Sometimes the narrator is upper-class, sometimes he is middling, as are Cash's presumed readers; sometimes he is "the common white." Sometimes he is first-person plural — Cash plus reader. But fundamentally this is a book written in the singular about a single character of indeterminate but relatively intimate identity. The confusion of the subject's and the narrator's identity makes the speaker Cash and/or southerners and/or us and lends the book much of its attraction for readers who recognize themselves in its pages in a way they can accept.

Rather than the history of a society, Cash has written a biography of a character named "the South," in which the use of singular constructions conveys unity and continuity, as Woodward so clearly understood.[11] A singular, anthropomorphic subject also invites language that is psychological rather than social, economic, or political. As his biographers and critics have long noted, Cash's vocabulary owes much to the popular work of Sigmund Freud.

Cash's framework features key words and phrases that are not merely psychological, but Freudian; for example, "subconscious," "ego," "defense mechanisms," "pleasure principle," "sublimated," "hysterical," and "taboos."[12] Such terminology declares *The Mind of the South* not only biography, but Freudian psychobiography. In this sense, the book resembles a sort of psychoanalysis of "the South"/"the Southerner."

I cannot name which, exactly, of Freud's works Cash knew, for his book lacks notes and his biographers, Joseph Morrison and Bruce Clayton, provide no citations.[13] If Cash had actually read Freud, as one of his letters would indicate — rather than absorbing general Freudian notions from American popular culture — I would expect him to have been familiar with Freud's most famous essay, *Civilization and Its Discontents*, which mentions all of the concepts that appear in *The Mind of the South. Civilization and Its Discontents* was first published in 1929; the first English translation appeared in 1930.

The parallels between *The Mind of the South* and psychoanalysis run deeper than borrowed terminology. Both Cash and Freud use the singular collective. Where Cash favors "the Southerner" and "the Negro," Freud speaks of "the male" and "the child." Both Freud and Cash tend to generalize from the individual case to the social, so that Cash can conflate "the Southerner" and "the South" while Freud speaks of the "cultural super-ego."[14]

Cash and Freud had something else in common that appears in Freud's writings in German and the ways in which others have interpreted Cash's concerns. Bruno Bettelheim reminds Freud's readers in translation that Freud's fundamental concern was more with the human soul than the mind—that for Freud, "psyche" meant the soul. Similarly, Richard King, one of Cash's more sympathetic critics, notes that *The Mind of the South* represents a counterpart to W. E. B. Du Bois's *Souls of Black Folk*.[15] In light of these insights and Joel Williamson's famous University of North Carolina at Chapel Hill course on southern race relations and white soul, Cash seems as much to be peering into the soul of the (white) South as its mind, which returns him to Freud.

### "On the Universal Tendency in the Sphere of Love"

Considering Cash's personal experience and individual needs and taking at face value his claim to have read Freud, I would suspect that, in addition to the more famous works (*The Interpretation of Dreams, Civilization and Its Discontents*), Cash probably also encountered a less-known essay that begins by addressing one of his own most poignant disabilities and also speaks to private worries that were common in the United States South. Again, the preoccupations of Cash and of his "the South" resist partition.

This essay, the second of Freud's "Contributions to the Psychology of Love," entitled "On the Universal Tendency to Debasement in the Sphere of Love," was first published in German in 1912.[16] Both Freud and Cash knew that many educated men in their societies found it difficult to achieve sexual fulfillment with well-brought-up (Freud) or respectable white (Cash) women. Freud, of course, discussed the matter in far greater depth and with more sensitivity than Cash or his biographers even hint at, but the disparity should not obscure the relevance of Freud's essay. Despite the imbalance in rhetorical sophistication between Cash and Freud, this piece of psychoanalytic writing is worth a closer look in connection with *The Mind of the South*.[17]

Freud begins "On the Universal Tendency to Debasement in the Sphere of Love" with the prevalence of the problem of male impotence, which may stem from psychological causes. Men thus afflicted often split the two currents of their feelings so that the same love object cannot inspire in them both affection and sensuality. According to Freud, well-brought-up women who have been taught not to enjoy sex tend to be inexperienced, inhibited, and frigid, and their husbands relate to them more as judges than as joyous physical partners. At the

same time, only love objects that seem to these men to be debased —
prostitutes, women of the lower class — can inspire full sensual feelings
and a high degree of pleasure. In a statement that has become famous,
Freud says; "Where such men love they have no desire and where they
desire they cannot love." Freud sees this problem as a consequence of
Western civilization and the motive behind the widespread practice
of middle- and upper-class men's taking as mistresses working-class
women whom they do not respect. Deep in their hearts, Freud adds,
such men regard the sex act as degrading and polluting.[18]

If Cash's analysis of such themes convinced masses of his readers, his
writing benefited from both its relevance to many of his fellow southerners and from the passion of autobiography. Morrison reveals that
Cash suffered from impotence and that his sexual experience was limited to only two women, or, at least, to two respectable white women: a
young woman identified only as Peggy Ann and Mary Ross Northrop,
whom he married in December, 1940.[19] His friend Lillian Smith described Cash as a man who was very much "involved with his own
taboos," and the Morrison and Clayton biographies show Cash as a
prig who was obsessed by sex.[20] In *The Mind of the South*, Cash deplores
the modern Western "collapse into barnyard morality," the "collapse of
old standards," and the "eternal and blatant concern with the theme of
sex" that followed World War I.[21] A close reading of *The Mind of the
South*, particularly of the pages on prostitutes and bellboys, suggests
that Cash (as well as many respectable white southern men about and
to whom he was writing) fits the pattern that Freud laid out in the
second of his "Contributions to the Psychology of Love."

### White Prostitutes and Black Bellboys

The second chapter of Book Three, entitled "Of Returning Tensions —
and the Years the Cuckoo Claimed" contains two numbered sections
that deal with what other authors have termed the "New Negro" of the
post–World War I era.[22] As in other parts of *The Mind of the South*,
Cash cannot begin a discussion of "the Negro" (*i.e.*, black men) without bringing in white women. In other parts of the book, where "the
Negro" is discussed in relation to political activities, "the Southern
woman" belongs to a more elevated moral order. But here the white
women are prostitutes.

Section 20 begins with Cash's narrative of black soldiers' experiences in France during World War I, which made them prone to what he calls "insolence or provocation on the slightest pretext or sometimes none at all." Cash calls France a "topsyturvy land," in which white prostitutes entertained and sometimes even preferred "the Negro."[23] This section continues with a page-long discussion of blacks who had lived in the North and returned to the South full of citified notions; the discussion then segues into another page on black bellboys working in southern hotels. Considering where his narrative would take him, Cash is relatively dispassionate about black soldiers with French prostitutes. His indignation erupts in the discussion of black bellboys and white prostitutes back home.

During Prohibition in the South, he says, black bellboys came to monopolize the marketing and distribution of bootleg whiskey through the hotels where they worked, which respectable white men patronized for the satisfaction of unacknowledged desires. These hotels had become whorehouses as a consequence of the crackdown on red-light districts; bellboys then added the vocation of pimp to that of bootlegger. The great damage, for Cash, starts with the fact that as pimps, black bellboys take much of the earnings of the white prostitutes they control. Worse, they also enjoy the pimp's right to sexual intercourse with his prostitutes. Worse yet, bellboys wield the power that comes with knowledge, here the secret knowledge associated with Freud's essay on the tendency to debasement in love. Like World War I France, southern hotels became a world turned upside down.

In one exasperated paragraph, Cash depicts the "horde of raffish blacks, full of secret, contemptuous knowledge" that white men who pretended to be respectable members of society have another, disreputable side. He repeats the word *contempt* as he describes the grinning bellboys, who, beneath the thinnest veneer of subservience, are "hugging to themselves with cackling joy their knowledge of the white man's women" (321). The mortification Cash betrays in this idiosyncratic passage reinforces the pertinence of Freud's observations about "degradation in erotic life" and corroborates the suspicion that Cash wrote out of his own experience of hypocritical embarrassment.

Although the resemblance between Cash's actual and rhetorical sexual conundrums and Freud's discovery of the "tendency to debasement in the sphere of love" is noteworthy, I stress it without intimating that

Freud's observations pertain to Cash alone. In her *Killers of the Dream* Lillian Smith links class and race and religion and sex perceptively. Others connected race and sexuality in political writing — angry, conflicted Thomas Dixon springs to mind — so that race, sex, and gender together represent an important theme in white supremacy. This intertwining explains both Cash's reliance in *The Mind of the South* on terms that implicate sexuality (puritanism, hedonism, romanticism) and the book's enduring attraction to readers who consume it as fact.

More Freud does not help explicate *The Mind of the South*, for Cash seems not to have intended to take the psychoanalysis of "the South" very far. First, Cash's use of Freudian concepts is not very rigorous, so that even though he borrowed the pleasure principle and the ego, he leaves aside Thanatos (the death instinct), the id, and the rule of law as an essential characteristic of civilization. He is not interested in the Oedipus complex, even though his use of southern women as the mothers of the race is central to his analysis of southern culture. Second, and just as important, Cash and Freud generalize from individuals to families to societies very differently. With a circumspection that is nowhere in Cash, Freud warns that civilizations are not individuals and that comparisons between them are no more than useful analogies.[24]

Another, less direct approach to Freudian insights illuminates Cash's thinking, for Freud (and his more recent followers) realized, as Cash may or may not have, that sexuality is central in the formation of human identity.[25] In Cash's case, the coincidence of his preoccupations with race and gender led to his configuration of sexuality and power.

## Cash's Maps of Sexuality and Power

By now it is well understood that the notion of *woman* often serves men as a sign of political power. We remember, too, with Michel Foucault, that sexuality is full of power relations.[26] In southern history race functions in a similar manner so that the least powerful people in southern society, African-Americans, have always been sexualized in white-supremacist writing. This convention continues in *The Mind of the South*, in which race and women appear together in discussions that invariably end up with or pass through sex.

Cash conjoins race and sex often in *The Mind of the South*. His maps of sexuality and power overlap, but they do so in reverse. The figures who are more powerful are less sexualized, those who are powerless are very sexualized. A closer look at the book's characters begins with "the Negro woman," the figure who makes this point with maximum clarity.

Cash reduces the least powerful figure in the South, "the Negro woman," to nothing but sex. Writing about her at length, he calls her the "all-complaisant [i.e., inclined to comply] Negro woman," who was "to be had for the taking" and whom plantation boys (white, one assumes) "inevitably learned to use." As is common in gendered discussions in which men stand for reason and culture and women stand for nature, Cash's Negro woman is "natural" and can "give herself up to passion in a way impossible to wives inhibited by Puritanical training."[27]

In comparison with his figure of the southern white woman, who is the source of physical and social reproduction and a symbol of political "mastery," "the Negro woman" is an important possession in only one particular aspect, the sexual. After she makes a quick appearance as mammy, "the Negro woman" is not allowed to play any role other than that of sex partner. Cash plays down her role as surrogate mother to emphasize her role as a sexual partner to white men and boys. Standing for the poorest, least educated, most-disfranchised group in his South, "the Negro woman" in *The Mind of the South* is sex, full stop, no more.

As suits Cash's thoroughly patriarchal vision, even white women receive little attention in *The Mind of the South*. With the exception of Harriet Herring, Lucy Randolph Mason, and a few others whose names appear briefly, Cash's white southern women lack both individuality and agency. They fall under the designation of "his women" or "his womanfolk," and they serve two closely related functions: they are the mothers of the white race and signifiers of men's social standing. Cash says that as "perpetuator of white superiority in legitimate line" the white woman "inevitably became the focal center of the fundamental pattern of proto-Dorian [white supremacist] pride."[28] He sexualizes this figure in terms that the Nazis carried to extremes. In the guise of "his women," white wives and daughters mark the rising status of the male *nouveaux* or the inability of the cotton-mill worker to clothe his dependents in style.[29] Lacking other roles in society, Cash's southern white women are simply wives and mothers, the embodiment of what Cash calls legitimate sex, and they belong to white men. In life, southern white women, though wealthier than their black counterparts, seldom numbered among the entrepreneurs who brought progress to the South or who wielded political power. Cash's figure of the southern white woman stands for people who had gained the vote only in 1920 and who were not considered likely to be officeholders or otherwise to wield political or economic power.

The figure of "the Southern woman" is also defined by the political dynamics of race. As the well-bred wife who is left alone while her husband pursues a "mulatto wench," she discovers that being placed upon a pedestal is her compensation as the victim of adultery.[30] From the other side, "the Southern woman" is a trope in white supremacist political ideology, in which she figures as the forbidden counterpart to "the Negro."

A crucial character in Cash's book is "the Negro" (not the same as the less abstract black bellboys), who, paradoxically, is not part of "the South." Cash emphatically places "the Negro" apart from "the South," going so far as to identify this figure as "a special alien group," whose presence assures enduring white unity.[31] Nonetheless, in the second paragraph of *The Mind of the South*, Cash mentions the presence of Negroes as an apparent but not decisive factor distinguishing the South from the North. He also cites the enormous impact of "the Negro" on "the Southerner" (and vice versa) and admits that "the Negro" has influenced the way the white man thinks, feels, speaks, and moves. Throughout the book Cash underlines the centrality of race and white supremacy in phrases such as "the hypnotic Negro-fixation" and "the ancient fixation on Negro."[32]

Alien though he may be, Cash's Negro functions as a compelling notion in the mind of the South. At the same time, however, Cash is not interested in "the Negro" as an autonomous historical actor; Cash creates a potent force in the experience of white people, then denies it agency in its own. "The Negro," therefore, represents an ambiguous character, an influential cipher, whom Cash thoroughly sexualizes.

"The Negro" stands for a virtually powerless people, for only black women were more oppressed than black men. The poverty and political impotence of black men prevented Cash from imagining them in political roles. Black political action seems so farfetched that when Cash broaches the subject, he veers off into ridicule. Cash could not imagine black men as political actors who would be a positive force in the South, although he did discern that certain black men were becoming wealthy. These tiny exceptions do not diminish the pungency of Cash's treatment of "the Negro," which deals more in sexuality than power.

A long, lurid passage portrays the Negro slums as they are glimpsed, overheard by the narrator, and, presumably, imagined by a white bourgeois. Although it deserves quotation in full as an illustration of Cash's hysteria over the secret lives of the black poor, this section is too long to reproduce here. In it Cash describes neighborhoods that are "dark, mysterious, and ominous." From the churches and dance halls of these "half-hidden" regions emanate "the jungle beat of drums . . . high, floating laughter; sudden screams," which the white man hears when he is at home with his family or when these noises bring him to "nightmarish awakening" in the middle of the night. At daybreak the denizens of these mysterious slums hide their secrets beneath masks of servility as they go about their work in the white man's home. He fancies he knows them, but in the back of his mind he wonders what "whispering, stealthy, fateful thing might they be framing out there in the palpitant darkness?"[33]

All this libidinous fantasy masquerades as a discussion of politics, as an explanation of why southern blacks would never join the Communist party, in which Cash cannot untangle the personal from the political. He is too riveted by the situation's lust and violence — his words — to analyze the South's political economy objectively. Cash probably intended to produce such an analysis, though I reckon his publishers knew better and wanted his book all the more for its preoccupation with lust and violence.

As is the case in other white-supremacist writing, Cash's political anxieties coalesced around the concept of Reconstruction, which he presents in the image of emancipated, enfranchised, self-confident black men, as seen through the eyes of erstwhile slaveowners. Depicting the figure of "Cuffey" in town of a Saturday, Cash shows him having a few drinks, letting his "ego a little out of its chains," and relapsing into self-confident Reconstruction manners. "Cuffey" hogs the sidewalk and swaggers about in razor-flashing, pistol-brandishing, "guffawing gangs."[34] In a discussion of politics that repeats the word *mastery*, Cash puts himself and the reader in the position of those forced to endure the sight of "their late slave strutting about full of grotesque assertions, cheap whisky, and lying dreams, feeling his elbow in their ribs, hearing his guffaw in high places."[35] However ludicrous, the image of independent black men leads Cash directly to white women, this time to the crime of lynching.

Ever since 1941, Cash has been complimented for presenting an enlightened — for a white southerner — discussion of lynching. He admits that rapes might be imaginary or trumped-up and that lynch mobs, which had been unjustly blamed on white trash, were led or manipulated by men of unimpeachable respectability and standing.[36] Although Cash deserves credit for moving past thoughtless recapitulation of the figure of the black-beast-rapist, he does not go far enough; he speaks of "the rape complex," not the rape-lynch syndrome or the phenomenon of lynching, and once again, his Southern woman functions as a sign in the heavily gendered, white-supremacist political ideology. As he explains how lynching is related to politics, Cash invokes concepts such as natural laws and inevitability. Speaking of rape rather than of lynching, Cash concentrates on the sexual and the personal rather than on the public and the quasi-judicial aspects of vigilante violence. In Cash's framework, rape (sexualized assault) is the most salient cause of lynching. Lynching's political and economic functions recede.

The sexuality permeating Cash's discussion of politics even spreads to the figure he presents most fully: "the Southerner" in all his various guises. Because Cash spends so many words on "the Southerner," this figure is less susceptible to a neat summing up; omnipresent in *The Mind of the South*, the various versions of "the Southerner" do all sorts of things. But who, for Cash, is "the Southerner"?

### *"The Southerner" in Many Guises*

Several characters appear repeatedly in this book under the rubric of "the Southerner": "the Virginians," "the old Irishman," "the *nouveaux*," "the yeoman farmer," "the common white," "the mill worker." These men, rather than historical events, lend the book its distinctive character. The very ambiguity and tension in Cash's writing about his male characters enliven his arguments but make his southern white males run together. These figures more or less collapse into two classes. Together, the Virginians, the old Irishman, and the *nouveaux* represent the better class.

The values and way of life of "the Virginians" laid the groundwork for all succeeding southern aristocracies.[37] Without challenging the enormous prestige of "the Virginians," Cash points out that there were simply not enough of them to engender all the succeeding aristocrats who claimed them as ancestors. He introduces another source of respectability in the figure of "the old Irishman," modeled on his grandfather, who stands for the likable new rich of the antebellum era.

The transformation from hardworking yeoman farmer to aristocrat occurs within one generation, yet the family of "the old Irishman" is not to be confused with "the *nouveaux*," whom Cash regards with tremendous scorn. The *nouveaux* appear at the same time as the old Irishman's generation (for instance, in the story of George Washington Groundling, modeled on the New South Duke and Reynolds families). But Cash exempts "the old Irishman" from his repeated accusations of coarseness.[38] The old Irishman achieves his standing through thrift, hard work, and high cotton prices, so that he deserves the respect that comes to him in his maturity. "The *nouveaux*," by contrast, are characterized by grasping ambition and bad taste.

Three other characters meld together to form the more modest and yet greater half of "the Southerner": "the yeoman farmer," "the common white," and "the mill worker." They are the core of the book, and the muddled relations between and among them lend *The Mind of the South* its ring of truth. Renouncing the commonplace formula that in other southern writing obliterates the existence of poor whites, Cash touches upon class conflict among whites and reveals the shallowness of claims of universal aristocracy. Throughout the book, Cash calculates "the common white's" chances for economic mobility, which with the exception of the antebellum era, he sees mostly as very limited. This concern does not translate into very much sympathy, for the slaveless ancestor of these three is not an attractive character. At his worst, he is idle and shiftless and degenerate. At best, he is the unreflective prisoner of his passions.[39] In the post–Civil War period this personage blends into "the common white," about whom Cash has a great deal to say.

Cash's late nineteenth-century "common white" is an unfortunate figure, for his shabby cultural inheritance compounds his difficulties in economic hard times of the Great Depression. Hobbled by his physical background, which Cash depicts in Lamarckian and Social Darwinist terms, "the common white" is the victim of low cotton prices and Populism. His instincts are romantic and hedonistic; he is blind to his "real interests"; he is "perhaps the least fitted" of southerners to get ahead. "Descending from those who in the beginning had had the smallest portion of industry and thrift and acquisitive will" and losing more and more of these characteristics over the generations, "the common white" has only whiteness, the badge of his superiority over "the Negro," as a basis for his self-esteem. With so much riding on that single trait, "the common white" resorts to violence to preserve his sense of racial supremacy.[40]

When the depression of the 1890s threatens to bring "the common white" into close competition (Cash speaks purposefully of "intimate" competition) with "the Negro," wealthy southerners, although "men of a generally coarser kind," step in with a capital P "Progress," in the form of cotton mills. Employment in the mills saves "the common white" from descent into a fate worse than death: social equality with "the Negro." Such work also transforms "the common white" into "the cotton-mill worker," who retains "romantic-hedonistic impulses" and hatred of "the Negro." "The common white" and "the mill worker" are connected to aristocrats by what Cash (pointing vaguely toward ancient Greek history) terms the "proto-Dorian bond" of white supremacy. By the time the cotton-mill worker arrives on the scene, the closely related figure of the yeoman farmer has begun to recede.

Viewed from above, the social characteristics of Cash's yeoman farmer, the common white, and the mill worker are essentially the same.[41] At one point Cash speaks through an expert who knows exactly how farmers waste their money. Then, in his own voice, Cash adds that the characterization also holds for mill workers: they squander their earnings on "whiskey, gambling, indulgence in sexual pleasures, purchase of useless articles of luxury, and excursions to distant towns."[42] For all the time spent on "the common white"/"the mill worker," their actions seem somehow futile. Cash paints them as hedonistic, and one section in particular reveals the ways in which he sexualizes poor whites.

In his depiction of the mill workers' Saturday night, Cash's writing turns steamy. Discharging (and here Cash's language of "egress" echoes Freud's hydraulic theory of emotions) their "old romantic-hedonistic impulses," his cotton-mill workers indulge in drunken sex with girls they pick up in town. Left to their own devices, his mill workers concentrate on three things only: casual sex, violence, and "orgiastic religion."[43] Whenever they try to accomplish anything constructive — to strike, to organize, to get ahead — their ineptness dooms them to failure. Sex and fighting, unadulterated wastes of human energy, are their natural resort.

The squandered Saturday becomes the hallmark of Cash's southern poor, the means by which he ridicules their use of their own time. What he has to say about "the mill worker" on Saturday repeats images of "the Negro" on Saturday. With their minds fixed on their pitiful Saturday dissipation, neither poor whites nor poor blacks in *The Mind of the South* are able to realize their political or economic potential.

The southern poor whom Cash sexualizes were relatively (if white) or virtually (if black) powerless in the southern political economy, for he finds things for the better classes to do beyond sex and violence. As the Virginians, the old Irishman, and the *nouveaux*, they amass wealth, hold office, and build factories. Wealth and power have Cash's respect in the sense that he accords to the figures with some autonomy a regard that he cannot offer members of the working classes. As much as Cash seems to want to sympathize with the poor, he finds it hard to take them seriously. This is not an accident.

The whole labor history of the South, with its utter degradation of workers through racial slavery and its closely related contempt for anyone else engaged in manual labor, devalued people who do work. Cash does not recognize that the early legalization of racial slavery and its attendant white supremacy segmented the southern work force and made the solidarity fundamental to practically impossible. labor politics extremely difficult. Just as slavery acquired a racial character, so black workers carried a racial taint into freedom that marked them as ineligible for solidarity with white workers, no matter how useful such solidarity would have been for both in the long run. A segmented work force was the result of white supremacy among southern workers, and workers so deeply divided could forge no enduring unity based on class. With the status of laborer so closely identified with blackness during and after slavery, white supremacists succeeded again and again in preventing the formation of farmer or labor parties across the color line.[44]

No working-class republicanism appears in *The Mind of the South*. The lack of enduring labor politics in the South and the absence of a strong, countervailing worker-centered sensibility deprived Cash of images of wise and sturdy workers. So one-sided a class culture meant that, by default, Cash wrote out of class prejudice as well as white supremacy; he never scrutinized his deep-running contempt for the southern poor. Rural and urban, farmer and worker, black and white, he saw them as the childish prisoners of their carnal appetites. Only toward the end of the book does he begin even tentatively to envision workers' cooperating across the color line.[45]

Until the very last chapter, Cash segregates his discussion of the mind of the South according to race, which means that although he never concludes that southerners of both races are hedonists, he can say that "the Southerner" is hedonistic and "the Negro" is hedonistic, as though hedonism were a racial characteristic in either case.[46] The one, like the other, is impotent politically because he misused the vote during Reconstruction, when he was the dupe of unscrupulous outsiders, or because he lacked a sense of his economic self-interest and thoughtlessly voted for demagogues. At one point Cash realizes that the southern polity is hierarchical, but he fails to understand what racial slavery and disfranchisement did to southern politics and to his own mapping of power and sexuality.

## The Great Depression

The Great Depression alters Cash's historical reckoning. He notes that planters had called the tune in southern states before the Civil War and is willing to concede that in the late nineteenth and early twentieth centuries the white poor were never able to realize the power of their numbers; but the picture is no longer clear after southerners embrace the New Deal. Once the old political verities fail, Cash begins to write differently. Earlier in the book he draws a strict color line, even when he reaches identical conclusions about the weaknesses of the poor, black and white. Toward the end of the book, however, Cash begins to look on both sides of the racial divide.

His poor are still "laughing, sleeping, drinking cheap wine or corn whisky, or dreaming restlessly of violence" regardless of color. But toward the end of the book, Cash sees repeatedly that social and economic ills are not bounded by race.[47] By extension — here Cash is not explicit — effective remedies cannot be race-specific. He speaks instead of the tragedy of his South, whose political leaders do not heed the counsel of intelligent and analytical thinkers (like W. J. Cash?). Because the politicians cannot transcend race or surmount white supremacy, they cannot even serve all southern white people effectively.

It is not clear whether Cash realizes that the southern tragedy he sees around him during the Great Depression represents the political impotence of the poor or that this impotence is directly related to the enslavement, disfranchisement, and subjugation of a large portion of the southern laboring population. I suspect not. And I suspect, too, that Cash's confusion, springing from white supremacy and characterized by the sexualization of even "the Southerner," paralyzed him intellectually.

### The Tragedy of Southern Politics

*The Mind of the South* ends with a long passage on the political and economic needs of the South in 1940. Even though those needs were long-standing, Cash saw that the Great Depression exacerbated the region's poverty. Yet Cash cannot pursue his glimmerings of insight. After indicting the lack of effective political leadership as the great tragedy of the South, he ends his book with a return to anthropomorphism. Why does he abandon the analysis? Why does Cash ultimately move away from the vision of pages 394–439, which is social and economic, rather than psychological? Why, in the last two pages (439–40) does he fall back on the figure of "the South" as individual and write of individual traits such as pride, bravery, courtesy, personal generosity, and loyalty?

Cash realizes that economic remedies require political change, and he already knows that the region's elected officials cannot meet the challenge of the Great Depression. The problem is that envisioning solutions would mean embracing remedies too radical for a segregationist like Cash. As Radical Republicans discovered in the wake of the Confederate defeat, fundamental change would mean enfranchising all the poor. But for Cash, as for so many white southerners of his generation, the confusion of race with class precludes real consideration of the enfranchisement of the poor. Racism, therefore, led segregationists into a political cul-de-sac.

So dramatic a remedy as extending the franchise to the poor who were black lay beyond a segregationist's ken. Like so many of his time, Cash could not see past segregation, a system built on black disfranchisement that, as a phrase, encapsulated black political impotence. In Cash's conventional, "common sense" reckoning of politics, extending the franchise, for whatever reason, would permit what was called "social equality"—meaning sex between "the Negro" and "the Southern woman." Social equality symbolizes everything threatening about desegregation and black enfranchisement. Thus the logical remedy for problems in the political economy entailed other dilemmas, of gender and hence of sex. Increasing the political clout of the southern poor might have remedied the economic ills that distressed Cash, but that remedy involved something that tormented him on the gut level: the sexualization—and therefore the disempowering—of the entire polity, not just of the poor and the black and the female. This peril brings us back to his sexualization of the other, richer half of Cash's figure of "the Southerner," even though he is the most effective and autonomous figure in the book.

In much of *The Mind of the South* "the Southerner" appears as an amorphous amalgam of white men. Ultimately the real "Southerner" is differentiated from "the mill people" whom the poor become.[48] Cash sexualizes the Southerner, and in the long discussion of Negro women's "easy complaisance," Cash admits that the rulers of the South did their share of race mixing; race mixing means sex.[49]

In the end, southerners of the better class are also fatally flawed, for they, too, betray the weakness that symbolizes powerlessness. In Cash's analysis, in which even elite white southern men are prisoners of lust, the root of the political tragedy of "the South"/"the Southerner" lies in sexuality. "The Southerner," even when wealthy, even when educated, cannot be effective in the public realm.

In *The Mind of the South* sexuality means impotence, for Cash's map of sexuality is an inverse map of power. This identification may be mainly autobiographical in its literal meaning, but it also relates to the network of power that characterized southern culture in the eras of slavery and segregation. At the same time, and without realizing it, Cash is pointing to the social and political repercussions of a hierarchical society in which only a few men held enormous, multivalent power. Having monopolized public agencies, including the legislatures, the police, and the courts, the few white men in power freely deprived everybody else of whatever they wanted, from decent wages, to the ability to organize their workplaces or vote their own interests, to sex.

As Foucault remarked, sexuality expresses all sorts of power relations, and here they were private and public, actual and symbolic.

Realizing however hazily that sexuality and power are linked, Cash still backs away from the implication of his intimation that the answer to economic distress lay in the empowering of the southern poor. That last step — away from segregation into something that Cash could only see as "social equality" — is not possible to take. His South remains tragic, his southerners tainted. The only people who emerge from the pages of *The Mind of the South* with unimpaired agency are Yankees, male and female.

## Potent Yankees

Unlike Cash's southern figures, "the Yankee" appears only sporadically. In some places Cash seems to confound "the Yankee" with "the tariff gang," as though protective tariffs were as significant an issue in the forging of white southern identity as antislavery and Radical Reconstruction. Cash concedes enormous power to "the Yankee," who is undiminished by sexuality and plays a crucial role in Cash's conventional version of southern history. During the antebellum era and during Reconstruction, which for Cash unaccountably covers the thirty years following the Civil War and is characterized by Yankee occupation, "the conflict with the Yankee" creates and intensifies southerners (185). As a powerful Other, "the Yankee" defines by opposition what is southern, or, in Cash's words, he "really created the concept of the South as something more than a matter of geography . . . in the minds of the Southerners."[50]

"The Yankee" is a symbol of modernity, one of the most compelling concepts in the book. More than once Cash admits that he practically uses the terms *Yankee* and *modern* interchangeably.[51] Yankees are the originators of Progress, so that when local capitalists take it upon themselves to provide "the common white" a sanctuary, Cash says that they have decided to copy "Yankeedom." Both factories and schools are the brainchildren of Yankees.[52]

Although she appears on only one page, "the Yankee schoolma'am," who stands for northern teachers to the southern freedpeople right after the Civil War, does something. The inspiration for the schooling of the masses comes from a figure whom Cash detests but allows considerable autonomy, which is all the more remarkable because this figure is a woman who is not sexualized. Quite to the contrary, Cash tries to desexualize her by disparaging her femininity. With the disdain of a man who more easily envisions white women as breeders and ornaments, Cash subjects "the Yankee schoolma'am" to stereotypical ridicule and blame. Judging her femininity and gauging her success by the degree to which she appears attractive to men, he finds nothing worth admiring in her physiognomy or her mission: "Generally horse-faced, bespectacled, and spare of frame, she was, of course, no proper intellectual, but at best a comic character." This woman was "at worse a dangerous fool, playing with explosive forces which she did not understand. She had no little part in developing Southern bitterness as a whole, and [with Yankee journalists] . . . contributed much to the growth of hysterical sensibility to criticism."

As much as Cash dislikes her — and to show his disdain he puts her vocation in quotation marks — the Yankee schoolma'am teaches people something. And she inspires strong emotions, even though they are negative, in the mind of the South.[53] She is the only active, educated female type in *The Mind of the South.*

These Yankees are able to push around everyone in the South. They dupe "the Negro," outrage "the Southerner," but set an example that Southerners feel impelled to follow. Standing at the edge of Cash's maps of sexuality and power and unfettered by sexuality and the weaknesses it entails, "the Yankee" and "the Yankee schoolma'am" manipulate the southern scenario from a position that is only half on the terrain of *The Mind of the South.*

## Conclusion

Wilbur Cash was more perceptive than most of his contemporary southern commentators: he saw through the moonlight and magnolias tradition of southern aristocracy and brought poor whites into his South. But his was only half-sight; he was blind to the power dynamics that led him to ridicule poor whites and define "the Negro" out of what was essentially southern. Cash recognizes hierarchy and calls it that. But he does not see that his comments on race and gender spring directly from his limited understanding of southern class relations. He can decipher the difference between "the Southerner" and "the common white," between "the South" and "the mill worker," but he does not perceive that his definition of the South reaches only as far as voters. On some level, he knows that women had only recently gained the vote and that poor people do not vote (much) in the South, but he does not recognize that their powerlessness makes them ridiculous in his eyes.

Lillian Smith saw how Cash's taboos blocked his vision and kept his discussion close to the conventions of southern life and history. Even so, *The Mind of the South* persists as a phenomenon more than a half-century after its publication. The enduring popularity of this quirky big book bears witness to the degree to which Americans to this day share Cash's conflicts, his blindness, and his complexes. Southerners and Americans of all races still confuse race with class and political power with sex so that their maps of power and sexuality are still likely to be as misleading as Cash's. Out of fear of the disabilities of the poor as expressed as racial failings, many still balk at allowing democracy to fulfill its whole promise. If *The Mind of the South* still reaches an audience, we may yet take some comfort in knowing that the revolution separating Wilbur Cash's time from our own has, at the very least, reworked the legal and hence the political foundations of his South. His confusion of gender, class, race, and sexuality no longer represents an enlightened view of a benighted region, and we are able to envision — if not yet to shape — a landscape of power that is less booby-trapped by history and prejudice than was his.

# NOTES

## INTRODUCTION

1. I'm thinking particularly of *The Militant South: 1800–1861* (Cambridge, Mass.: Harvard University Press, 1956); *Southern Odyssey: Travelers in the Antebellum North* (Baton Rouge: Louisiana State University Press, 1976); and *Land of the Free* (Pasadena, Calif.: Ritchie Press for Franklin Publications, 1965), the textbook Franklin wrote with John Caughey and Ernest May for use in the California schools.

2. See Glenda Gilmore, *Gender and Jim Crow: Women and the Politics of White Supremacy in North Carolina, 1896–1920* (Chapel Hill: University of North Carolina Press, 1996); Walter L. Johnson, *Soul by Soul: Life inside the Antebellum Slave Market* (Cambridge, Mass.: Harvard University Press, 2000); and Crystal N. Feimster, "'Ladies and Lynching': The Gendered Discourse of Mob Violence in the New South, 1880–1930," Ph.D. diss., Princeton University, 2000.

3. My graduate students do not all write across the color line. Those writing dissertations in African American history do so because they find exciting topics in that field. Its freshness attracts them, and they share the mission of correcting the myriad distortions still in evidence.

4. By "psychoanalysis" I mean the thinking of Sigmund Freud and his followers, including Jacques Lacan and Nancy Chodorow. By "psychology" I mean mainly the ideas of object relations theorists, notably John Bowlby. Fuller citations can be found in the notes of the essays that follow.

5. Frank Freidel (1916–1993), to whom I dedicated *Standing at Armageddon: The United States, 1877–1919*, was my dissertation advisor at Harvard. However, he deferred to Gutman (1928–1985) when it came to African American history, and so Gutman influenced the choice of my dissertation topic almost as much as Freidel. On Herbert Gutman and American labor historiography, see Ira Berlin's introductory essay in Herbert Gutman, *Power and Culture: Essays on the American Working Class* (New York: New Press, 1989). For a discussion of Herbert Gutman, African American history, and African American historians, see Nell Irvin Painter, "Remembering Herbert Gutman and Afro-American History," *Labor History* 29, no. 3 (Summer 1988): 336–43.

6. I am very grateful to Nellie McKay for helping me get started in gender theory, a topic outside my graduate education.

7. I use the term "white supremacy" to indicate a belief structure that assumes that white people are better than nonwhites. White supremacy need not always find violent expression. Black people and other people of color as well as whites can believe in it, by taking white people's superiority for granted.

8. "Honest Abe and Uncle Tom," *Canadian Review of American Studies/Revue canadienne d'études américaines* 30, no. 3 (2000): 245–72.

### 1. SOUL MURDER AND SLAVERY

Thanks to Carole Beal, Jean Layzer, Glenn Shafer, Constance and Preston Williams, and Elaine Wise for suggestions, encouragement, and assistance.

1. Fox Butterfield, "Why America's Murder Rate Is So High," *New York Times*, 26 July 1998, sec. 4, 1.
2. Philip Greven is exceptional among historians in investigating child abuse carefully. However he does not focus upon child abuse associated with enslavement. See Philip Greven, *The Protestant Temperament: Patterns of Child-Rearing, Religious Experience, and the Self in Early America* (New York: Knopf, 1977) and *Spare the Child: The Religious Roots of Punishment and the Psychological Impact of Physical Abuse* (New York: Knopf, 1991).
3. Daniel Paul Schreber, *Memoirs of My Nervous Illness*, translated and edited by Ida Macalpine and Richard A. Hunter, with a new introduction by Samuel M. Weber (Cambridge, Mass.: Harvard University Press, 1988), xii–xiii. See also Sigmund Freud, "Psycho-Analytic Notes on an Autobiographical Account of a Case of Paranoia (Dementia Paranoides)" [1911], in *The Standard Edition of the Complete Psychological Works of Sigmund Freud*, edited and translated by James Strachey (London: Hogarth Press, 1958), 9–82; Jacques Lacan, "On a Question Preliminary to any Possible Treatment of Psychosis" [1955–56], in *Ecrits*, translated by Alan Sheridan (New York: W. W. Norton, 1977); and Leonard Shengold, *Halo in the Sky* (New York: Guilford, 1988). The great legal reformer Anselm von Feuerbach was the father of philosopher Ludwig Feuerbach. My thanks to Ulrich Struve for help in sorting out the story of Kaspar Hauser.
4. Leonard Shengold, *Soul Murder: The Effects of Childhood Abuse and Deprivation* (New Haven: Yale University Press, 1989), 1–5; James A. Chu, "The Repetition Compulsion Revisited: Reliving Dissociated Trauma" (paper presented at the International Conference on Multiple Personality and Dissociative States, November 6, 1987), 1. I am grateful to Becky Thompson for bringing this paper to my attention.

   See also Leonard Shengold, *Soul Murder Revisited: Thoughts about Therapy, Hate, Love, and Memory* (New Haven: Yale University Press, 1999).
5. Ian Hacking, "Memoro-politics: Trauma and the Soul" (Davis Center Seminar Paper, Princeton University, September 25, 1992; used with the permission of the author), and "The Making and Molding of Child Abuse," *Critical Inquiry* 17 (Winter 1991): 253–88; Carol Tavris, "Beware the Incest-Survivor Machine," *New York Times Book Review*, January 3, 1993.
6. See Louis Althusser, "A Letter on Art," in *Lenin and Philosophy and Other Essays*, translated by Ben Brewster (New York: Monthly Review Press, 1971), 221–27, and Pierre Macherey, *A Theory of Literary Production* (1966), translated by Geoffrey Wall (London: Routledge and Kegan Paul,

1978), esp. 82–97; Judith Lewis Herman, *Trauma and Recovery: The After-math of Violence — From Domestic Abuse to Political Terror* (New York: Basic Books, 1992) and *Father-Daughter Incest* (Cambridge Mass.: Harvard University Press, 1981).

7. Elkins, *Slavery: A Problem in American Institutional and Intellectual Life*, 1, 122–23 (Elkins's emphasis). See also Ann J. Lane, ed., *The Debate over Slavery: Stanley Elkins and His Critics* (Urbana: University of Illinois Press, 1971); Peter Kolchin, *American Slavery: 1619–1877* (New York: Hill and Wang, 1993), 135–39; and Peter J. Parish, *Slavery: History and Historians* (New York: Harper and Row, 1989), 7, 67–70.

8. Herbert Gutman, *The Black Family in Slavery and Freedom, 1750–1925* (New York: Oxford University Press, 1976).

9. Karl Marx and Frederick Engels, "Feuerbach: Opposition of the Materialist and Idealist Outlook," in *The German Ideology, Part One* [written 1845–46], edited by C. J. Arthur (New York: International Publishers, 1947, 1970), 47–49 (emphasis in the original).

10. Alexis de Tocqueville, *Democracy in America*, edited by J. P. Mayer (Garden City, N.Y.: Doubleday, 1969), 345, 375–76, 585–88.

11. Althusser sees the family as one of the potent "ideological state apparatuses" that silently inculcate ideology alongside whatever coercion the state may employ. Lacan speaks of the "paternal metaphor" and "the name of the father" as means by which children are initiated into the conventions and power relations of social life. Althusser, *Lenin and Philosophy*, 143–45, 150–58, 189–220; Jacques Lacan, *Ecrits*, 65–73, 142–43, 196–97, 201–20, 252.

12. Quoted in Brenda Stevenson, "Distress and Discord in Virginia Slave Families, 1830–1860," in *In Joy and in Sorrow: Women, Family, and Marriage in the Victorian South, 1830–1900*, edited by Carol Bleser (New York: Oxford University Press, 1991), 111.

13. Kenneth Stampp, *The Peculiar Institution: Slavery in the Ante-Bellum South* (New York: Knopf, 1959, Vintage ed.), 141.

14. William Wells Brown, *Narrative*, quoted in John Blassingame, *The Slave Community: Plantation Life in the Antebellum South*, rev. ed. (New York: Oxford University Press, 1979), 186; Nell Irvin Painter, ed., *Narrative of Sojourner Truth* (originally published, 1850; New York: Penguin Books, 1998), 26.

15. Theodore Rosengarten, *All God's Dangers: The Life of Nate Shaw* (New York: Knopf, 1974), 6–11.

16. Stampp, *Peculiar Institution*, 144 (irregular capitalization in original); Alice Miller, *For Your Own Good: Hidden Cruelty in Child-Rearing and the Roots of Violence* (New York: Farrar, Straus, Giroux, 1983, 1990), 58, 65, 88.

17. Concerning attachment, the three-volume work of John Bowlby is crucial: *Attachment* (London: Tavistock Institute of Human Relations, 1969; reprint, New York: Basic Books, 1982), *Separation: Anxiety and Anger* (New

York: Basic Books, 1973), and *Loss: Sadness and Depression* (New York: Basic Books, 1980).

18. Michael Tadman, *Speculators and Slaves: Masters, Traders, and Slaves in the Old South* (Madison: University of Wisconsin Press, 1996), 12, 26. See also Parish, *Slavery*, 86; Kolchin, *American Slavery*, 96–98, 125–39. The dust jacket of Kolchin's book shows a slave auction in which a black mother on her knees reaches vainly for her baby, whom the auctioneer holds up for sale by one arm and on whom a gentleman bids. In the lower right corner, a soon to be sundered slave family huddles in tears.

19. Harriet A. Jacobs, *Incidents in the Life of a Slave Girl, Written by Herself*, edited by Jean Fagan Yellin (Cambridge, Mass.: Harvard University Press, 1987), 27–28, 33. See also Nell Irvin Painter, ed., *Incidents in the Life of a Slave Girl* (New York: Penguin, 2000), xv–xvii.

20. Mary Chesnut quoted in Lee Ann Whites, "The Civil War as a Crisis in Gender," in *Divided Houses: Gender and the Civil War*, edited by Catherine Clinton and Nina Silber (New York: Oxford University Press, 1992), 6.

21. Gayle Rubin, "The Traffic in Women: Notes on the 'Political Economy' of Sex," in *Toward an Anthropology of Women*, edited by Rayna R. Reiter (New York: Monthly Review Press, 1975), 157–210.

22. Andrew Jackson, *Narrative and Writings of Andrew Jackson of Kentucky* (Syracuse, N.Y.: Daily and Weekly Star, 1847), 24. I thank Walter Johnson for bringing this anecdote to my attention.

23. Herman, *Father-Daughter Incest*, 81–83, and *Trauma and Recovery*, 106.

24. Catharine A. MacKinnon, *Sexual Harassment of Working Women: A Case of Sex Discrimination* (New Haven: Yale University Press, 1979), 29, 40, 45. MacKinnon also notes that "racism is deeply involved in sexual harassment" (31).

25. David Finkelhor with Sharon Araji, Larry Baron, Angela Browne, Stefanie Doyle Peters, and Gail Elizabeth Wyatt, *A Sourcebook on Child Sexual Abuse* (Newbury Park, Calif.: Sage Publications, 1986), 152–64.

26. Benjamin Mays, *The Negro's God as Reflected in His Literature* (Boston: Chapman and Grimes, 1938), 22, 87.

27. John Hope Franklin, "Slavery and Personality: A Fresh Look," *Massachusetts Review* 2 (Autumn 1960), and Earl E. Thorpe, "Chattel Slavery and Concentration Camps," *Negro History Bulletin* 25 (May 1962), both quoted in August Meier and Elliott Rudwick, *Black History and the Historical Profession, 1915–1980* (Urbana: University of Illinois Press, 1990), 140, 248.

28. Unfortunately, due to the state of the historiography, I cannot elaborate on the cultural and psychological situation of the millions of slaves who lived outside black communities, for this, like much in studies of the psychology of households that included whites and blacks, remains to be investigated. Historical scholarship on nonplantation southern blacks is virtually nonexistent. Historians writing on northern slavery have tended to examine those slaves' conditions of life rather than their actual experiences. One

exception to this rule is Shane White, *Somewhat More Independent: The End of Slavery in New York City, 1770–1810* (Athens: University of Georgia Press, 1991). The first two chapters of my biography of Sojourner Truth, *Sojourner Truth: A Life, A Symbol* (New York: W. W. Norton, 1996), deal with the personal experience of slaves in New York State.

29. Blassingame, *Slave Community*, 191; Deborah Gray White, *Ar'n't I a Woman? Female Slaves in the Plantation South* (New York: W. W. Norton, 1985), 119–41.

30. Gail Elizabeth Wyatt and M. Ray Mickey, "The Support by Parents and Others as It Mediates the Effects of Child Sexual Abuse: An Exploratory Study," in *Lasting Effects of Child Sexual Abuse*, edited by Gail Elizabeth Wyatt and Gloria Johnson Powell (Newbury Park, Calif.: Sage Publications, 1988), 211–25.

31. Albert Raboteau, *Slave Religion: The "Invisible Institution" in the Antebellum South* (New York: Oxford University Press, 1978); Gayraud S. Wilmore, *Last Things First* (Philadelphia: Westminster Press, 1982), 42, 77; James H. Cone, *God of the Oppressed* (San Francisco: Harper San Francisco, 1975), 32, 57, 175.

32. Arthur A. Stone, Lynn Helder, and Mark S. Schneider, "Coping with Stressful Events: Coping Dimensions and Issues," in *Life Events and Psychological Functioning: Theoretical and Methodological Issues*, edited by Lawrence H. Cohen (Newbury Park, Calif.: Sage Publications, 1988), 187–88.

33. Catherine Clinton, *The Plantation Mistress: Woman's World in the Old South* (New York: Pantheon, 1982), 165.

34. Caroline [Howard] Gilman, *Recollections of a New England Bride and of a Southern Matron* (new edition, rev.; New York: Putnam & Co., 1852 [*Southern Matron* originally published 1837, *New England Bride*, 1834]), 297, 384.

35. Elizabeth Fox-Genovese notes that the family "figured as a central metaphor for southern society as a whole." "Family and Female Identity in the Antebellum South: Sarah Gayle and Her Family," in *In Joy and in Sorrow*, 19.

36. On white women in the fields, see Stephanie McCurry, "The Politics of Yeoman Households in South Carolina," in *Divided Houses*, 28–31.

37. Painter, ed., *Narrative of Sojourner Truth*, 36–39.

38. [Theodore Dwight Weld], *American Slavery as It Is: Testimony of a Thousand Witnesses* (New York: American Anti-Slavery Society, 1839), 51–52.

39. Elizabeth Fox-Genovese, *Within the Plantation Household: Black and White Women in the Antebellum South* (Chapel Hill: University of North Carolina Press, 1988), 24, 97, 308–14.

40. Quoted in [Weld], *American Slavery*, 54–55 (emphasis in the original).

41. Thomas Jefferson, *Notes on the State of Virginia* (originally published, 1787; New York: W. W. Norton, 1972), 162. Similarly, an advice manual for slave-owning mothers published in 1830, *Letters on Female Character*,

noted that slave owning encouraged "all the most malignant vices of his nature" in the child. Quoted in Clinton, *Plantation Mistress*, 91.

42. Philip G. Ney, "Triangles of Abuse: A Model of Maltreatment," *Child Abuse & Neglect* 12 (1988): 363–73.

43. See Virginia Walcott Beauchamp, ed., *A Private War: Letters and Diaries of Madge Preston, 1862–1867* (New Brunswick, N.J.: Rutgers University Press, 1987).

44. Stephanie McCurry, *Masters of Small Worlds: Yeoman Households, Gender Relations, and the Political Culture of the Antebellum South Carolina Low Country* (New York: Oxford University Press, 1995), 86–91.

45. A. Leon Higginbotham Jr., *In the Matter of Color: Race and the American Legal Process: The Colonial Period* (New York: Oxford University Press, 1978), 40–47; Peter W. Bardaglio, *Reconstructing the Household: Families, Sex, and the Law in the Nineteenth-Century South* (Chapel Hill: University of North Carolina Press, 1995), 37–78.

46. Daniel Blake Smith, *Inside the Great House: Planter Family Life in Eighteenth-Century Chesapeake Society* (Ithaca, N.Y.: Cornell University Press, 1980).

47. Carol Lawson, "Violence at Home: 'They Don't Want Anyone to Know,'" *New York Times*, 6 August 1992.

48. Ronald C. Summit, "Hidden Victims, Hidden Pain: Societal Avoidance of Child Sexual Abuse," in *Lasting Effects of Child Sexual Abuse*, 40.

49. Jeffrey Moussaieff Masson, *The Assault on Truth: Freud's Suppression of the Seduction Theory* (New York: HarperCollins, 1984, 1992).

50. Richard L. Bushman, *The Refinement of America: Persons, Houses, Cities* (New York: Knopf, 1992), xiv, 55, 288; Jay Fliegelman, *Declaring Independence: Jefferson, Natural Language, and the Culture of Performance* (Stanford: Stanford University Press, 1993), 79–129, 189–200.

51. Lillian Smith, *Killers of the Dream* (rev. ed.; New York: W. W. Norton, 1961), 83–89, 121–24.

## 2. THE JOURNAL OF ELLA GERTRUDE CLANTON THOMAS

The original version of this essay was completed while I was a fellow at the Center for Advanced Study in the Behavioral Sciences at Stanford, California, with the generous support of the National Endowment for the Humanities (grant #FC-20060-85) and the Andrew W. Mellon Foundation. I am grateful to colleagues at the Center and to other scholars in southern history for their help in sorting out Gertrude Thomas's society. I also wish to thank the staff of the Special Collections of the Duke University Library.

This essay is based on the Ella Gertrude Clanton Thomas journal housed in the Special Collections of the Duke University Library, as corrected by Virginia Burr. Burr, the great-granddaughter of Thomas and granddaughter of Mary Belle Thomas Ingraham, corrected the typescript Mary Elizabeth Massey had had prepared in the late 1960s in preparation for the publication of *The Secret Eye: The Journal of Ella Gertrude Clanton Thomas, 1848–1889* (Chapel Hill: University of North Carolina Press, 1990), an edited version of the Thomas journal. This essay draws on the entire journal rather than merely the published edition; therefore occasional citations may refer to entries not included in the published version.

1. Thomas's history recalls those of southern suffragists like Rebecca Latimer Felton and Caroline Merrick. See Rebecca Latimer Felton, *Country Life in Georgia in the Days of My Youth* (Atlanta: Index Printing Co., 1919), and Caroline E. Merrick, *Old Times in Dixie Land: A Southern Matron's Memories* (New York: Grafton Press, 1901). See also Shari Benstock, "Authorizing the Autobiographical," in Shari Benstock, ed., *The Private Self: Theory and Practice of Women's Autobiographical Writings* (Chapel Hill: University of North Carolina Press, 1988), 20.

2. Myrta Lockett Avary, *Dixie after the War: An Exposition of Social Conditions Existing in the South, during the Twelve Years Succeeding the Fall of Richmond* (New York: Doubleday, Page, 1906); Isabella D. Martin and Myrta Lockett Avary, eds., *A Diary from Dixie, as Written by Mary Boykin Chesnut, Wife of James Chesnut, Jr., United States Senator from South Carolina* (New York: D. Appleton & Co., 1905); Ben Ames Williams, ed., *A Diary from Dixie. The Most Famous Single Source of Information about the Heroic, Tragic, and Romantic Life of the Women at Home under the Stars and Bars* (Boston: Houghton Mifflin, 1949); C. Vann Woodward, ed., *Mary Chesnut's Civil War* (New Haven: Yale University Press, 1981).

3. I am prevented from offering a more critical discussion of Thomas's life here by two factors: First, no letters to or from Thomas survive, making the diary virtually the only source for information on her life; second, Carolyn Curry's unpublished 1987 Georgia State University dissertation, the sole full-length biography of Thomas, has not been made available for purchase from University Microfilms by anyone but the author.

4. In 1860 some 400,000 southern white families owned slaves, usually only one or two. Planter families, by definition, owned twenty or more slaves. The proportion of white families owning slaves decreased during the antebellum era, from 36 percent in 1830 to 31 percent in 1850 and 26 percent in 1860. Further, the proportion of slaveowners in the white population varied throughout the South, there being relatively few in the upcountry and more in the low country Black Belts such as the Georgia and South Carolina hinterlands of Augusta. See James Oakes, *The Ruling Race: A History of American Slaveholders* (New York: Alfred A. Knopf, 1982), 225, 229.

5. Information on the Luke, Clanton, and Thomas families comes from Virginia Burr and Mary Elizabeth Massey, "The Making of a Feminist," *Journal of Southern History* 39, no. 1 (Feb. 1973): 3–22.

6. Anne Firor Scott, *The Southern Lady: From Pedestal to Politics, 1830–1930* (Chicago: University of Chicago Press, 1970), 68–74; Catherine Clinton, *The Plantation Mistress: Woman's World in the Old South* (New York: Pantheon, 1982), 124–28; Jane Turner Censer, *North Carolina Planters and Their Children, 1800–1860* (Baton Rouge: Louisiana State University Press, 1984), 44; and Donald G. Mathews, *Religion in the Old South* (Chicago: University of Chicago Press, 1977), 89–91, 96–97.

7. Concerning Mat Oliver, the most interesting entries from Thomas's journal are: 2 Feb. 1849, 5 Jan., 19 Apr., 9 June, 9 July 1852, 11 Apr. 1855, 9 Feb. 1858. Thomas and Jule Thomas remained friends, even when Jule moved to North Carolina after having married Nathaniel Scales. In 1860 sibling exchange reinforced the close bonds between the Thomas and Clanton families when Jule and Jeff's younger brother Pinckney married Gertrude's younger sister Mary.

8. John D'Emilio and Estelle B. Freedman, *Intimate Matters: A History of Sexuality in America* (New York: Harper & Row, 1988), 94; Steven M. Stowe, "Courtship: Sexuality and Feeling," in *Intimacy and Power in the Old South: Ritual in the Lives of the Planters* (Baltimore: Johns Hopkins University Press, 1987), 50–121; and Thomas Journal, 26 Feb., 16 Mar., 15, 18, 30, 31 May, 5 Nov. 1852. Entries from Thomas's journal will hereafter be cited by date only.

9. 27 Apr., 9 July, 20 Aug., 29 Sept. 1855, 10 Mar. 1856, 1 Jan. 1857, 7 Feb. 1858.

10. 13, 16 July 1861.

11. 15, 16 July 1861, 1 Jan. 1862. In the use of the first-person plural Thomas had a good deal of company, as illustrated in the journal of Susan Cornwall of Burke County, Georgia, quoted in LeeAnn Whites, *The Civil War as a Crisis in Gender: Augusta, Georgia, 1860–1890* (Athens: University of Georgia Press, 1995). Jean Bethke Elshtain mentions Jean-Jacques Rousseau's and Machiavelli's celebration of military values in *Women and War* (New York: Basic Books, 1987), 55. See also journal entries for 15, 16 July 1861, 7 Oct. 1862. For a discussion of Confederate nationalism that accords well with Thomas's experience, see Drew Gilpin Faust, *The Creation of Confederate Nationalism: Ideology and Identity in the Civil War South* (Baton Rouge: Louisiana State University Press), 1988.

12. 27 June, 17 Sept. 1862. Both Thomas W. Thomas (of Elbert County, Georgia, in the Augusta hinterland) and Robert Toombs, who had been a U.S. senator from Georgia, resigned their commissions in early 1862. In April 1862 the Confederacy resorted to conscription in order to supply the necessary manpower. See J. William Harris, *Plain Folk and Gentry in a Slave Society: White Liberty and Black Slavery in Augusta's Hinterlands* (Middletown, Conn.: Wesleyan University Press, 1985), 144–47.

13. 18 Aug. 1861, 17 Jan. 1862.

14. 22 Oct., 21 Nov. 1864.

15. James L. Roark, *Masters without Slaves: Southern Planters in the Civil War and Reconstruction* (New York: W. W. Norton, 1977), 61, 77, 196, 208.

16. See Elizabeth Fox-Genovese, *Within the Plantation Household: Black and White Women of the Old South* (Chapel Hill: University of North Carolina Press, 1988), 15, 22–27.

17. 5 May 1865.

18. See also entries for 1 Jan. 1862, 31 Dec. 1863, 12 Feb. 1865, 3 Dec. 1868.

19. Scott, *Southern Lady*, 98–99; Mary Elizabeth Massey, *Bonnet Brigades* (New York: Alfred A. Knopf, 1966), 153, 174–75, 242, 260. Other scholarship on women in war — for instance, on women in World War I — indicates that wars liberate women even as they debilitate men. See Sandra M. Gilbert, "Soldier's Heart: Literary Men, Literary Women, and the Great War," in Margaret R. Higonnet, Jane Jensoln, Sonya Michel, Margaret Collins Weitz, eds., *Behind the Lines: Gender and the Two World Wars* (New Haven: Yale University Press, 1987), 199, 201, 214, 223.

20. 22 Sept., 22 Nov. 1864, 29 Mar., 5 May 1865, 9 July, 12 Oct. 1866.

21. 25 Oct. 1864, 9, 22 July 1866, 20 Sept. 1869, 29 Sept., 30 Nov. 1870, 9 Feb. 1879, 21 Feb. 1880. Thomas shared this aspiration with many other southern women who had kept journals during the Civil War.

22. This use of her own (as opposed to her husband's) first name merits two mentions in the journal, on 25 March and 15 May 1880. See also 14 Dec. 1870, 2 Jan. 1871.

23. 1, 2 Nov. 1868.

24. The quote is from 29 May 1865. See also 1 Feb., 10 Apr. 1871, 5 Jan. 1881.

25. 29 Nov. 1868.

26. See particularly 10 Jan., 6 Mar., 5 Dec. 1870, 23 June 1880.

27. 12 Dec. 1870, 2 Jan. 1871, 9 Feb. 1879, 22 Jan. 1880.

28. 14 May 1869, 10 Jan. 1870, 18 Dec. 1879, 19 May 1880.

29. 10 Aug. 1879; 2 Jan., 13 June 1880.

30. 3 Apr. 1888.

31. E.g., 8 Feb. 1879, 3 Apr. 1888.

32. 10 Jan., 5 Dec. 1870.

33. 29 Nov. 1868; 9 Mar. 1871.

34. 29 Nov., 4, 20 Dec. 1868; 3, 4 May 1869, 9 Jan., 5, 12 Dec. 1870. The Thomases' other creditors exerted more pressure than their families for the repayment of debt. The Georgia homestead law of 1868 had been tailored to meet the needs of planters as well as yeoman farmers, hence the generous limits on real and personal property (Jonathan M. Bryant, "'The Work of Negroes and Thieves': Georgia's Homestead and Exemption Laws, 1868–1877," unpublished paper, University of Georgia, 1986).

35. 29 Mar. 1865, 4 Dec. 1868, 19 June 1869, 22 Jan., 5 Dec. 1870, 9 Mar. 1871, 31 Dec. 1878.

36. E.g., 2 Nov. 1868, 28 Jan., 7 Mar. 1869, 3 Oct. 1882.

37. E.g., 10 Jan. 1870.

38. 23 June 1880.

39. 10 Jan., 30 Nov., 12 Dec. 1870, 8 Jan. 1880, 3 Oct. 1883.

40. Gertrude projected the opening of her own school for the winter of 1865–66 on 8 May 1865, and in her journal she speaks of wanting to teach from time to time over the next several years. On 30 Nov. 1870 she records Jeff's continuing opposition to her working.

41. E.g., 12 Apr. 1871, 4 Jan., 8 Feb. 1879. In February 1879 her salary was increased to $35 per month.

42. 8 Jan. 1880, 3 Oct. 1883.

43. 18 Dec. 1879. When Clanton died in 1879 he was a few days from turning seven. In 1879 Turner was twenty-six; Mary Belle, twenty-one; Jeff, eighteen; Cora Lou, sixteen; Julian, eleven; and Kathleen, four.

44. 3 Apr. 1888.

45. Theodore Rosengarten, *Tombee: Portrait of a Cotton Planter* (New York: William Morrow, 1986), 299.

46. Scott, *Southern Lady*, 139–52.

47. Marjorie Stratford Mendenhall, "Southern Women of a 'Lost Generation,'" *South Atlantic Quarterly* 33, no. 4 (Oct. 1934): 341; and John Patrick McDowell, *The Social Gospel in the South: The Woman's Home Mission Movement in the Methodist Episcopal Church, South, 1886–1939* (Baton Rouge, La., 1982), 1–11.

48. Anne Scott cites 1884–87 as the period of explosive growth of women's clubs in the South. Thomas's Hayne Circle, named for Paul Hamilton Hayne, a local poet, does not quite fit this pattern, however, as it was formed during the 1870s and also included men.

49. 18 Mar. 1852, 17 Aug. 1879.

50. Jean E. Friedman, *The Enclosed Garden: Women and Community in the Evangelical South, 1830–1900* (Chapel Hill: University of North Carolina Press, 1985), 111–21.

51. See Rebecca Ragsdale Lallier, "The Woman's Christian Temperance Union, Frances Willard, and the South," unpublished paper, 1988, 13.

52. The NAWSA had been formed in 1890 with the merger of the National Woman Suffrage Association, led by Elizabeth Cady Stanton and Susan B. Anthony and based in New York, and the American Woman Suffrage Association, led by Lucy Stone and her husband, Henry Blackwell, and based in New England.

53. For example, the journal of Samuel Agnew of Mississippi, housed in the Southern Historical Collection of the University of North Carolina at Chapel Hill, is longer but less detailed.

54. For *The Secret Eye*, Virginia Burr checked every page against the manuscript and corrected omissions and inaccuracies.

55. Shari Benstock aptly terms "'writing the self' . . . a process of simultaneous sealing and splitting" (Benstock, "Authorizing the Autobiographical," in *The Private Self*, 29). The clearest statement of the dramaturgy of self-

presentation is found in Erving Goffman, *The Presentation of Self in Every-day Life* (Garden City, N.Y.: Doubleday, 1959), esp. 17–76, 209, 252–55.

56. Stowe, *Intimacy and Power*, 1–2. See also Journal, 1 Aug. 1870, 17 Aug. 1879.

57. The quote is from 14 Nov. 1848. On 1 Aug. 1852 she apologizes for writing informally because others are in the room and distracting her. In the early years of her journal, Gertrude Clanton speaks repeatedly of not having written regularly: 17, 29 Nov. 1848, 27 May 1851, 24 Jan., 6 Feb., 20 June [n.d.], 22 Aug., 2 Sept. 1852.

58. Thomas's struggle for open self-expression extended over many years. See particularly the entries for 26 May 1852, 26 June 1856, 5 May 1865. See also 2 June 1855, 20 Feb. 1857, 4 July 1864, 18 Sept. 1864.

59. E.g., 12 Apr., 12 May 1856.

60. Censer, *North Carolina Planters and Their Children*, 52. Journal, 5 Feb. 1852, 19 Apr., 1 Jan. 1859, 31 Dec. 1863, 16 Oct. 1865, 2 Sept. 1880. See also Sander L. Gilman, *Difference and Pathology: Stereotypes of Sexuality, Race, and Madness* (Ithaca, N.Y.: Cornell University Press, 1985), 20–24.

61. Elisabeth Muhlenfeld, *Mary Boykin Chesnut: A Biography* (Baton Rouge: Louisiana State University Press, 1981), 41–49; Stowe, *Intimacy and Power*, 162.

62. 29 May–3 June 1855, 1 Jan. 1859, 17 May, 22 July, 16 Oct., 31 Dec. 1865, 20 Sept. 1866, 30 July 1870, 2 Jan., 2 Sept. 1880.

63. 22 July 1865, 17 Aug. 1879, 5 Dec. 1870. See also Arno Gruen, *The Betrayal of the Self: The Fear of Autonomy in Men and Women*, trans. Hildegarde and Hunter Hannum (New York: Grove Press, 1988), xv, 30, 34, 59, 61–64.

64. See Mathews, *Religion in the Old South*, 113–14; and Journal, 1 Jan. 1858, 31 Dec. 1865. See also 27 July 1856, 25 Dec. 1864, 1 Aug. 1870, 8 Jan., 2 Apr. 1871.

65. Anne C. Loveland, *Southern Evangelicals and the Social Order, 1800–1860* (Baton Rouge: Louisiana State University Press, 1980), 68.

66. Albert J. Raboteau, *Slave Religion: The Invisible Institution in the Antebellum South* (New York: Oxford University Press, 1978), 57–60, 67, 127.

67. 4 July 1864, 3 Sept. 1870, 22 Sept. 1882.

68. 8 Oct. 1848, 9 May 1851, 2 May, 24 June, 12, 22, 25, 27 July 1855.

69. 30 July 1870.

70. In one unusual instance, Thomas records that one of the instructors at Wesleyan, the Reverend Myers, "was very happy and shouted" at a prayer meeting. During that same period, she also mentions children making "a great deal of noise shouting and screaming" in church (9, 13 May 1851).

    See Mathews, *Religion in the Old South*, xvii; and David Edwin Harrell, Jr., "The Evolution of Plain-Folk Religion in the South, 1835–1920," in Samuel S. Hill., ed., *Varieties of Southern Religious Experience* (Baton Rouge: Louisiana State University Press, 1988), 24–33.

71. 10, 15 Apr. 1851, 27 Aug. 1864.

72. 17 May 1855. Whereas women's shouting was acceptable, although unusual, women's speaking in church was questionable. In the former case,
religion presumably overwhelmed the worshiper; in the latter, the woman
addressed men as well as women with authority in a public space.

73. 17 May 1855, 25 Oct., 26 Dec. 1864. The quote is from 13 Dec. 1861.

74. 1 Feb. 1849, 8, 11, 15, 17 Aug. 1851, 25 Apr., 2, 15 May, 12 July 1855, 17
Sept. 1864, 1 Aug., 3 Sept. 1870, 31 Dec. 1879, 15 May 1880, 22 Sept. 1882.
Jeff goes to the altar: 29 Aug. 1870. He has left the church: 17 Aug. 1879.

75. 6 Sept. 1857, 28 Aug. 1861, 12 July 1864, 22 July 1866, 12 Feb. 1871, 6 Sept.
1882. See also Censer, *North Carolina Planters and Their Children*, 18.

76. R. Laurence Moore, *In Search of White Crows: Spiritualism, Parapsychology,
and American Culture* (New York: Oxford University Press, 1977), 3.
Other mid-century Americans fascinated by spiritualism included William
Lloyd Garrison, Harriet Beecher Stowe, Sarah Grimké, Horace Greeley,
Sojourner Truth, and Frances Willard.

77. The writings of the Swedish philosopher Emanuel Swedenborg, who died
in 1772, circulated in the United States in the 1840s and paved the way for
the spiritualist movement of the 1850s. Swedenborg described a series of
spiritual spheres, through which the dead moved steadily farther away
from earth. His views on the ability of the living to communicate with
God, the dead, and other spirits were institutionalized in the American
denomination known as the Church of the New Jerusalem and became
fundamental tenets of American spiritualism. Thomas discovered spiritualism early in the movement's period of greatest influence, roughly 1850–75
(Moore, *In Search of White Crows*, xv, 7, 9–10).

78. 28 Feb. 1857, 15 Apr., 27 Aug., 25 Dec. 1864, 20 Sept. 1869, 27 Jan., 29
Sept., 2 Oct. 1870, 2, 12 Apr. 1871, 16 Nov., 18 Dec. 1879, 1 Jan., 21 Feb.
1880.

79. 27 Aug., 25 Dec. 1864, 14 Oct. 1865, 3 Aug. 1870, 4 Jan. 1887.

80. 15 Apr., 27 Aug. 1864.

81. 27 Aug. 1864, 8 Oct. 1865.

82. 8 Oct. 1865.

83. Ibid. The northern and southern Methodist Episcopal churches had split
over the issue of slavery in 1845.
    Looking back on the antebellum era from a later date, a leading south-
ern Baptist minister, Jeremiah Jeter, wrote that slavery was divinely sanctioned, that Moses had allowed the Israelites to own slaves, and that Jesus
and his apostles had preached on the responsibilities of masters and slaves
(Jeter, *Recollections of a Long Life* [Richmond, Va., 1891], cited in Loveland, *Southern Evangelicals and the Social Order*, 188).

84. 3 Aug. 1870.

85. 20 May 1855, 25 Oct. 1864, 3 Sept. 1870. "Dame Nature": 12 July 1864;
"the dear and gracious Mother": 22 July 1866.

86. 1 Jan. 1859.

87. Not happy to be pregnant: 26 June 1855, 11 June 1856, 29 Dec. 1862. The need to space children: 13 June 1855, 11 June, 26 July 1856, 29 Dec. 1862.

88. See D'Emilio and Freedman, *Intimate Matters*, 57–58.

89. 9 Mar. 1865.

90. 18 Aug. 1856, 20 Jun 1869.

91. On women's role: 16 Sept. 1857, 9 Feb. 1858, 1 Jan. 1859, 4 July 1864, 9 July 1866. On solidarity with other women: 18 Aug. 1856, 4, 12 July, 27 Dec. 1864.

92. E.g., 5 Dec. 1870.

93. On separations: 13 June 1855, 8 Feb. 1858. On divorces: 27 Apr. 1856, 4, 22 Nov. 1858, 14 Mar. 1859, 7 Mar. 1869.

94. Quotes are from 11 Apr. 1855. Other comments on women's inferiority and men's superiority are found in the entries for 9 July 1852 and 1 Jan. 1856.

95. 13 Dec. 1861, 26 June 1869.

96. 23 July 1852, 30 Mar. 1856.

97. On the need for women's purity: 18 Aug. 1856, 16 Sept. 1857, 9 Feb. 1858. On men's depravity: 12 Apr. 1856, 2 Jan. 1859, 7 May 1869. See also Linda Gordon, *Woman's Body, Woman's Right: A Social History of Birth Control in America* (New York: Grossman, 1976), 116–17.

98. See D'Emilio and Freedman, *Intimate Matters*, 152–54. Even though southern Methodists had sponsored temperance organizations as early as the 1820s and 1830s, Thomas did not abstain from consuming or serving wine (itself a source of some controversy) until well after the Civil War.

99. 2 Jan. 1859.

100. 26 Dec. 1858, 16 July 1861, 31 July 1863.

101. E.g., 10 June 1852, 11 Apr. 1855. See also Marli F. Weiner, *Mistresses and Slaves: Plantation Women in South Carolina, 1830–80* (Urbana: University of Illinois Press, 1997), 81–82, 227–229. Janet Cornelius notes that slaveholders monitored slave marriages closely for discipline as well as to show support in "Slave Marriages in a Georgia Congregation," in Orville Vernon Burton and Robert C. McMath, Jr., eds., *Class, Conflict, and Consensus: Antebellum Southern Community Studies* (Westport, Conn.: Greenwood, 1982), 129.

102. The quote is from 12 July 1855. For other examples of slaves as mothers, see 11 Jan. 1855, 11 May, 18 Aug. 1856.

103. Quote is from [n.d., late] Nov. 1857; other, longer entries are 19 Aug. 1855, 13 Jan. 1859. Brief mentions: 8, 11 Apr., 30 May, 24 June, [n.d., early] Nov. 1855.

104. [N.d.] Nov. 1857; 13 Jan. 1859.

105. 25 Oct. 1864, 7 May 1869. In the latter entry, Thomas mentions the Reconstruction-era married women's property bill passed by the Georgia legislature in 1868 and strengthened by the state supreme court in 1869. See Suzanne Lebsock, "Radical Reconstruction and the Property Rights

of Southern Women," *Journal of Southern History* 43, no. 2 (May 1977): 201-2, 209-10.

106. 29 Sept. 1855, 1 Aug. 1870, 21 Dec. 1868, 3, 14 May 1869, 5, 12, 19 Dec. 1870, 8 Jan. 1871.

107. 1 Jan. 1859, 4 July 1864, 16 Sept. 1857.

108. 14, 17 Apr. 1862.

109. 1 Jan. 1859; the quotes are from 9 Mar., 14 Oct. 1865. In the 1830s, another southern diarist and young mother, Sarah Haynsworth Gayle, also rejected the idea of her successor. She asked her husband not to marry again in the event of her death, but she did die young, and he took a second wife (Fox-Genovese, *Within the Plantation Household*, 25-26).

110. 1 Jan. 1859; 3 Jan., 9 Mar., 27 May, 14 Oct. 1865, 7 May 1869, 13 Jan. 1870.

111. 3 Jan. 1865.

112. Ibid. Thomas decided not to send the letter after learning that the Shermans' baby had died.

113. 26 June 1869, 17 Feb. 1871, 24 Nov. 1880.

114. 27 May 1865.

115. 16 Sept. 1866, 7 May 1869.

116. 26 June 1869, 13 Jan. 1870.

117. Quote is from 3 Jan. 1865. See also 12 Oct. 1866.

118. 11 Apr., 24 June 1855.

119. Pierre L. van den Berghe notes that racism of what he calls the "paternalistic" type often seems superficially to resemble economic or social rather than racial discrimination, because the members of the reputedly inferior race are also poor and unschooled. See *Race and Racism: A Comparative Perspective* (New York: J. Wiley, 1967), 27.

120. 12 July 1855. Thomas often ascribes emotion to blacks in settings in which she, herself, has been touched emotionally (see also 2 May 1855, 29 July 1861).

121. 31 July 1863. This entry also speaks of African Americans as "naturally religious."

122. Particularly 18 Sept. 1861, but also 17 Sept. 1866, 30 Dec. 1870.

123. 30 Nov. 1858. Rejects "Ariel" doctrine: 7 May 1869, 30 July 1870.

124. On her own lack of fear: 1 Jan. 1857, 1, 2 Nov. 1868, 10 Apr. 1871. On frightened whites: 1 Jan. 1857, 23 July 1865, 1, 2 Nov. 1868, 10 Apr. 1871. Mt. Vesuvius image: 25 Dec. 1858, 1 Nov. 1868.

125. 12 Feb. 1858.

126. 2 Jan. 1859.

127. 17, 23 Sept. 1864, 26 June 1869. Fredrika Bremer, *The Homes of the New World: Impressions of America*, trans. Mary Howitt (New York: Harper & Brothers, 1853), 1:382; C. Vann Woodward and Elisabeth Muhlenfeld, *The Private Mary Chesnut: The Unpublished Civil War Diaries* (New York: Oxford University Press, 1984), 21 (4 Mar. 1861), 42-43 (18 Mar. 1861).

Catherine Clinton notes that southern aristocrats who objected to slavery because of miscegenation deplored the immorality of the slaves rather than that of the owners. See "Caught in the Web of the Big House," in Walter J. Fraser, Jr., R. Frank Saunders, Jr., and Jon L. Wakelyn, eds., *The Web of Southern Social Relations: Women, Family, and Education* (Athens: University of Georgia Press, 1985), 22.

128. 31 July 1863, 17, 27 May 1865, 1 Nov. 1868, 7 May 1869, 30 July 1870.

129. 17, 23 Sept. 1864; this is the first time that Thomas makes so systematic an attempt to depict what had been the normal antebellum routine. Further purposeful thinking about slavery: 17 Nov., 26 Dec. 1864, 31 Dec. 1865, 4 May 1871.

130. 7, 8, 17 May 1865.

131. 4 May 1871.

132. 12 June 1865. This is an example of what psychologists term reaction formation, in which Thomas cannot admit to any positive feelings and responds by going completely over into hatred, so as to keep her psyche intact in a time of upheaval.

133. 17, 29 May, 12 June 1865, 3 Dec. 1868.

134. 1, 2 Nov. 1868, 14 May 1869.

135. 28 Jan. 1869.

136. Glenda Gilmore, *Gender and Jim Crow: Women and the Politics of White Supremacy in North Carolina, 1896–1920* (Chapel Hill: University of North Carolina Press, 1996), 91–146, and Leon F. Litwack, *Trouble in Mind: Black Southerners in the Age of Jim Crow* (New York: Alfred A. Knopf, 1998), 217–325, describe the phenomenon of successful blacks and the panic they inspired in white southerners in the late nineteenth and early twentieth centuries.

137. 26 June 1869, 30 July 1870.

138. 26 June 1869, emphasis in original.

139. An observer in northern Louisiana also noticed the increased occurrence of mixed unions after the war; see Nell Irvin Painter, *Exodusters: Black Migration to Kansas after Reconstruction* (New York: Alfred A. Knopf, 1976), 73.

140. 2 Jan. 1859, 17, 23 Sept. 1864. The quoted phrase is from 26 June 1869, but Thomas uses virtually the same wording on 13 January 1870.

141. 26 June 1869.

142. See also Marli F. Weiner, *Mistresses and Slaves*, 224–231, 212–215.

143. 11 Apr. 1855, 20 Feb. 1857.

144. As Orlando Patterson points out in *Slavery and Social Death: A Comparative Study* (Cambridge, Mass.: Harvard University Press, 1982), the whole point of slavery is to create a class of people who lack self-interest. Slaves are by definition extensions of their owners' wills.

145. For instance, Mary Boykin Chesnut's housemaid, Mollie, kept herself and

her former mistress in cash with a butter-and-egg business in which Chesnut had invested; see Muhlenfeld, *Mary Boykin Chesnut*, 128.

146. 27, 29 May 1865, 26 June 1869, 14 Dec. 1870, 3, 8 Jan., 4 May 1871.

147. On inexperienced help: 29 May 1865, 21 Dec. 1868, 12 May, 1, 20 June, 20
Sept. 1869, 10 Jan., 7 Feb., 12 Dec. 1870, 2 Jan., 10 Apr., 4 May 1871. On
respect: 17 May 1865, 23 Feb., 7 May, 20 June 1869, 30 Dec. 1870, 1 Feb.
1871, 16 Aug. 1880, 5 Jan. 1881.

148. 19 Dec. 1870.

149. 27, 29 May 1865, 3 Dec. 1868, 1 Aug. 1870.

150. 29 May 1865, 7, 17 May, 1 June 1869.

151. 29 Mar., 26, 29 May 1865, 1 Jan. 1866, 21 Dec. 1868, 20 Sept. 1869, 1
Aug., 30 Nov., 12 Dec. 1870. See also Weiner, *Mistresses and Slaves*, 81–82,
227–229.

152. 10 Apr. 1871.

153. Paul Ekman, "Self-Deception and Detection of Misinformation," in Joan
S. Lockard and Delroy L. Paulhus, *Self-Deception: An Adaptive Mechanism?* (Englewood Cliffs, N.J.: Prentice-Hall, 1988), 231–32.
  Building on Sigmund Freud's observations that individuals provide
nonverbal clues that undermine what they are saying, psychologists have
usually looked for deception clues and leakage in the realm of nonverbal
communication, which, of course, is not available in the present case.
Thomas, however, provides verbal clues and verbal leakage that undermine the conventions she expresses in her writing.

154. Goffman, *Presentation of Self*, 81; Adrienne Rich, *On Lies, Secrets, and
Silence: Selected Prose, 1966–1978* (New York: W. W. Norton, 1979), 188.

155. 4 July 1864.

156. 7 Feb. 1869. Unfortunately, the journal(s) from the difficult years 1871–
78 no longer exist(s). Sue King mentioned the Thackeray incident in
both her published novels, *Lily* (1855) and *Gerald Gray's Wife* (1863).

157. 4 Nov. 1852, 2 June 1855, 26 June 1856, 10 Jan. 1870, 4 November 1852.

158. 11 Apr., 13 June 1855. See also 4 July 1864.

159. See also 12 May 1856, 7 May 1869.

160. 2 Jan. 1859.

161. E.g., Harriet Beecher Stowe, *A Key to Uncle Tom's Cabin: Presenting the
Original Facts and Documents upon Which the Story Was Founded. Together
with Corroborative Statements Verifying the Truth of the Work* (Boston: J. P.
Jewett & Co., 1853), 63, 142–43; L. Maria Child, *An Appeal in Favor of
Americans Called Africans* (originally published 1836; reprint, New York:
Arno Press and the New York Times, 1968), pp. 23–24. Historian Ronald
G. Walters quotes abolitionists who wrote of the antebellum South as
"ONE GREAT SODOM" and of the male slaveowner as one who "totally
annihilates the marriage institution" (Walters, "The Erotic South: Civili-
zation and Sexuality in American Abolitionism," *American Quarterly* 25,

no. 2 [May 1973]: 183, 192). See also James L. Leloudis II, "Subversion of the Feminine Ideal: The *Southern Lady's Companion* and White Male Morality in the Antebellum South, 1847–1854," in Rosemary Skinner Keller, Louise L. Queen, and Hilah F. Thomas, eds., *Women in New Worlds*, vol. 2 (Nashville: Abingdon, 1982), esp. 67–68.

162. Harriet Martineau, *Society in America* (New York, 1837), 2:112, 118; Bremer, *Homes of the New World*, 1:382; Woodward and Muhlenfeld, *Private Mary Chesnut*, 42 (18 Mar. 1861). See also Deborah Gray White, *Ar'n't I a Woman?: Female Slaves in the Plantation South* (New York: W. W. Norton, 1985), 27–47; Clinton, *Plantation Mistress*, 203–4, 210–22; James Hugo Johnston, *Race Relations in Virginia and Miscegenation in the South, 1776–1860* (Amherst: University of Massachusetts Press, 1970), 165–90, 243; Kenneth M. Stampp, *The Peculiar Institution: Slavery in the Ante-Bellum South* (New York: Alfred A. Knopf, 1956), 350–61; Eugene D. Genovese, *Roll, Jordan, Roll: The World the Slaves Made* (New York: Pantheon, 1974), 413–29; Bertram Wyatt-Brown, *Southern Honor: Ethics and Behavior in the Old South* (New York: Oxford University Press, 1982), 307–24; Weiner, *Mistresses and Slaves*, 131–39, 177–90; bell hooks, *Ain't I a Woman?: Black Women and Feminism* (Boston: South End Press, 1981), 26–41; Angela Y. Davis, *Women, Race, and Class* (New York: Random House, 1981), 25–29, 173–77; Fox-Genovese, *Within the Plantation Household*, 325–26.

163. E.g., Harriet A. Jacobs, *Incidents in the Life of a Slave Girl, Written by Herself*, edited by Jean F. Yellin (Cambridge, Mass.: Harvard University Press, 1987). See also James M. McPherson, "The War of Southern Aggression," *New York Review of Books* 35, nos. 21–22 (19 Jan. 1989), 19; Carol Bleser, ed., *Secret and Sacred: The Diaries of James Henry Hammond, a Southern Slaveholder* (New York: Oxford University Press, 1988), xvi.

164. Clinton, *Plantation Mistress*, 213–21.

165. Herbert Fingarette, in his classic *Self-Deception* (London: Routledge & Kegan Paul, 1969), explains the tactic of not spelling out, or hiding, uncomfortable truths (see esp. 43–50). Fingarette's not-spelling-out is analogous to Jean-Paul Sartre's *mauvaise foi*, which is translated as "bad faith," in the context of self-deception. See Sartre, *Being and Nothingness: An Essay on Phenomenological Ontology*, translated by Hazel E. Barnes (New York: Citadel Press, 1967), 47–56.

On the antebellum South's great secret, see also Ann Taves, "Spiritual Purity and Sexual Shame: Religious Themes in the Writings of Harriet Jacobs," *Church History* 56 (1987): 65–66.

The term "toxic" is Annette Lawson's, in *Adultery: An Analysis of Love and Betrayal* (New York: Basic Books, 1988), 12, 30–31, 53. Robert S. Weiss stresses the symbolic meaning of sexual relationships in defining the damage that adultery inflicts in *Marital Separation* (New York: Basic

Books, 1975, 31–33). Frank Pittman prefers "infidelity" to "adultery" but retains the connotations that I have used in connection with adultery; see *Private Lies: Infidelity and the Betrayal of Intimacy* (New York: W. W. Norton, 1989), 20, 53. Mark A. Karpel stresses the shame, guilt, and loss of relational resources, i.e., violation of trust and reciprocity, that secrets cause within families. See "Family Secrets: I. Conceptual and Ethical Issues in the Relational Context," *Family Process* 19, no. 3 (Sept. 1980): 300. See also Judith A. Libow, "Gender and Sex Role Issues as Family Secrets," *Journal of Strategic and Systemic Therapies* 4, no. 2 (1985): 32–33; and Sissela Bok, *Secrets* (New York: Pantheon, 1982), 25, 59–72. A late-twentieth-century southern autobiography by Sallie Bingham reveals the toxic nature of lies in modern family secrets in *Passion and Prejudice: A Family Memoir* (New York: Alfred A. Knopf, 1989).

166. Bleser, *Secret and Sacred*, 170, 234–44, 254–69.

167. Rebeca Latimer Felton (1855–1930), *Country Life in Georgia in the Days of My Youth, also Addresses Before Georgia Legislature Woman's Clubs, Women's Organizations and other Noted Occasions* (Atlanta: Printed for the author, 1919; Arno Press reprint, New York, 1980), 79, 93.

168. See Lawson, *Adultery*, 10, 35, 56–59, 221, 260; Pittman, *Private Lies*, 261, 281; Philip E. Lampe, ed., *Adultery in the United States: Close Encounters of the Sixth (or Seventh) Kind* (Buffalo: Prometheus Books, 1987), 3–9, 13. Sue M. Hall and Philip A. Hall point out that adultery is often cited as a reason for denying child custody to one parent or the other. An adulterer appears to be unfit to care for children and unable to serve the child's best interests ("Law and Adultery," in Lampe, ed., *Adultery in the United States*, 73–75). Thomas discusses parents who own or sell their own children (2 Jan. 1859). See Lillian Smith, *Killers of the Dream*, rev. ed. (New York: W. W. Norton, 1961), 83–89, 121–24.

169. Harriet Jacobs, *Incidents in the Life of a Slave Girl*, Nell Irvin Painter, ed. (New York: Penguin Classics, 2000), 34.

170. Thomas on morality, sex, and slavery: 12 Apr. 1865, 2 Jan. 1859, 17, 23 Sept. 1864, 26 June, 7 May 1869. For Mary Chesnut's comments on the low morals of black women, see Woodward and Muhlenfeld, *Private Mary Chesnut*, 42–43 (18 Mar. 1961).

171. 18 Aug. 1856. See also 9 Feb. 1858, 2 Jan. 1859.
     It is possible that Thomas's opinions about sexually vulnerable slave women and white men's unreliability and lack of morals contributed to her later advocacy of woman suffrage.

172. Thomas often censors herself by ceasing to write about distressing lines of thought, which she calls digressions, investigations of forbidden subjects, or potential harangues (12 May 1856, 9 Feb. 1858, 4 July 1864, 7 Feb., 7 May 1869, 17 Aug. 1879).

173. 1 Jan. 1859, 28 Jan. 1864, 9 Mar., 14 Oct. 1865, 13 Jan. 1870.

## 3. THREE SOUTHERN WOMEN AND FREUD

1. I come to Freud's writing from a direction different from that of the literary critics and most Lacanians. Although Freud's work is the starting place for object relations theory, it, too, would be more useful to me than certain Lacanians (notably Jane Gallop, whose insights are valuable here) if object relations analysts were not so relentlessly focused on the mid-twentieth-century middle class. The family structure that objects relations scholars — such as Nancy Chodorow — envision is strictly nuclear, whereas many nineteenth-century southern families included parental figures not related to children by birth.

2. Caroline [Howard] Gilman, *Recollections of a New England Bride and of a Southern Matron* (new edition, rev.; New York: Putnam & Co., 1852 [*Southern Matron* originally published 1837, *New England Bride*, 1834]). Gilman never mentions owner-ownee sexuality, but she does deplore "*ungovernable passions*" and the "temptations which assail the other sex," 171–72, 183. Abram Kardiner and Lionel Ovesey, *The Mark of Oppression: A Psychological Study of the American Negro* (New York: W. W. Norton, 1951).

3. E.g., Leonore Davidoff, "Class and Gender in Victorian England: The Diaries of Arthur J. Munby and Hannah Cullwick," *Feminist Studies* 5 (Spring 1979), and Maria Ramas, "Freud's Dora, Dora's Hysteria," in Judith L. Newton, Mary P. Ryan, and Judith R. Walkowitz, ed., *Sex and Class in Women's History*, (London: Routledge and Kegan Paul, 1983).

4. Sue Petigru King Bowen, *Lily* (New York, 1855) and Jean Fagan Yellin, *Incidents in the Life of a Slave Girl, Written by Herself, by Harriet A. Jacobs* (Cambridge, Mass.: Harvard University Press, 1987). Although I am aware the controversy surrounding the designation of genre of *Incidents*, I am treating it here as autobiography.

5. Orlando Patterson, *Slavery and Social Death: A Comparative Study* (Cambridge, Mass.: Harvard University Press, 1982), 50, 229, 230, 261.

6. Catherine Clinton, *Fanny Kemble's Civil Wars* (New York: Simon & Schuster, 2000), 124; Catherine Clinton, ed., *Fanny Kemble's Journals* (Cambridge, Mass.: Harvard University Press, 2000), 15, 157–159. Hortense Spillers makes some tantalizing observations in this regard in "Mama's Baby, Papa's Maybe: An American Grammar Book," *Diacritics* 17 (Summer 1987).

7. Susan Petigru King, *Gerald Gray's Wife and Lily: A Novel*, Jane H. Pease and William H. Pease, eds. (Durham: Duke University Press, 1993), vii, xiii–xiv.

8. Jane H. Pease and William H. Pease, *A Family of Women: The Carolina Petigrus in Peace and War* (Chapel Hill: University of North Carolina Press, 1999), 80, 83.

9. King, *Gerald Gray's Wife and Lily*, 6

10. Ibid., 10, 17, 28, 31.

11. Ibid., 45, 57, 64, 116.

12. Ibid., 15–18, 31. "Sallow" served as the favorite characterization of the complexion of poor whites in the nineteenth and twentieth centuries. Although King is not impugning Angelica's social class, she is using a word full of negative connotations.

13. Ibid., 18, 31, 127. King (Bowen), *Lily*, 206, 227–28. W. J. Cash also utilizes Spanishness to hint at the blackness within white southerners. See W. J. Cash, *The Mind of the South* (New York: Alfred A. Knopf, 1941), 25.

14. King, *Gerald Gray's Wife and Lily*, 37, 53, 55, 110.

15. Ibid., 196.

16. Ibid., 160–61.

17. Pease and Pease introduction to King, *Gerald Gray's Wife and Lily*, xii–xiii.

18. Pease and Pease, *A Family of Women*, 71–86. Rebeca Latimer Felton, *Country Life in Georgia in the Days of My Youth, also Addresses Before Georgia Legislature Woman's Clubs, Women's Organizations and Other Noted Occasions* (Atlanta: Printed for the author, 1919; Arno Press reprint, New York, 1980), 147, 153–55, 266–67, 280–82.

19. King, *Gerald Gray's Wife and Lily*, 172–73.

20. King (Bowen), *Lily*, 278. *Sigmund Freud: Collected Papers*, trans. Joan Riviere (New York: International Psycho-analytical Press, 1959), 4, 207, 210–211.

21. For a longer introduction to Harriet Jacobs stressing themes of family and sexuality, see Harriet A. Jacobs, *Incidents in the Life of a Slave Girl Written by Herself*, ed. Nell Irvin Painter (New York: Penguin Classics, 2000).

22. Ibid., 4.

23. Ibid., 57.

24. Yellin, ed., *Incidents in the Life of a Slave Girl*, by Harriet A. Jacobs, 27–28, 33.

25. Ibid., 37.

26. Moses Roper, *A Narrative of the Adventures and Escape of Moses Roper from American Slavery*, 5th ed. (1843), 9–10, quoted in Frances Smith Foster, *Witnessing Slavery: The Development of Antebellum Slave Narratives* (Westport, Conn., 1979), 78; and Frederick Douglass, *Narrative of the Life of Frederick Douglass an American Slave* (1845), 4, quoted in Foster, *Witnessing Slavery*, 79. Clinton, ed., *Fanny Kemble's Journals*, 15, 158–159.

27. Painter, ed., *Incidents in the Life of a Slave Girl*, 58.

28. See Jane Gallop, "Keys to Dora," in *The Daughter's Seduction: Feminism and Psychoanalysis* (Ithaca, N.Y.: Cornell University Press, 1982), 137, 141–145, 147; Elisabeth Young-Bruehl, ed., *Freud on Women: A Reader* (New York: W. W. Norton, 1990); Jim Swan, "Mater and Nannie: Freud's Two Mothers," *America Imago* 31, no. 1 (Spring 1974); Hannah S. Decker, *Freud, Dora, and Vienna 1900* (New York: Free Press, 1991); Maria Ramas,

"Freud's Dora, Dora's Hysteria," in Newton et al., eds., *Sex and Class in Women's History*; and Mary Poovey, "The Anathematized Race: The Governess and *Jane Eyre*," in *Uneven Developments: The Ideological Work of Gender in Mid-Victorian England* (Chicago: University of Chicago Press, 1988).

29. Jeffrey Moussaieff Masson, *The Complete Letters of Sigmund Freud to Wilhelm Fliess, 1887–1904* (Cambridge, Mass.: Harvard University Press, 1985), 241.

30. Decker, *Freud, Dora, and Vienna 1900*, 109.

31. See also Freud's "'Civilized' Sexual Morality and Modern Nervous Illness" (1908) and *Civilization and Its Discontents* (1930), in which he surveyed what he saw as the psychosexual dysfunctions associated with civilization. In "'Civilized' Sexual Morality" Freud makes some observations that might be useful in southern history: "In her [the girl's] mental feelings [as she marries] she is still attached to her parents, whose authority has brought about the suppression of her sexuality; and in her physical behaviour she shows herself frigid, which deprives the man of any high degree of sexual enjoyment. I do not know whether the anaesthetic type of woman exists apart from civilized education, though I consider it probable. But in any case, such education actually breeds it. . . . In this way, the preparation for marriage frustrates the aims of marriage itself." In Young-Bruehl, ed., *Freud on Women*, 176.

32. Deborah Gray White, *Ar'n't I a Woman? Female Slaves in the Plantation South* (New York: W. W. Norton, 1985), 15–17, 27–28, 58.

33. Catherine Clinton, *The Plantation Mistress: Woman's World in the Old South* (New York: Pantheon, 1983), 6–15, 35, 222.

34. Elizabeth Fox-Genovese, *Within the Plantation Household: Black and White Women of the Old South* (Chapel Hill: University of North Carolina Press, 1988), 29–30, 34–35, 43–45, 63–64, 313–315.

35. "Caught in the Web of the Big House: Women and Slavery," in Walter J. Fraser Jr., ed., *The Web of Southern Social Relations: Women, Family, and Education*, R. Frank Saunders Jr., and Jon L. Wakelyn, (Athens: University of Georgia Press, 1985), 19–34; "'Southern Dishonor': Flesh, Blood, Race, and Bondage," in Carol Bleser, ed., *In Joy and in Sorrow: Women, Family, and Marriage in the Victorian South, 1830–1900*, (New York: Oxford University Press, 1991), 52–68; Eugene Genovese, "'Our Family, White and Black': Family and Household in the Southern Slaveholders' World View," in Bleser, ed., *In Joy and in Sorrow*, 69–87, grasps the reality of slaveholders' ideology of the family almost as though to substitute it for reality and without following its significance in family relations.

36. Mary Frances Berry, "Judging Morality: Sexual Behavior and Legal Consequences in the Late Nineteenth-Century South," *Journal of American History* 78 (December 1991): 835–56; Martha Hodes, *White Women, Black Men : Illicit Sex in the Nineteenth-Century South* (New Haven: Yale Uni-

versity Press, 1997); *Sex, Love, Race : Crossing Boundaries in North American History*, Martha Hodes, ed. (New York: New York University Press, 1999).

## 4. "SOCIAL EQUALITY" AND "RAPE" IN THE FIN-DE-SIÈCLE SOUTH

I would like to acknowledge the support of the Russell Sage Foundation, Nellie McKay, Mary Kelley, George Shulman, Orlando Patterson, and the New School CSSC and CHS "Think, Then Drink" Seminar.

1. See Pete Daniel, "The Metamorphosis of Slavery, 1865–1900," *Journal of American History* 66 (June 1979); Harold D. Woodman, "Postbellum Social Change and Its Effect on Marketing the South's Cotton Crop," *Agricultural History* 56 (January 1982): 215–30; and "Sequel to Slavery: The New History Views the Postbellum South," *Journal of Southern History* 43 (November 1977): 523–24.
2. Pete Daniel, "The Metamorphosis of Slavery," 95.
3. Joel Williamson, *The Crucible of Race: Black-White Relations in the American South Since Emancipation* (New York: Oxford University Press, 1984), 522.
4. For a comprehensive discussion of the political and economic changes wrought by Reconstruction, see Eric Foner, *Reconstruction: America's Unfinished Revolution, 1863–1877* (New York: Harper & Row, 1988), esp. pp. 346–411.
5. Edmund S. Morgan, *American Slavery, American Freedom: The Ordeal of Colonial Virginia* (New York: W. W. Norton, 1975), 295–337.
6. Myrta Lockett Avary, *Dixie after the War: An Exposition of Social Conditions Existing in the South, during the Twelve Years Succeeding the Fall of Richmond* (New York: Doubleday, Page & Company, 1906), 394.
7. My attention to sex and the psychological aspects of white supremacy and southern identity separate me from the position of Barbara J. Fields, who sees race as "ideological." She sees white supremacy as "a slogan, not a belief." I see it as a very deep belief, rooted in sex and personal, gendered identity. See Fields, "Ideology and Race in American History," in *Region, Race, and Reconstruction: Essays in Honor of C. Vann Woodward*, J. Morgan Kousser and James M. McPherson, eds. (New York: Oxford University Press, 1982), 151, 156, 158.
8. I do not mean to say, however, that racial violence and white supremacy were more acute at the turn of the twentieth century than at any other time following the institution of slavery in the South. Slavery itself was a brutal system, resting on violence and threats of violence, but there is no way of counting up how many men and women were beaten and how many women were raped in slavery. It is also not possible to know how many

blacks were the victims of rioters and lynchers before the Chicago *Inter-Ocean*, National Association for the Advancement of Colored People, and Tuskegee Institute began keeping lynching statistics in the late nineteenth and early twentieth centuries. My reading of congressional testimony indicates that the level of bloodshed was exceedingly high in the 1860s and 1870s. Lacking evidence to draw any but the most general conclusions about violence against blacks before the 1880s, I use turn-of-the-century rhetoric and violence as examples because the evidence is close at hand. I do see racial violence declining after the First World War, however, for reasons I explain at the end of the essay.

9.  In the 1850s Republicans in Louisiana exempted items of subsistence (bacon, corn) from debt seizure. In South Carolina in 1876 the knowledge that his constituency was poor agricultural workers prevented the Republican governor from sending troops to force striking rice workers back to work. In neighboring Georgia, the Democratic governor felt no such pressure, as black Republican voters no longer played a prominent part in the politics of that state.

I should add here that although blacks have suffered the most extreme disfranchisement, other blocs and coalitions of voters seeking to express the interests of the poor also have not lasted in this country. In the late nineteenth century, neither the Farmers' Alliances, Knights of Labor, or People's Party was able to translate class-based issues into durable political gains. Like other groups who expressed themselves politically as working people, the masses of black southerners lost their voice in politics.

10.  On the use of sex in post-war southern politics, see Jane Dailey, *Before Jim Crow : The Politics of Race in Postemancipation Virginia* (Chapel Hill: University of North Carolina Press, 2000), and Laura F. Edwards, *Gendered Strife and Confusion: The Political Culture of Reconstruction* (Urbana: University of Illinois Press, 1997).

11.  See Crystal N. Feimster, *Ladies and Lynching: The Gendered Discourse of Mob Violence in the New South, 1880–1930* (Ph.D. diss., Princeton University, 2000), 45–106.

12.  Orlando Patterson, *Slavery and Social Death: A Comparative Study* (Cambridge, Mass.: Harvard University Press, 1982), 261, points out that in the antebellum South, as in every other slave society, masters claimed the right to have sex with their female slaves.

13.  Rebeca Latimer Felton, *Country Life in Georgia in the Days of My Youth, Also Addresses Before Georgia Legislature Woman's Clubs, Women's Organizations and Other Noted Occasions* (Atlanta: Printed for the author, 1919; Arno Press reprint, New York, 1980), 79.

14.  Lillian Smith, *Killers of the Dream*, rev. ed. (New York: W. W. Norton, 1961), 121.

15.  See Stephen Kantrowitz, *Ben Tillman & the Reconstruction of White Supremacy* (Chapel Hill: University of North Carolina Press, 2000).

16. Josephus Daniels, *Editor in Politics* (Chapel Hill: University of North Carolina Press, 1941), 302.

17. Quoted in C. Vann Woodward, *Tom Watson, Agrarian Rebel* (New York: Oxford University Press, 1963 [1938]), 379.

18. Ray Stannard Baker, *Following the Color Line* (New York: Harper and Row, 1964 [1908]), 5.

19. One interesting case occurred in Murray County, Georgia, in 1893, when a band of eighty white men broke into jail and freed a white man convicted of raping a white woman. See Edward L. Ayers, *Vengeance and Justice: Crime and Punishment in the Nineteenth-Century American South* (New York: Oxford University Press, 1984), 259. For a thorough discussion of southern lynching of all sorts, see Stewart E. Tolnay and E. M. Beck, *A Festival of Violence: an Analysis of Southern Lynchings, 1882–1930* (Urbana: University of Illinois Press, 1995); W. Fitzhugh Brundage, *Lynching in the New South: Georgia and Virginia, 1880–1930* (Urbana: University of Illinois Press, 1993); and William Pickens, *Lynching and Debt-Slavery* (New York: American Civil Liberties Union, 1921).

20. For example, see Baker, *Following the Color Line*, 180, 186–87. It is difficult to draw a line between riots and lynching beyond the following two distinctions: riots occurred in urban areas, lynching mostly in the countryside; and riots rarely claimed that their many victims were the actual perpetrators of the supposed crimes that had touched off the riots in the first place. Lynchings had one or rarely two victims who were alleged to be connected to specific criminal acts, real or imagined. Otherwise my generalizations here about riots also apply to lynching, which was an aspect of the same phenomenon.

21. Lillian Smith, *Strange Fruit* (New York: Reynal and Hitchcock, 1944) and *Killers of the Dream*, rev. ed. (New York: W. W. Norton, 1961), 92, 144; Walter White, *The Fire in the Flint* (New York: Alfred A. Knopf, 1924) and *Flight* (New York: Alfred A. Knopf, 1926); Richard Wright, *Black Boy: A Record of Childhood and Youth* (New York: Harper and Row, 1945), 30–33; *Uncle Tom's Children* (New York: Cleveland the World Pub. Co., 1938); and interviews with Katherine Du Pre Lumpkin and Maya Angelou.

22. Ayers, *Vengeance and Justice*, 231, and Susan Brownmiller, *Against Our Will: Men, Women and Rape* (New York: Simon and Schuster, 1975), 216.

23. Baker, *Following the Color Line*, 15.

24. Ida B. Wells, *On Lynchings: Southern Horrors, A Red Record, Mob Rule in New Orleans* (Salem, N.H.: Ayer, 1993 [1895]); *A Red Record*, 16–19.

25. Ida B. Wells, *On Lynchings*, 14; Baker, *Following the Color Line*, 199.

26. Charles Manigault Memoranda, Manigault Papers, Southern Historical Collection, University of North Carolina at Chapel Hill (emphasis and erratic capitalization in the original).

27. Unwittingly Dixon (and other white supremacists and Anglo-Saxonists of the turn of the twentieth century) were tapping into stereotypes that had

been circulating since antebellum times and had done service against the Irish in the North. See Dale T. Knobel, *Paddy and the Republic: Ethnicity and Nationality in Antebellum America* (Middletown, Conn.: Wesleyan University Press, 1986), 32 and illustrations following 156.

28. Abolitionists also associated sexuality with women of mixed race, notably the famous fugitive Ellen Craft. See R. J. M. Blackett, *Beating Against the Barriers: Biographical Essays in Nineteenth-Century Afro-American History* (Baton Rouge: Louisiana State University Press, 1986), 98.

29. Avary, *Dixie after the War*, 197–98.

30. Alfred Holt Stone, *Studies in the American Race Problem* (New York: Doubleday, Page and Co., 1908), 431–35.

31. See Bertram Wyatt-Brown, *Southern Honor: Ethics and Behavior in the Old South* (New York: Oxford University Press, 1982), pp. 315–316, on miscegenation. White women intimate with black men had "defective notions of their social position," and "the blacks in question were unusually gifted — and good — lovers, whom a white man might well envy." Joel Williamson also sets the blame for race mixing on poor whites. See *New People: Miscegenation and Mulattoes in the United States* (New York: Free Press, 1980), 103–109.

32. Brownmiller, *Against Our Will*, 22–23, 124, chapters 3 and 4.

33. Kathy Peiss, "'Charity Girls' and City Pleasures: Historical Notes on Working-Class Sexuality, 1880–1920," in Ann Snitow, Christine Stansell, and Sharon Thompson, eds., *Powers of Desire: The Politics of Sexuality*, (New York: Monthly Review Press, 1983), 77, 83.

34. Quoted in Frances Foster, "'In Respect to Females . . .': Differences in the Portrayals of Women by Male and Female Narrators," *Black Literature Forum* 15 (Summer 1982): 67. Although the vulnerability of slave women to sexual assault from masters is a common source of resentment in slave narratives, William Craft, married to a woman who looked white and who therefore reminded British and American whites of the sexual abuse in slavery, had a personal motive for stressing this evil. See also Fanny Kemble's similar remarks regarding slave masters' abuse of slave women in Brownmiller, *Against Our Will*, 166.

35. Jacquelyn Dowd Hall, "'The Mind That Burns in Each Body': Women, Rape, and Racial Violence," in Snitow, Stansell, and Thompson, eds., *Powers of Desire*, 339, and *Revolt against Chivalry: Jessie Daniel Ames and the Women's Campaign against Lynching* (New York: Columbia University Press, 1979), 153, 194–96.

36. Susan Griffin, *Pornography and Silence: Culture's Revenge Against Nature* (New York: Harper and Row, 1981), 2, 15, 22, 46–47, 79. For a grisly pictorial record of such sadism, see James Allen, ed., *Without Sanctuary: Lynching Photography in America* (Santa Fe: Twin Palms, 2000).

37. See Wyatt-Brown, *Southern Honor*, pp. 458–461.

38. Although lynching no longer occurs with late nineteenth- and early

twentieth-century frequency, the practice has not ended, as events in Mobile, Alabama, in 1981, Howard Beach, New York City, in 1986, and Missoula, Montana, and Jasper, Texas, in 1998 indicate.

39. Williamson, *Crucible of Race*, 511–522. See also 180–233 and 224–258.

## 5. HOSEA HUDSON

Thanks to James E. Jackson and Herbert Aptheker for contributing information on the recent history of the Communist Party, and to Stewart Davenport for research assistance.

1. Autobiographical manuscript in Hosea Hudson's possession. This manuscript formed part of the basis for Hudson's *Black Worker in the Deep South* (New York, 1972); henceforth cited as Hudson MS, 1965.

2. Hudson MS, 1965, and Hudson-Painter tapes. The tapes are available to scholars at the Southern Historical Collection of the University of North Carolina at Chapel Hill. Unless otherwise indicated, all further unpublished Hudson quotations are from these tapes.

3. This listing of the family's moves from plantation to plantation, within a circle about 30 miles in diameter, is based on Hudson's memory. He has related the sequence to me more than once, and is consistent. I repeat it for what it shows both about Hudson and about the vicissitudes of black southern life at the time.

   Wilkes and Oglethorpe counties are located in northeastern Georgia, close to the Savannah River dividing Georgia and South Carolina, and roughly stretching between Athens and Augusta. Birmingham, Alabama, is almost a straight line to the west from Wilkes County, passing through Atlanta, a distance of some 105 miles.

4. Hudson MS, 1965.

5. James D. Vaughn Music Publishers (Lawrenceburg, Tennessee, 1946). Vaughn published shape-note songbooks between 1923 and 1946, at 35 cents a copy.

6. I have named the notes here according to Hudson's 1946 songbook. Hudson says he begins with fa at middle C.

   Today shape-note songbooks are written by both black and white composers for a market that is also black and white. The publishing houses are located in the South, several in Tennessee, and each house brings out at least one new shape-note songbook a year. In the best days of shape-note singing, between the end of the nineteenth century and the First World War, shape-note songbooks poured out of the publishers to a public that held singing contests, or "conventions," four times a year. Information from Joel Brett Sutton, "The Gospel Hymn, Shaped Notes, and the Black Tradition: Continuity and Change in American Traditional Music" (M.A.

NOTES TO PAGES 147–48 225

thesis, University of North Carolina, 1976). I am grateful to Sutton's adviser, Daniel W. Patterson, for bringing this thesis to my attention and for sharing with me his insights into southern Baptist life.

7. In March 1978, shortly before his death, Al Murphy wrote me a long autobiographical letter. This material comes from 7–9.

The meeting Murphy attended was held on 21 July 1930, at 2131 24th Court, North. Joe Carr was the organizer who addressed the meeting. On 25 July, a follow-up meeting was held at the same address for those who had joined on the 21st. Technically these were meetings of the Trade Union Unity League, which was closely related to the CP. *Investigation of Communist Propaganda. Hearings Before a Special Committee to Investigate Communist Activities in the United States of the House of Representatives*, 71st Congress, 2nd session, pt. 6, vol. 1, 96; henceforth cited as *Investigation of Communist Propaganda*. This committee spent one day each in Chattanooga, Birmingham, Atlanta, New Orleans, and Memphis, and in several northern and western cities. The committee sat in Birmingham on 14 November 1930. Only in Atlanta and New Orleans in the South did Negroes give testimony.

8. Ibid., 8.

9. The only participant's account of the adoption of the self-determination position at the Sixth Comintern Congress in 1928 is Harry Haywood's. According to Haywood, Lenin had written of Afro-Americans as an "oppressed nation" as early as 1917, but the process that actually led to the policy adopted in 1928 began with a visit to the United States by Haywood's friend Nasanov—evidently his whole name—in 1927. On his return to Moscow, where Haywood was a student, Nasanov spoke of Negroes as a nation with a need for self-determination. Haywood found the idea "far-fetched."

Early in 1928 a special subcommittee of the Anglo-American Secretariat of the Comintern was formed to prepare a report on blacks in the United States and South Africa. The six members were Nasanov, four American Negro students in Moscow, and one white American student in Moscow, plus two white American ex-officio members. After several long discussions, Haywood saw the correctness of Nasanov's position. But the rest of the subcommittee was not convinced. Otto Hall, Haywood's brother and also a member of the subcommittee, was implacably opposed to the "oppressed nation" and "self-determination" formula. The subcommittee reached no agreement, and the Negro question was debated in committee and on the floor at the Sixth Comintern Congress in the summer of 1928.

Haywood was the only black supporting the self-determination policy in the sixth congress as a whole and in the Negro Commission (a subcommittee of the Colonial Commission). "The strongest opposition to the self-determination thesis . . . was from the Black comrades James Ford and Otto Hall," Haywood says. Nonetheless, the position was ultimately adopted. Haywood says that it marked "a revolutionary turning point in the treatment of the Afro-American question." Harry Haywood [Haywood Hall], *Black Bolshevik, The Autobiography of an Afro-American Communist* (Chicago, 1978), 218–280.

10. James S. Allen [Sol Auerbach], *The Negro Question in the United States* (New York, 1936), 178–193. Allen taught briefly at the University of Pennsylvania before going South to edit the Chattanooga weekly *Southern Worker* in 1930. Although two other whites, Robert Minor and Robert Dunne, carried more weight in Party deliberations on the Negro question, Allen published widely on the subject. His two pamphlets, *The American Negro* (New York, 1932) and *Negro Liberation* (New York, 1932), and his book, *The Negro Question in the United States* (New York, 1936), set forth the CP position on the national question and self-determination for the Black Belt.

11. Robert Alperin, "Organization of the CPUSA, 1931–1938," dissertation, Northwestern University, 1959, 60, cited in Harvey Klehr, *Communist Cadre: The Social Background of the American Communist Party Elite* (Stanford, Calif., 1978), 80–81; Horace R. Cayton and George S. Mitchell, *Black Workers and the New Unions* (Chapel Hill, N.C., 1939), p. 338; Nathan Glazer, *The Social Basis of American Communism* (New York, 1961), p. 174.

12. The NAACP's branches have been virtually all-black since the 1920s. During the association's early period, in the 1910s, the officers were all white, with the exception of W. E. B. Du Bois. The tradition of white presidents continues. That means that in the 1930s, the NAACP was interracial only on the highest levels. Members of local branches knew it as a Negro organization.

13. In his 29 June 1977 interview with me in New York City, Aptheker noted that a black and a white walking together in the streets of New York in the 1940s were assumed to be Communists. No one else met across the color line. In *A Fine Old Conflict* (New York, 1977), Mitford wrote that FBI agents, "seeking evidence of Communist affiliation, would routinely ask a suspect's neighbors and co-workers, 'Do Negroes visit their home for meetings or social gatherings?'" (134). Genovese says that FBI agents asked the same of his acquaintances in the 1950s.

14. Even the FBI took cognizance of Hudson's growth in its way, noting the contrast between Hudson as he looked in 1934, when he was photographed in a Philadelphia jail, and his appearance in 1947. The informant found Hudson "a more polished and wideawake negro now." U.S. Department of Justice, FBI, Bureau File #100-24584, Dallas office to Director, 25 March 1947.

15. Letter from Hudson to me, Atlantic City, 26 January 1978.

16. Hudson had broken his leg in a motorcycle accident on his way to work. The Bible citation is actually from Ephesians 6:5–6.

17. Harvey Klehr writes that black leaders in the CP "were far less likely to leave the CPUSA by either resignation or expulsion than whites . . . blacks were

relatively unaffected by the major organizational schisms of the CPUSA. . . . Several blacks did leave the CPUSA at various times as a result of specifically racial issues. All — two were prominent figures, Angelo Herndon and Harry Haywood — were accused by the CPUSA of being black nationalists or ultra-leftists . . . there were far fewer opportunities of any kind for blacks in American society and this deterrent may have convinced some that their future outside the CPUSA was even dimmer than inside." Klehr, *Communist Cadre*, 91–92.

The only black ex-communist Vivian Gornick interviewed, whom she called "Hugh Armstrong" in her book, says he left the Party after Khrushchev's report on Stalin in 1956, which seemed to negate years of being patronized by white Communists: "All those years I always felt I wasn't being listened to as seriously as a white [section organizer] . . . it was never anything I could actually put my finger on, just a feeling that never left me." Vivian Gornick, *The Romance of American Communism* (New York, 1977), pp. 164–165.

18. A long-time black Communist and leader of the Southern Negro Youth Congress, Edward Strong died of leukemia in 1956. He was a member of the national committee of the CPUSA.

19. An example of this interpretation is James Weinstein's *Ambiguous Legacy: The Left in American Politics* (New York, 1975), which dismisses the "third period" for its policy of lumping liberals with fascists under the rubric "social fascists." Weinstein overlooks entirely the third period's push into the South and its attracting large numbers of black members for the first time. "The results of the Third Period," he says, "were horrendous" (43).

20. Hudson is much opposed to my mention of Haywood in his book, and he asked me to insert this statement of opposition to Haywood and his present politics: "I wants to make it clear to readers and friends that I take responsibility only for what I have to say on the Negro question. In particular, I differ with Harry Haywood and other black ex-Communist Party members, and their writings on the Negro question and position as I interpret it. [Nell Painter's] comments and interpretations on the question in reference to Harry Haywood and some of these other Negro ex-Communist Party member writers' positions are solely [hers], in [her] rights as [she] and I agreed to. I hope that I have made my position very clear and understood by all concerned." Letter from Hudson to me, Atlantic City, 21 September 1978.

21. Letter from Hudson to me, Atlantic City, 26 January 1978.


6. SEXUALITY AND POWER IN *THE MIND OF THE SOUTH*

1. "The Mind of the South" appeared initially in the October 1929 issue of the *American Mercury*. It is reprinted in Joseph L. Morrison, *W. J. Cash*,

*Southern Prophet: A Biography and a Reader* (New York, 1967), 182–92. In this essay, Cash writes that "the slaves spent most of their lives on their backsides, as their progeny do to this day" and that "the Southerner" is in a "perpetual sweat about the nigger" (183–84). The Knopfs also published many of the writers of the Harlem Renaissance, which would indicate that they saw a market for varying, even conflicting, expressions of opinion.

2. Lillian Smith claimed to have persuaded Knopf to reprint *The Mind of the South*, which became a steady seller in paperback in the 1960s (Smith to George Brockway, July 3, 1965, in *"How Am I to Be Heard?": Selected Letters of Lillian Smith*, ed. Rose Gladney [Chapel Hill, 1993]).

3. C. Vann Woodward, "The Elusive Mind of the South," in Woodward, *American Counterpoint: Slavery and Racism in the North-South Dialogue* (Boston, 1971), 261–84; Michael O'Brien, "A Private Passion: W. J. Cash," in O'Brien, *Rethinking the South: Essays in Intellectual History* (Baltimore, 1988), 179–89; Eugene D. Genovese, *The World the Slaveholders Made* (New York, 1970), 137–50. A far too generous analysis is found in Richard King, *A Southern Renaissance: The Cultural Awakening of the American South, 1930–1955* (New York, 1980), 146–72.

4. King, *Southern Renaissance*, 146, 163.

5. Wilbur J. Cash, *Mind of the South* (New York, 1941), 38–41, 43.

6. Lillian Smith said that *The Mind of the South* lacked "in-depth probing" (Smith to George Brockway, July 3, 1965, in *"How Am I to Be Heard?,"* ed. Gladney). In his prison notebooks, Antonio Gramsci distinguishes between the fragmented, contradictory, uncritical, and unconscious way that most people perceive the world, which he terms "common sense," and the thoughtful, critical, self-conscious approach to the world that he terms "good sense." Common sense includes all of a society's unexamined prejudices. See Quintin Hoare and Geoffrey Nowell Smith, eds. and trans., *Selections from the Prison Notebooks of Antonio Gramsci* (New York, 1971), 322, 325, 396, 419, 423. See also Stuart Hall, "Gramsci's Relevance for the Study of Race and Ethnicity," *Journal of Communication Inquiry*, X (Summer 1986), 20–21.

7. Cash, *Mind of the South*, 98, 112, 115, 371.

8. Ibid., 394, 429, 435.

9. Ibid., x.

10. Ibid., 265, 285, 382, 414.

11. Woodward, "The Elusive Mind of the South," 271–75.

12. Cash, *Mind of the South*, 31, 40, 64, 71, 86, 129, 136, 337, 387.

13. Morrison, *Cash*, 44; Bruce Clayton, *W. J. Cash: A Life* (Baton Rouge, 1991), 58, 60, 66, 78, 86, 93, 198–99, 206; Bruce Clayton, "A Southern Modernist: The Mind of W. J. Cash," in John Salmond and Bruce Clayton, eds., *The South Is Another Land* (Westport, Conn., 1987), 177.

14. Sigmund Freud, *Civilization and Its Discontents*, ed. and trans. James Strachey (New York, 1961), 91.

15. Bruno Bettelheim, *Freud and Man's Soul* (New York, 1983), xi, 12, 73, 32–33; King, *Southern Renaissance*, 164.

16. This essay is sometimes anthologized under the title "The Most Prevalent Form of Degradation in Erotic Life."

17. Sigmund Freud, "On the Universal Tendency to Debasement in the Sphere of Love," in Freud, *Collected Papers*, authorized translation under the supervision of Joan Riviere (New York, 1959), iv, 203, 207, 210; Cash, *Mind of the South*, 86–88.

18. Freud, "On the Universal Tendency to Debasement in the Sphere of Love," 207, 210–11. See also Cash, *Mind of the South*, 86.

19. Morrison, *Cash*, 38–39, 42, 46, 56, 108–109.

20. Smith to George Brockway, July 3, 1965, in *"How Am I to Be Heard?,"* ed. Gladney. Morrison says that Cash had a "particular brand of woman worship" and that he "harbored a strong Victorian streak" (*Cash*, 46, 52).

21. Cash, *Mind of the South*, 338–39.

22. Interestingly enough, Cash uses "black" to modify the plural "bellboys," even though elsewhere he usually speaks of "the Negro." This use of the plural may indicate a stepping out of abstraction and into the memory of actual people and events.

23. Cash, *Mind of the South*, 319.

24. Freud, *Civilization and Its Discontents*, ed. and trans. Strachey, 91.

25. See Jane Gallop, *The Daughter's Seduction: Feminism and Psychoanalysis* (Ithaca, 1982); Elisabeth Young-Bruehl, ed., *Freud on Women: A Reader* (New York, 1990); Mary Poovey, *Uneven Developments: The Ideological Work of Gender in Mid-Victorian England* (Chicago, 1988); Jane Flax, *Thinking Fragments: Psychoanalysis, Feminism, and Postmodernism in the Contemporary West* (Berkeley, 1990); Nancy J. Chodorow, *Feminism and Psychoanalytic Theory* (New Haven, 1989); Richard Feldstein and Judith Roof, eds., *Feminism and Psychoanalysis* (Ithaca, 1989).

26. E.g., Judith Butler, *Bodies That Matter: On the Discursive Limits of "Sex"* (New York, 1993); Mary Douglas, *Purity and Danger* (New York, 1966); Joan Scott, "Gender: A Useful Category of Historical Analysis," *American Historical Review* 91 (December 1986): 1053–75; Lynn Hunt, ed., *Eroticism and the Body Politic* (Baltimore, 1991); Michel Foucault, *The History of Sexuality: Volume 1: An Introduction*, trans. Robert Hurley (New York, 1978). Foucault speaks of sexuality as "an especially dense transfer point for relations of power" (103).

27. Cash, *Mind of the South*, 56, 87–89.

28. Ibid., 87.

29. Ibid., 245–56, 260.

30. Ibid., 88–89.

31. Ibid., 40.

32. Ibid., vii, 38, 51, 68, 132, 171.

33. Ibid., 325–27.

34. Ibid., 232. Charles Manigault also named his imaginary free black man Cuffy.

35. Ibid., 116.

36. Morrison, *Cash*, 173; Woodward, "The Elusive Mind of the South," 261; King, *Southern Renaissance*, 159, 165–66.

37. Cash, *Mind of the South*, 5–8, 11–14, 64–66, 70–81.

38. Ibid., 15–17, 77–79, 235–40.

39. Ibid., 27–29.

40. Ibid., 160, 170–72, 175–76.

41. Ibid., 175–76, 204–205, 279, 289, 295–99.

42. Ibid., 281.

43. Cash describes the hedonistic antebellum "common white" on pages 43–48, 52, 69–70, and the hedonistic "mill worker," on pages 249–50, 281. His description of the mill workers' Saturday night is on page 296: "maybe to have a drink, maybe to get drunk, to laugh with passing girls, to pick them up if you had a car, or to go swaggering or hesitating into the hotels with their corridors saturated with the smell of bichloride of mercury, or the secret, steamy bawdy houses; maybe to have a fight, maybe with knives or guns, maybe against the cops; maybe to end whooping and singing, maybe bloody and goddamning, in the jailhouse — it was more and more in the dream and reality of such excursions that the old romantic-hedonistic impulses found egress."

44. White supremacy defeated interracial working-class-farmer cooperation in Virginia in the early 1880s and in North Carolina in the late 1890s. Similar tactics helped disfranchise blacks in Georgia in 1906, and they succeed in winning elections to this very day.

45. Cash, *Mind of the South*, 428–29.

46. Ibid., 51, 56, 58.

47. Ibid., 418–20, 424–27, 438.

48. "They [the mill workers] had always met the narrow social contempt which the South visited upon them" (ibid., 399).

49. Ibid., 88.

50. Ibid., 68.

51. Ibid., 141–42.

52. Ibid., 177–79.

53. Ibid., 140–41.

# ACKNOWLEDGMENTS

I would like to thank Samuel K. Roberts Jr. and Malinda Alaine Lindquist for research assistance in preparing this volume. Thadious M. Davis and Linda K. Kerber midwifed this book into print. I thank Thadious Davis for ever-sustaining friendship. She and Carl Schorske gave the introduction thoughtful readings that I very much appreciate. My thanks also go to Elaine Wise, for so many kinds of help during the 1990s.

The following publishers have given permission for republication of material originally appearing under their imprints:

Baylor University Press for permission to reprint *Soul Murder and Slavery*.

"Introduction" from *The Secret Eye: The Journal of Ella Gertrude Clanton Thomas, 1848–1889* edited by Virginia Ingraham Burr. Copyright © by Virginia Ingraham Burr and Gertrude T. Despeaux. Used by permission of the University of North Carolina Press and the author.

"Soul Murder and Slavery" from *U.S. History as Women's History: New Feminist Essays* edited by Linda K. Kerber, Alice Kessler-Harris, and Kathryn Kish Sklar. Copyright © 1995 by the University of North Carolina Press. Used by permission of the publisher and the author.

"Preface to the 1994 Edition" of *Narrative of Hosea Hudson* from W. W. Norton & Company.

"Wilbur Cash" reprinted by permission of Louisiana State University Press from *W. J. Cash and the Minds of the South*, edited by Paul D. Escott. Copyright © 1992 by Louisiana State University Press.

"Of Lily, 'Linda Brent,' and Freud" courtesy of the Georgia Historical Society.

Introduction to *Narrative of Hosea Hudson* reprinted by permission of the publishers from *Narrative of Hosea Hudson: His Life as a Negro Communist in the South* by Nell Irvin Painter. Cambridge, Mass.: Harvard University Press. Copyright © 1979 by the President and Fellows of Harvard College.

"Social Equality, Miscegenation, Labor, and Power" reprinted by permission of the University of Georgia Press, from Numan V. Bartley, *The Evolution of Southern Culture*. Copyright © 1982 by the University of Georgia Press.

# GENDER & AMERICAN CULTURE

*Revising Life: Sylvia Plath's Ariel Poems*, by Susan R. Van Dyne (1993)

*Made From This Earth: American Women and Nature*, by Vera Norwood (1993)

*Unruly Women: The Politics of Social and Sexual Control in the Old South*, by Victoria E. Bynum (1992)

*The Work of Self-Representation: Lyric Poetry in Colonial New England*, by Ivy Schweitzer (1991)

*Labor and Desire: Women's Revolutionary Fiction in Depression America*, by Paula Rabinowitz (1991)

*Community of Suffering and Struggle: Women, Men, and the Labor Movement in Minneapolis, 1915–1945*, by Elizabeth Faue (1991)

*All That Hollywood Allows: Re-reading Gender in 1950s Melodrama*, by Jackie Byars (1991)

*Doing Literary Business: American Women Writers in the Nineteenth Century*, by Susan Coultrap-McQuin (1990)

*Ladies, Women, and Wenches: Choice and Constraint in Antebellum Charleston and Boston*, by Jane H. Pease and William H. Pease (1990)

*The Secret Eye: The Journal of Ella Gertrude Clanton Thomas, 1848–1889*, edited by Virginia Ingraham Burr, with an introduction by Nell Irvin Painter (1990)

*Second Stories: The Politics of Language, Form, and Gender in Early American Fictions*, by Cynthia S. Jordan (1989)

*Within the Plantation Household: Black and White Women of the Old South*, by Elizabeth Fox-Genovese (1988)

*The Limits of Sisterhood: The Beecher Sisters on Women's Rights and Woman's Sphere*, by Jeanne Boydston, Mary Kelley, and Anne Margolis (1988)